The Uses of Diversity

Polycentricity: Studies in Institutional Diversity and Voluntary Governance

Series Editors: Lenore T. Ealy and Paul Dragos Aligica

This interdisciplinary series explores the varieties of social institutions, processes, and patterns of governance that emerge through individuals' coordination, cooperation, and competition in governance systems based on freedom of choice, freedom of exchange, and freedom of association. Under conditions of relative freedom of association, human diversity leads to institutional diversity and polycentric structures. In contrast to monocentric, unitary, and hierarchical command and control systems, polycentric social systems comprise many decision centers interacting freely under an overarching set of common rules. First introduced by Michael Polanyi as a descriptive and normative feature of free societies and further elaborated by Nobel Prize in Economics recipient Elinor Ostrom and public choice political economy co-founder Vincent Ostrom, the notion of polycentricity has proven itself able to offer a powerful analytical framework for expanding our understanding of the operation of governance regimes, constitutional federalism, law, public administration, private ordering, civics and citizenship, subsidiarity, nonprofit organization, cultural pluralism, civil society and entrepreneurship. Studies in this series will refine the conceptual framework of polycentricity and its governance theory implications, while expanding their application in the study of what Alexis de Tocqueville called the art and science of association. These studies should be of interest to scholars, policymakers, executives, social entrepreneurs, and citizens working to devise ways of living together harmoniously in civil societies.

Cryptodemocracy: Blockchain Technology and Democratic Governance by Darcy W.E. Allen, Chris Berg, and Aaron Matthew Lane

The Uses of Diversity: Essays in Polycentricity by David Ellerman

The Uses of Diversity

Essays in Polycentricity

David Ellerman

LEXINGTON BOOKS
Lanham • Boulder • New York • London

Published by Lexington Books
An imprint of The Rowman & Littlefield Publishing Group, Inc.
4501 Forbes Boulevard, Suite 200, Lanham, Maryland 20706
www.rowman.com

6 Tinworth Street, London SE11 5AL, United Kingdom

British Library Cataloguing in Publication Information Available

Library of Congress Control Number: 2020934290

ISBN 978-1-7936-2372-0 (cloth)
ISBN 978-1-7936-2373-7 (electronic)

Contents

List of Figures and Tables

FIGURES

TABLES

Preface

This book is a collection of chapters, some unpublished and some revised versions of published articles, that focus on a common theme. But that common theme is best seen as a "cluster concept" involving such ideas as the following:

- diversity,
- the logic of commitment in organizations,
- parallel experimentation,
- contestation,
- indirect methods of autonomy-respecting help,
- the "how" of social learning in development assistance,
- localism,
- pragmatism and piecemeal social change,
- democratic decision-making.

Stated negatively, the chapters argue against the following:

- monocentric modes of organization,
- experimentation that assumes one knows where the "Truth" lies,
- views based on authoritative and bureaucratic diktat or social conformity to "correct" views instead of views born out of contestation and debate,
- modes of "help" the override or undercut autonomy,
- "globalization" as a euphemism for hegemonic or imperialistic investment and control in developing or transition economies,
- organizations based on the logic of exit,
- big bangery, shock therapy, or engineered social change,

- autocratic-technocratic decision-making based on the logically fallacious methodologies of cost-benefit analysis and the social wealth maximization school of juridical thought.

Many of the chapters were written during my tenure at the World Bank as the senior adviser and speechwriter for Joseph Stiglitz as the chief economist (1997–1999). The World Bank could be seen as a model of the authoritative uncontested establishing of "The World Bank View" on topics of economic and social development. The World Bank, IMF, and the US Agency for International Development (USAID) also supported shock therapy and social engineered types of institutional change in the post-socialist economies much to the detriment of the latter. Given the structural impediments to basic change, I had to conclude that the World Bank should be wound up and shut down under a policy of "decentralization with extreme prejudice" (see Ellerman 2005).

I have also benefited over the years from a series of conferences and workshops organized by Lenore Thomas Ealy, who, together with George Mason University professor Paul Dragos Aligica, is the editor of this series on polycentricity. Those conferences also collected together people from many disciplines. I have tried to maintain that multidisciplinary approach in the chapters by emphasizing how essentially the same concepts can be developed in what at first seem to be disparate areas of study. This concordance and coherence between disciplines increases the power and importance of the common ideas. All the chapters are written in a nontechnical humanistic style, although the chapter on cost-benefit analysis includes some numerical examples.

Chapter 1

Jane Jacobs

The Diva of Diversity

INTRODUCTION

Jane Jacobs (1916–2006) is probably best known for her first book, *The Death and Life of Great American Cities* (1961). But she did not consider that as her most important work (personal communication). That was her later work on the study of economies and their development (she never referred to it as "economics"[1]) such as *The Economy of Cities* (1969), *Cities and the Wealth of Nations: Principles of Economic Life* (1984), and *The Nature of Economies* (2000).[2]

Why is her work on economies and development so little known and understood? Partly it is her "own fault"; she does not utilize the received presuppositions or concepts of economics. She writes about firms but takes no pains to repackage the ideas for economists who think of firms as being modeled by production functions. She writes about growth and development but does not try to build bridges with economists who think in terms of increases in K and L along with an expanding black box labeled "total factor productivity." It is not a matter of jargon; there are also basic differences in ideas.

One of the overarching themes in Jane Jacobs's thought is the importance of diversification. This is a leitmotiv in evolutionary biology as emphasized by Stephen Jay Gould:

> Evolutionary biologists (I am one) tend to equate goodness with what we view as the agent and the result of evolutionary change: the correlation between unconstrained smallness and innovation (for new species usually arise in tiny populations separated from larger parental groups), and the sheer exuberant diversity of life. If an evolutionist believes in any *summum bonum*, it can only be diversity itself. (Gould 1987, 204)

After quoting Gould, Jacobs notes that this "sort of view has worked a strong influence upon me; it did so long before I was conscious of its source in the thinking of naturalists. . . . Three cheers for the dogged persistence and mysterious vitality of diversity" (Jacobs 1980, 113–15).

But from Adam Smith onward, a leitmotiv of economics has been the (static) efficiency returns to specialization in the division of labor both in the small and in the large (i.e., the principle of comparative advantage). Efficiency improves by specializing in what one does best, not in diversifying. But, in spite of the weight of that orthodox tradition, the importance of diversity has started to creep into economics through the consideration of knowledge spillover effects. For instance, in Robert E. Lucas's work on endogenous growth theory, he noted "I will be following very closely the lead of Jane Jacobs, whose remarkable book *The Economy of Cities* seem to me mainly and convincingly concerned (although she does not use this terminology) with the external effects of human capital" (Lucas 1988, 37).

Edward Glaeser and colleagues (1992) have constructed and tested three models of knowledge spillovers in cities. Roughly, the Marshall-Arrow-Romer (MAR) model (Marshall 1920; Arrow 1962; Romer 1986) emphasizes the grouping of firms in the same industry and predicts that local monopoly would outperform local competition due to better internalization of the rewards to innovation. A model associated with Michael Porter (1990) also focused on groupings or clusters of like firms but emphasized local competition. The Jacobs model agrees with Porter on the importance of local competition rather than monopoly but disagrees on the clustering of like firms. As Glaeser writes:

> Jacobs (1969), unlike MAR and Porter, believes that most important knowledge transfers come from outside the core industry. As a result, variety and diversity of geographically proximate industries rather than geographical specialization promote innovation and growth. (Glaeser et al. 1992, 1128)

Glaeser and colleagues use a data set on the growth of large industries in 170 US cities between 1956 and 1987 to test the models and find that the "evidence is . . . negative on MAR, mixed on Porter, and consistent with Jacobs" (Glaeser et al. 1992, 1129). In qualitative terms, they

> find that local competition and urban variety, but not regional specialization, encourage employment growth in industries. The evidence suggests that important knowledge spillovers might occur between rather than within industries, consistent with the theories of Jacobs. (Glaeser et al. 1992, 1126)

Empirical results that favor Jacobs's emphasis on diversity continue to come in. Jean Imbs and Romain Wacziarg (2003) report quite robust findings in a bastion of orthodox thought, the *American Economic Review*, in an article entitled "Stages of Diversification." They relate sectoral concentration (as a proxy for nondiversification) to per capita income (as a proxy for development) in a variety of settings and find a robust U-shaped relationship. As per capita income increases, sectoral concentration drops over the lower part of the U-shaped curve and then may rise once income reaches a developed country level. Instead of specializing to comparative advantage being the path of development, they find: "Countries diversify over most of their development path" (Imbs and Wacziarg 2003, 64; quoted in Rodrik 2007, 103).

And some theoretical work in growth theory (Weitzman 1992; 1998) has rediscovered the importance of diversity in growth and has exploited some of the biological metaphors. Similar conclusions have emerged from the recent work on complex adaptive systems (often associated with the Santa Fe Institute). For instance, Stuart Kauffman concludes that

> diversity should be a major predictor of economic growth. This is not a new idea. Canadian economist Jane Jacobs advanced the same idea on different grounds two decades ago. (Kauffman 1995, 295)

Indeed, for over a third of a century, Jane Jacobs has not only noted these facts about diversity but has developed a theory of economic development that helps to explain those facts. Reading and rereading her books to see how she arrives at those conclusions is its own reward. I will only try here to sketch some of the arguments and tease out some of the policy implications.

DEVELOPMENT AS GROWTH THROUGH DIVERSIFICATION

The notions of "growth" and "development" are sometimes used almost interchangeably, but it would be useful to our purposes to make a sharp distinction. Jacobs points out that there was a sharp distinction even in biology. In the history of embryology, there were two schools about the process of change from an embryo to a mature organism. The "preformation" school (e.g., Aristotle) saw the embryo as just a tiny version of the mature organism so the process of embryonic change was simply one of quantitative growth. The epigenesis school saw the process of change in the embryo as a qualitative process of differentiation and transformation.

Aggregate growth theory in economics does a disservice to the understanding of *development* by abstracting away from the difference between growth (figure 1.1) and development (figure 1.2).

The biologist, C. H. Waddington, described the "epigenetic landscape" of development through diversification as being more like a branched and

Figure 1.1 Growth without Diversification.

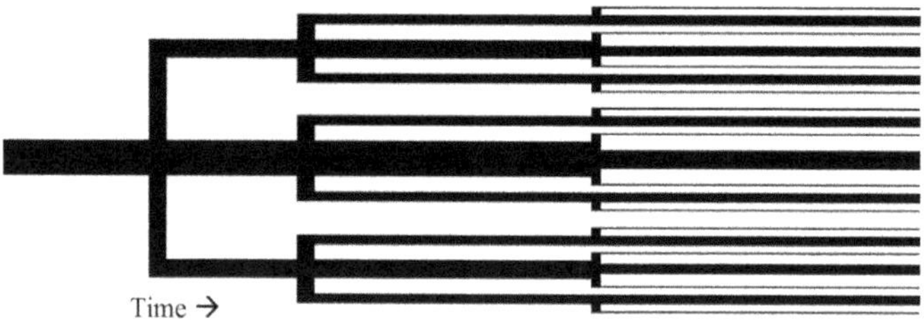

Figure 1.2 Development.

differentiated river delta than just a wider and deeper river. "One visual illustration would be the very final edge between the land and the sea in a great river delta like those of the Mississippi and the Nile—there are almost innumerable little separate rivulets of the fresh water running down to the sea, separated quite definitely but only by low banks of mud" (Waddington 1977, 116).

Development involves not just "growth" but diversification and the continuing ramifications of different products and different kinds of work. These might take place, in part, within firms but also through spin-offs, breakaways, split-ups, and the like within a city and its region. A preformation theory of city growth would picture a "city" just as a quantitatively bigger version of a small town, like a number of towns located together in a geographical area. But that is not what vibrant cities are nor how they grow. According to Jacobs, it is more like the process of epigenetic transformation, not blowing up a small balloon—with more capital and labor—to make a big balloon.

JACOBS'S BASIC ECOLOGICAL ANALOGY: THE TANGLED BANK VISION

The use of biological metaphors and analogies, both good and bad, is hardly new in economic thought. But Jacobs goes on to use a quite specific set of biological or rather ecological analogies that to my knowledge have not been emphasized elsewhere in the economics of development literature. The economic unit for development, for Jacobs, is not a country but a city and its surrounding region. To set up an analogy between a city and an ecological system, she gives a sketch of the energy flows in an ecological system.

Organized energy comes free from the sun but its trajectory within an ecology will depend on the complexity of the system. The two extremes could be taken as a desert and a rain forest. A rain forest and a desert at the same latitude would have about the same amount of solar energy arriving per unit area. In the case of the desert, it is essentially a sterile conduit; the energy comes in during the day and is dissipated at night. Little is captured; it is a throughput operation. The opposite is the case for the rain forest. Much energy is captured through the photosynthesis of its plants. Then the stored energy is passed around in a complex diversified web of relationships until it is finally dissipated through leakages. Plants die and decay to feed other plants. Plants are eaten by herbivores who are eaten by carnivores. All animals give off waste products and eventually die to feed other organisms directly or through decay.

At first glance, the economic analogue to incoming energy would seem to be incoming money either as payments for exports, as proceeds in a loan, or as remittances from abroad. The funds would then have a multiplier effect on the local economy seemingly similar to the cascades of energy going from one stage to another until finally dissipated. But Jacobs specifically does not use that analogy.

Rather, Jacobs constructs the ecological analogy by taking the *imports*—as incoming bundles of embodied knowledge and know how—coming into an economic settlement as being analogous to the incoming organized energy. If development is conceptualized as a form of social learning, then it is clearer why it is imports—like new useful books arriving in the mail—that are key to developmental learning, not exports. Lacking the free energy of the sun, there must still be some exports of commodities or services to fund the imports. The exports could originally be natural resource based as with oil, gas, or minerals or they could be derived from agriculture. The exports could be manufactured goods that might range all the way from just the assembly of imported parts or kits to goods that result from an extensive chain of domestic value-added operations. Or the exports could be some form of services, as in a community supported by remittances from migrant workers,[3] a community supported by tourism, an Indian reservation funded by a casino, a retirement community living off pension income (past services), or a Bangalore-type operation (selling software services) which might be part of a more complex operation of products and by-products. One way or another, an economic settlement needs to fund its imports.

It is the way imports are used—primary, intermediate, final, or producer goods—that separate the economic "deserts" from the "rain forests." A settlement is more like a desert when the imports are dissipated in consumption or are incorporated directly into the (enclave) production of what is exported. The settlement is a rather straightforward economic conduit.

A settlement is more like a rain forest when the imports feed into a diversified web of local value chains—some goods being inputs into many other products or spawning import replacements. The imports spread out like a river delta to directly and indirectly feed a diverse weblike "ecology" of economic activities.

Jacobs's vision of a developed economy recalls the famous "tangled bank" (i.e., "bank" of a stream) passage in the closing paragraph of Darwin's *Origin of Species* (sixth edition):

> It is interesting to contemplate a tangled bank, clothed with many plants of many kinds, with birds singing on the bushes, with various insects flitting about, and with worms crawling through the damp earth, and to reflect that these elaborately constructed forms, so different from each other, and dependent upon each other in so complex a manner, have all been produced by laws acting around us. (Darwin 2009)

With the tangled bank image, Darwin surpasses older imagery to arrive at a modern ecological vision of life that Jacobs has reimported into the study of economies (in considerable contrast to the crude competition-as-survival-of-the-fittest analogies that have appealed to so many economists):

> The image of the great Chain of Life if ordered, hierarchic, and static, essentially medieval; the great Tree of Life is ordered, hierarchic, but dynamic and competitive, a Renaissance vision; but the great Tangled Bank of Life is disordered, democratic, and subtly interdependent as well as competitive, essentially a modern vision. (Hyman 1966, 33)

The most sterile or inert desert-like settlements are the settlements based essentially on direct consumption of imports such as communities living off migrant worker remittances, retirement communities living off pensions (and income from capital invested elsewhere), and military bases. Not far behind are the settlements based on one stage of production with little local value-added such as agricultural- or natural-resource-based towns, tourist centers, casinos on Indian reservations, company towns, and labor-intensive assembly or processing enclaves. These are more like economic deserts—perhaps with one variety of cactus—than economic rain forests.

Thus, we get a clear contrast in definitions of development. By a living standards or consumption-oriented definition of development (e.g., gross domestic product [GDP]), an economic settlement made rich by pumping out oil would be "developed." For instance, in the World Bank, the oil-rich Gulf States qualify as Part 1 "developed" countries, not as Part 2 developing countries. But by Jacobs's productivist definition, such an economy is just a big pipe—an economic conduit—not a tangled bank. The oil exports fund imports which are then consumed, that is, dissipated, rather than feeding into a web of value-added activities and manufactured products some of which might be exported for the oil-independent funding of future imports. A city built in the desert just by oil is still a "desert" from Jacobs's productivist or capabilities-based viewpoint.[4]

To become more ramified and complex, an economic settlement should have multiple uses for imports to produce diversified and multistaged products with a significant part for local use. Each specialization to achieve some static efficiency should be accompanied by the diversification of outputs into various product niches, by backward integration to produce previously imported inputs, and perhaps by unexpected recombinant matings with nearby processes and products to produce novel offspring.[5] These are the innovations from "human capital externalities" that tend to happen when diverse people with various skills and complementary knowledge jostle together in companies and when a symbiotic web of sectorally diverse companies jostle together in cities.

HOW ADAM SMITH GOT IT WRONG

The jostling together of diverse people and skills spawns the diversifying sideways jumps from specialized old work to new work in a nearby field. "For instance, making forgings for one purpose develops skills and enterprises that can be drawn upon for other purposes. An economy that can produce improved fish-canning machinery can feasibly produce improved furniture-making machinery" (Jacobs 1980, 60). Paul Bairoch supports Jacobs on this point that "the diversity of urban activities quite naturally encourages attempts to apply or adopt in one sector (or in one specific problem area) technological solutions adopted in another sector" (Bairoch 1988, 336).

This combinatorial view of innovation[6] was key to the contagious innovation that made the Industrial Revolution. As one of the leading historians of the Industrial Revolution wrote:

> All these gains, plus the invention of machines to build machines, came together in the last third of the eighteenth century—a period of contagious novelty. Some of this merging stream of innovation may have been a lucky harvest. But no. Innovation was catching because the principles that underlay a given technique could take many forms, find many uses. If one could bore cannon, one could bore the cylinders of steam engines. If one could print fabrics by means of cylinders (as against the much slower block printing), one could also print wallpaper that way; or print word text far faster than by the up-and-down strokes of a press and turn out penny tabloids and cheap novels by the tens and hundreds of thousands. Similarly, a modified cotton-spinning machine could spin wool and flax. (Landes 1998, 191–92)

Those who bore cannon may themselves not be interested in steam engines, and those who print fabrics may hardly be interested in printing wallpaper, not to mention penny tabloids and cheap books. But in a diverse environment and with flexible or "fissionable" economic organizations, these spin-offs and recombinations to go from old work to new work might take place.

Adam Smith didn't get it quite right in *The Wealth of Nations*; it is not a process driven by increasing specialization. Deepening the division of labor increases operating efficiency and thus may expand old work, but it is not the dynamics of development of new work. Jacobs criticizes Smith on seeing the division of labor and increasing specialization as being key to development.

> Dividing existing work into tasks is by no means confined to advancing economies. It is also practiced in the most stagnant economies, where men and women spend their entire working lives at very specialized tasks: tapping rubber trees, or herding goats, or loading bananas, or twisting fibers, or dancing in temples, or mining salt, or crushing ore, or carrying baskets of dirt for public works, or cultivating corn and beans. A stagnant economy may lack almost everything, but not division of labor. (Jacobs 1969, 83)

One key to dynamics is when the process of deepening the division of labor in the old work leads to a new type of work, a new branch on the tree. Jacobs illustrates with Smith's own example of pin making (Smith 1994, Chapter 1). The story of the improvements in pin making started on an earlier branch of the tree, the making of wire bristles to card wool. Specialization in making carding combs lead to people "who bought iron ingots from smiths, drew them into wire, made the wire into bristles and sold the bristles to cardmakers" (Jacobs 1969, 82). But the operations of making the shaft of the wire bristle were the same as those needed to make the shaft of a pin; the Carders and Pinners were associated guilds. Hence, some bristle makers could branch off with the further steps to add heads to the wire bristles to make pins. "They were adding a new complexity, pin making, to an older simplicity, bristle making. From this addition came the rest of the divisions of labor in pin making that Smith describes" (Jacobs 1969, 82).

The story of the *dynamics* of development is not the static efficiency of greater specialization but the branching off of new kinds of work. Carrying the pin-making story further, about fifty years after Smith's exposition, the hand-making of pins was rendered obsolete in a stroke by a pin-making machine. That machine, however, did not develop from the specialization of labor in the pin-making business; rather, it developed from a new branch on another tree, a new application made by a designer of machines for other industries.

EXAMPLE OF "DEVELOPMENT IN ONE COMPANY"

Jane Jacobs uses the development of the Minnesota Mining and Manufacturing Company (3M company) as a modern example to illustrate how innovation turns mere growth ("expanding old work") into diversified and ramified development ("adding new work") in a process where "one sort of work leads to another" (1969, 53). The 3M company started with two proprietors and some workers gathering and processing sands used for abrasive purposes. Then they decided to make sandpaper but had trouble with the adhesives to stick the sand to the paper. After experimenting with adhesives, they developed a gummed paper to use as masking tape for painters and eventually a whole line of tapes: "shoe tape, electrical tape, acetate tape, pressure-sensitive adhesive tape (better known as Scotch tape), acetate fiber tape, cellophane tape, printed cellophane tape, plastic tape, filament tape, sound recording magnetic tape, nonwoven synthetic fibers" (1969, 53). Today, we could add a host of other spin-off products such as the post-it notes and magnetic disks for computers.[7]

Other uses of adhesives were not forgotten. The diversification continued with "sandblasting stencils, automotive adhesives, industrial adhesives, marine adhesives, marine calking compounds, tile and construction adhesives, construction compounds" (1969, 53). The original product of sand also sent out its branches on the ramifying tree of products: "coated sand for polishing, then wax and varnish coatings, finely ground paint pigments, roofing granules, nonslip cleats and strips, abrasive cloth, reflective sheeting, reflective compounds, paving materials, and welding fluxes. . . . This process in which one sort of work leads to another must have happened millions of times in the whole history of human economic development" (Jacobs 1969, 53).

This is an example of the dynamics of development that goes beyond increases in labor and capital and that goes on inside the expanding black box of "total factor productivity."

JACOBS'S LADDER: CLIMBING TOWARD DEVELOPMENT

In graduate school, it often seems that future economists are trained using modernized Pavlovian methods to intellectually "growl" whenever they hear the phrase "import substitution." Being without the benefit of such professional training, Jacobs rethought the idea of "import substitution" to arrive at an alternative viewpoint. For her own reasons, in fact, she agrees with most of the orthodox critique of state-planned import substitution programs. As she writes:

> The import-substitution programs fixed upon items selected abstractly, from statistics on imports. Factories were located in semi-rural economic deserts because jobs were most needed there. Although labor costs were low, the factories and their imported equipment and imported managers and supervisors were expensive. Markets weren't at hand; co-developments were missing; nothing meshed. When the intended substitutes for imports could actually be produced with reasonable speed and reliability—an expectation seldom realized—the products cost more than equivalent imports. (Jacobs 2000, 81)

But instead of stopping with this critique and urging economies to specialize in their current comparative advantage, Jacobs looked at how city economies that do develop use import replacement as a key part of the process.

Cities can grow through a process of dynamic interaction with each other through direct or indirect rivalry. To play in the "game," a city must produce something which it can export—perhaps based on its natural endowment. The export earnings can then buy imports from other cities that were not produced in the given city. In the rivalry between cities, a manufactured import is like a "slap in the face," an "insult," or a challenge; the city has to buy the import because it cannot produce it itself. If the other exporting cities were not too advanced, then the import will present a plausible challenge to be replaced through learning and improvisation (the process of moving beyond old work to new work outlined previously) and perhaps improved upon by the importing city. Since the wealth to buy the imports might have been earned productively (not a gift), the city might already have some productive capacity that might begin to improvise and differentiate to produce and replace the import.

In the meantime, the other cities might be replacing the original exports of the city; its temporary advantage might be competed away. Now the domestic and perhaps improved version of the originally imported products can then be reexported perhaps to the original supplier city or more likely to other cities "down the line" that are less developed or have different specializations. The new export earnings will then purchase other more challenging imports, and the process can repeat itself ratcheted up at a higher level. In this matter, a diversified group of innovative and versatile cities can through trade learn from each other and not only grow but *develop* "on one other's shoulders" (Jacobs 1984, 144)—which we might call climbing *Jacobs's Ladder*.

It should be particularly noted that the Jacobs's Ladder mechanism works best between competitors at a roughly comparable level of development.[8] Her theory provides a rationale for regional trading blocs between countries at roughly the same level of development, not for free importing from the most advanced countries. "Science fiction" imports from advanced countries (largely to feed the conspicuous consumption habits of the elites[9]) would stop the rivalrous process in the same way that allowing a heavyweight to box in a lightweight class would stop the rivalry and stop the associated process of learning and improvement through competition—leaving aside any other damages. Enforcing "level playing field" competition between "heavyweights" and "lightweights"—that is, between advanced and underdeveloped countries—would be tantamount to "kicking away the ladder" (Chang 2002) that the developing countries could climb.

JACOBS'S LADDER AS A SCHEME OF PARALLEL EXPERIMENTATION FOR SOCIAL LEARNING

In the presence of genuine uncertainty, innovation and learning progresses best by conducting diverse concurrent experiments with a common goal—for instance, toward the most economical car or the most effective mean of treating AIDS.

> The use of a parallel-path strategy for the solution of difficult development problems is standard practice in several of our outstanding industrial laboratories. It is extremely common in agricultural and medical research. And in the atomic-bomb project, one of the most spectacularly successful military projects the United States has ever undertaken, the parallel-path strategy was employed. (Nelson 1961, 353)

It is the opposite of specializing one's resources in what is currently considered as the One Best Way. As the parallel experiments score successes, there must be some mechanism so that those successes are transmitted to the other experiments and thus the whole group is ratcheted up.

The international community of scientists in any field furnishes an excellent example of such scheme of discovery and learning through parallel experimentation. Rather than "avoiding duplication" and "increasing efficiency" by putting all resources on what seems the most promising way, a diversity of centers of research is ideally fostered. As Jacobs writes:

> Development work is a messy, time-, and energy-consuming business of trial, error and failure. The only certainties in it are trial and error. . . . Indeed, development work is inherently so chancy that by the law of averages, chances of success are greatly improved if there is much duplication of effort. . . . Just so, when Pasteur, that wise old man, begged for enlarged support of the biological sciences, he begged for multiplication of laboratories. (Jacobs 1969, 90–91)

Evolutionary biology provides a natural example of parallel experimentation. There are two opposing moments in an evolutionary process: variation (exploration or diversification) to expand the range of possibilities and selection (exploitation or specialization) to whittle down the given possibilities to the best ones. Thus, specialization and diversification are seen as two opposing moments in one overall process. Think of a species as trying to climb to a higher level of evolutionary fitness on a "fitness landscape" that has multiple peaks. But the species might be on a low hill. From Darwin up until Sewall Wright's work in the early 1930s, evolutionary theory focused on selection which by itself is only a hill-climbing mechanism. If the main population is climbing a low "dead-end" hill, then there needs to be some alternative way to go downhill against selective pressures, cross a valley of low fitness, and start climbing a higher hill. Mutation in one large interbreeding population was not enough. Sewall Wright was the first evolutionary thinker to focus on that problem of variation, exploration, and diversification. "The problem of evolution as I see it is that of a mechanism by which the species may continually find its way from lower to higher peaks in such a field" (Wright 1932; reprinted in Wright 1986, 163–64).

The solution[10] was again diverse semi-isolated experiments (subpopulations or "demes" in different niches) run in parallel with enough migration of genes between the subpopulations so that successes would ratchet up the whole population. Since there was always a balance to be struck between the semi-isolation of the subpopulations to encourage novelty, and communication between the groups to share successes, Wright called it the "shifting balance theory."

As a general scheme of parallel experimentation for learning under uncertainty (where you really don't know the One Best Way to go), the "Wright stuff" are different experiments running concurrently

- with some common goal (rather than focusing resources on what currently seems like the best option),
- with some semi-isolation from the pressure of immediate success,
- with benchmarking comparisons made between the experiments, and
- with the "migration" of discoveries between experiments wherever possible to ratchet up the performance of the whole population.[11]

The Jacobs' Ladder mechanism is, of course, an example of a parallel experimentation scheme. The different cities (or countries) within a vibrant trading bloc are each carrying on various experiments and then exporting their successes to others in the group. Each member tries to incorporate and improve upon the "challenging" imports and then to reexport their successes so that they develop "on each other's shoulders" ratcheting up the level of development (knowledge and productive capacity) of the whole group.

Such a scheme of mutual challenges and import replacements ratcheting up and continuously improving the whole trading bloc is in striking contrast to the scheme promoted by comparative advantage theory in which each city, region, or country in the trading bloc specializes in "what it does (relatively) best" and then exports that product (perhaps ever-improving through more specialization) to the other specialized trading partners who, in turn, supply their ever-improving specialized products as imports to the others in the bloc. Jacobs sees this scheme of specialization as a recipe for long-term stagnation. People with specialties can further dynamic improvements if they jostle together with people of other specialties within a company. Or companies with specialties can promote dynamics if they jostle together with other companies within a versatile city. But when a whole city specializes and trades with other specialized cities, then that locked-in pattern of static efficiency is a recipe for stasis and long-term decline.

JACOBS UNIVERSITY: A SCHOOL FOR LIFETIME LEARNING

It is not easy to explain Jacobs's theory in terms of conventional economic models. Perhaps one key is to focus on her theory of development as a type of social learning and then to construct a purely educational analogue as an aid to understanding. That is the purpose of this section.

Imagine a school of people who are both students and teachers. They earn chits by teaching some topic to their fellow students, and then they can use the chits to pay for courses offered on other topics by their fellow student-teachers. For simplicity, we assume that the student-teachers' other needs are taken care of by other means, for example they are like students living at home. As students learn and can recombine knowledge and innovate, they may offer new courses to their fellows if they can find enough takers. The student-teachers play the role of the cities with the courses they teach being their "exports" and the courses taken being their "imports." Thus, Jacobs University is a simplified educational model of the Jacobs' Ladder mechanism. The student-teachers learn (develop) on each other's shoulders. Many of her basic arguments can be modeled and perhaps clarified within the Jacobs University model. The arguments are developed in parallel in table 1.1.

The Jacobs University analogue clarifies some difficult points. Conventionally, the emphasis is on export-driven growth, but Jacobs puts the emphasis more on imports and the process of stretching and replacing them. Seeing an import as a crystalized packet of codified knowledge and tacit production know-how, learning to replace an import is analogous to taking a course and assimilating the knowledge perhaps improving on it and then being able to

Table 1.1 An Educational Analogy for Jacobs's Economic Theory

Theme	*Economic Model: Jacobs' Ladder Mechanism*	*Educational Model: Jacobs University for Lifetime Learning*
Players	Cities.	Student-teachers.
Inputs	Imports.	Courses taken by students.
Outputs	Exports.	Teaching fellow students.
Means of obtaining inputs	Exports earning imports.	Teaching other students to earn chits to pay other student-teachers to teach one a new topic.
Original endowment	Endowment of natural resources to start process (as original unearned resources to buy imports).	Inherited chits to start taking a course.
How success forces players to next level	Exports to a creative city will soon be replaced forcing a city to generate new exports.	Courses successfully taught will dry up the students willing to take the same course, so teacher has to learn something new to teach.
Desert	Imports (however funded) are just consumed with no attempt to stretch or replace them.	Course taken (however funded) but no learning and no subsequent teaching.
Rain forest	Imports are assimilated, stretched, and modified in a diversity of products. City is in an excellent position to innovate and export goods. This is easier in a diverse city with many entry points to assimilate and creatively use imports.	Course knowledge feeds into a number of "hooks" or "entry points" so a student has an in-depth understanding of topic and is in an excellent position to teach—perhaps in new courses. This is easier in a student with more diverse knowledge.
Export processing zone	Imports get a little processing and are then reexported.	Courses not really learned but mechanically used to teach others with little real understanding oneself.
Advanced-backward trade	Science fiction import cannot be stretched or replaced. Not assimilated in that sense. Stops the dynamic.	Course at too advanced level so little is learned or assimilated. Stops the dynamic.

Supply regions	Regions that produce something, natural resources, agricultural outputs, or a military supplier that is not part of a Jacobs' Ladder dynamic (inert partners with steady demand) so it is lulled into just using its earnings to buy imports and has lost the necessity and capacity to replace the imports. It has stopped learning and becomes specialized.	Finds that teaching in a specific field goes on and on so one can take other courses but it is not really necessary to learn them to teach in the new topics. Slides outside the dynamic of teaching, students learning to teach, teacher needing to learn a new topic, and so forth.
Unearned imports	Unearned imports paid for with subsidies given perhaps for charitable or political reasons.	Getting unearned chits to take a course—perhaps for charitable or political reasons.
Transactions of decline	Even though it may be an advanced creative city ultimately providing subsidies (through the government) to backward regions that turn around and give demand for the city's exports, there is no creative partner, so the city gets locked into becoming a supply region to inert subsidized partners. Sustained use of taxes for military expenditures on a city's products is the same type of pattern locking the city into becoming an industrialized supply region.	Good student-teachers provide some scholarship chits for backward students who can thus pay for the better teachers' courses. But the backward students might not learn or progress (since the chits were unearned by their own learning and teaching). One is outside the positive dynamics of teaching students who learn so teacher uses fees to take another course, which can then be used for teaching, and so forth. Teachers may fall into an inert pattern of teaching to subsidized unlearning students.
Remittances	Remittances, being unearned where they are spent on imports back home, do not lead to learning, import stretching, or replacement.	Getting chits unearned by teaching (earned in some other way elsewhere) so the student would have little capacity to learn anything to kick off the learning-teaching dynamic.
Specialization to comparative advantage	Each city specializes so it does not learn from imports, and other cities similarly don't learn from its exports. They are in a static "equilibrium" until the products are obsolete and competition from outside the specialized trading group exposes their inertness.	Some students decide to specialize and then take in each other's laundry (each teaching their own specialty to unlearning students). The situation repeats itself. When new knowledge finally comes from outside, neither will be able to learn it.

(*Continued*)

Table 1.1 An Educational Analogy for Jacobs's Economic Theory *(Continued)*

Theme	*Economic Model: Jacobs' Ladder Mechanism*	*Educational Model: Jacobs University for Lifetime Learning*
How transplants can attenuate the dynamics on the importer-student side	Exporters who transplant a factory to the importing city so product will be "produced locally" are in fact attenuating the dynamic as it forestalls genuine import replacement. Importing cities might compete to get the transplant factories so they could quickly get into the "producing-and-exporting" business without going through the time-consuming process of learning to produce themselves.	If teacher offers to teach (with lower return) "for" the students, then the students get some return (as student-assistants) but don't learn in order to teach the topic themselves. Students might even compete to offer deals to teacher to teach for them so they can quickly get in the "teaching" business without going through the time-consuming process of learning to teach the topic themselves.
How transplants can attenuate the dynamics on the exporter-teacher side	Since previously exporting city is now benefiting (owners, not workers) from having the product produced locally in the previously importing city, there will be no real import replacement, so the partner has become inert. The exporting city can thus sterilize potentially creative import-replacing partners so that it can continue doing the same thing.	If the teacher can teach "for" the student, the student will not replace the demand for teaching that topic by learning, so the student-partner has become a relatively inert student-assistant. By doing this for the potentially learning students, the teacher can render their learning to teach unnecessary so the teacher can continue doing the same thing.

Source: Author.

teach others (reexport the improved product). Thus, the exports are basically the means to pay for the imports, and the important thing is what happens in between—learning to replace the imports and developing new exports.

Another difficult point for those accustomed to "static" models of growth is the inherent dynamism of the Jacobs model. The school analogy captures this nicely since a school that just keeps on repeating the same courses to the same unlearning students is a clear failure even though it might have an increasing volume of repeating students in its circular flow. In the Jacobs University model, imagine two initial sets of "specialized" student-teachers. One set teaches mathematics to the other set and that other set teaches postmodernism to the math set. Each set finds the other topic totally incomprehensible, so they keep repeating the taking and teaching of the courses in a static equilibrium. Each repeats its comparative advantage. But there might be some unemployed members of each set. The university administrators could have a one-time pump-priming injection of chits into both groups so that the unemployed members could now be employed to teach their topic and to thus pay for being students of the other topic. The system would then have "growth" to a higher-level equilibrium—like giving a one-time push to a frictionless wheel to leave it spinning with increased angular momentum. But such "growth" is only the failure to learn on a broader scale. Now we turn from the macro-model of the Jacobs' Ladder mechanism to Jacobs's micro-level analysis of innovation in the firm.

HOW NEW WORK MIGHT BE SPAWNED FROM OLD WORK

Jane Jacobs's micro-level analysis of how old work can lead to new work in firms has interesting and powerful implications for economic policy about job and enterprise creation. New work arises out of old work in a variety of ways. One way is simply that old products might be stretched to find new applications; old services might be stretched to find new categories of clients. But a deeper source of innovation lies in the multiple uses and recombinations of a technology. Once a company learns the technology W to produce product X, the economically rewarding path and "path of least resistance" is probably to continue in the same groove (or rut) to produce more and better X instead of using the technology W to produce noncompeting products Y and Z.[12] In a diverse environment, the additional knowledge to use the technology to produce the other products Y and Z might be readily available. But the filling out of the possibilities of each technology might fail for other reasons than an overly specialized environment. Management would become a nightmare in this "strange hive." Each new kind of work might be in a different sector and would have its own customers, input and space needs, financing and staffing requirements, and growth rate all not in any coordination with the original work of the company. It probably is not worth the distraction to the original company. Given the limitations on the scope and attention span of unified management, the company might decide to just "stick to its knitting" with the original products. The new job creation possibilities would be squandered.

EVERY COMPANY'S TWO PRODUCTS

Here Jacobs's thought meets up with some older observations by Cambridge economist Arthur C. Pigou (1877–1959). Every company produces two products. One product is its products. The other product is the organization of people (always with some turnover) trained in the technologies used by the company and trained in the general business capabilities needed to carry on the business. Pigou noted that the businesses in a country provided this *potential* positive externality (meaning their potential social product exceeded their private product) of training people in technologies and business capabilities:

> One very important indirect service is rendered by the general economic organisation of a country in so far as, in addition to fulfilling its function as an instrument of production, it also acts, in greater or lesser degree, as a training ground of business capacities. (Pigou 1960, 204)

What are the policy implications of this fundamental point that existing businesses are major training grounds for entrepreneurial, managerial, and technological capability and potential incubators for new businesses? The extent to which this widespread potential positive externality is exploited to create new jobs—or new work from old work—depends crucially on the form of the business. The additional job creation that could follow from a corporation's "second product" (its training of people in technologies and business capabilities) is typically not a part of the company's goals; that is why it is an externality.

PUTTING JANE JACOBS TO WORK: NEW JOB AND ENTERPRISE CREATION

First, we consider the conventional corporate form of business. How might the externality be internalized through private or public action? While unitary corporate management typically tries to maximize the size of its empire, the diseconomies of scale and scope will soon extract their price.[13]

One counterstrategy is the multidivisional firm (e.g., Chandler 1990). The example of the 3M company shows that a multidivisional structure (together with a very special corporate culture) can be used to try to fill out the plenum of possibilities offered by each technology mastered by a company. But 3M is more the exception than the rule; larger organizations usually mean deeper ruts to imprison the older work.

Here again, a biological example might be instructive. There are two ways that biomass can be increased: by existing organisms getting bigger (like multidivisional growth in a firm) and by existing organisms spawning new life by having offspring.[14] Nature gives little choice between these options. There are powerful structural limits to physical growth in each type of organism, and the grim reaper imposes even stricter time limits. Hence, the biological "principle of plenitude" (Lovejoy 1960, 52) by which biomass has increased is principally by old life spawning new life through fission and reproduction. Incidentally, the orthodox "dream world" of perfectly enforced intellectual property rights would tend to shut off the second option of spawning new economic life—while the "grim reaper" of limited patent life is an attempt to (belatedly) bring the second option back into play.

For an economy to be more like a rain forest than a desert, it must increase its "economic mass." But corporations do not have a limited lifetime and the diseconomies of scale and scope seem to place little natural limit on the ambitions of management to try to grow directly or to grow indirectly through acquisitions and mergers. Hence, conventionally organized companies do not tend to follow an economic principle of plenitude by deliberately spawning new offspring. Indeed, where new life gets going on its own, large corporations try to compensate for their lack of innovation and oncoming senility by gobbling up the previously successful start-ups (reverse spin-offs) in a process of "destructive corporate cannibalism" (Jacobs 2004, 170).

One possibility is realized by franchising. Often a business has natural geographical limits (e.g., a restaurant). But the business' "second product"—its capacity to train people in the specific business—could be used to "replicate the DNA" to other geographical locales. If there are enforceable intellectual property rights to the "concept" and perhaps property rights to some unique inputs, then the positive externality might be internalized as a franchise operation. If successful, then the company's second product becomes the main product—the use of the company's training capacity to replicate the business DNA in the franchisee operations. Even when some of the prerequisites are not present for a full-blown master franchiser operation, each business still has the potential to replicate its successful DNA—it just lacks the means to recoup the benefits (which is why positive externalities tend to be underrealized). For instance, with some temporary doubling up of staff, new people could be trained to replicate the business in a noncompetitive locale.

It is also possible for a company to use spin-offs of partial subsidiaries (rather than new divisions) to develop new products out of the old products and technologies. One interesting example of systematic spin-off promotion is the Thermo Electron Group in and around Boston.[15] The original company Thermo Electron was started by an MIT physics professor George Hatsopoulos in 1956. Once a company has mastered a technology to produce one product, there are often many nearby products that beckon to be produced. Thermo Electron established the principle that new nearby products would be produced in new companies that were "spin-outs" from the original company. The mother company would keep a majority of the shares (to address the incentive problem) but the other shares would be held by the people in the spin-out or would be sold to the public. Operational control would be in the hands of the spun-out company whose name would always begin with "Thermo" to signify membership in the Thermo Group (with over sixty companies). Now the children have begun to have children since the ramification through spin-outs is a principle for all the companies of any generation.

But here again, the Thermo Group is more the exception than the rule (see Peters 1992 for more exceptions). When asked why others have not copied his ideas, Hatsopoulos said:

> People who head large companies are not venturesome enough. The CEOs of established companies are afraid to lose control because we are turning a lot of decision-making over to the individual manager. (Quoted in Bailey and Syre 1996, 45)

The example of the Thermo Group is quite instructive on several counts. It shows one way that the externality problem can be addressed by fostering partially owned spin-offs (or "spin-outs").[16] But it also shows the severity of the incentive problem since the Thermo example has not been imitated. Corporate management wants to expand the empire directly under its thumb; spin-outs to an associated group do not seem to fit the bill. After Hatsopoulos died, these empire-building proclivities set in and many of the Thermo companies were combined in the Fisher Scientific Company that brags about having 70,000 employees worldwide.

Yet another possibility arises when most of the technology is embodied in highly mobile "human capital," where independent venture capital is available, and where the economic environment has reached a certain critical mass of diversity. Then as in California's Silicon Valley, Boston's Route 128, or Taiwan's Silicon Gulch[17] (not to mention the fervent period of the Industrial Revolution in England), many of the technological possibilities can be fulfilled by breakaways and spin-offs that cannot be prevented by empire-building management in the original company—management that sees "Big things turning into smaller things" as "decay and disintegration" rather than "birth and renewal of vigor" (Jacobs 1980, 68).

And finally, there are many service sector enterprises with small capital requirements where management cannot stop spin-offs and breakaways. In these last two cases, spin-offs are possible not because they are compatible with the legal form of the enterprise but because much of the business is embodied in the human knowledge and skills of the staff who walk out the door at the end of each working day and have the choice of not coming back.

THE DIFFERENCE DEMOCRACY MAKES

The enemies of diversification are not just one-sided economic theories that emphasize the deepening of old work rather than the creation of new work (to put it in Jacobs's terms). Empire-building proclivities also thwart diversity, and those tendencies are evident both politically and economically. But the political grip of those proclivities will depend on the form of government. In an autocracy where power comes from above, the sovereign will seek to maintain and perhaps even expand the realm.[18] But if power comes from below as in a political democracy (leaving aside the half-free and half-slave antebellum America), there are few grounds to deny the expressed wish of the bulk of the population in a part of a country to become autonomous or to secede. Jacobs cites the early twentieth-century peaceful secession of Norway from Sweden as an example (the separation of Singapore from Malaysia might also be mentioned), and she viewed the possible secession of Quebec with equanimity, if not support (see Jacobs 1980).[19]

The same dynamics of power and legitimacy are at work in an economic polity. In a conventional company, where power comes from above, management has little reason to sponsor spin-offs and would have little cause to accede to any expressed desires coming from below to use the firm's technological and business capabilities for new enterprise creation through spin-offs and breakaways. When the preconditions of a Silicon Valley are present or in labor-intensive service sectors, then it may happen anyway—not because of the form of business but in spite of it.

In a democratic company (e.g., an industrial cooperative) where power comes from below, then management has less of a leg to stand on to oppose new enterprise creation through spin-offs and breakaways.[20] Pigou specifically mentioned that "associations of workers combined together in small co-partnership workshops" would constitute the "first school in which this capacity can be developed," and thus such companies would contribute to the community not just "boots and shoes" but the second product of "well-trained competent" people (Pigou 1960, 205–06).

That has certainly been the experience of today's best example of cooperative development, the Mondragon group of cooperatives in the Basque region of Spain.[21] The companies known collectively as "Mondragon Cooperative Corporation" produce a rather full variety of high-valued added consumer products, intermediate goods, and capital goods including the first robots and computer numerically controlled (CNC) machinery designed and built in Spain. Since the firms are all cooperatives, it was all done with no foreign ownership. The group started with a single company in the mid-1950s producing a kerosene heater. Then it systematically implemented the economic principle of plenitude by filling out the backward linkages, producing the machines to make the heaters and then the machines to make those machines. Through multiproduct diversification, it started producing other consumer durables (stoves, refrigerators, and washing machines) and all the things to produce those things. Each bottleneck called forth new energies to solve problems, for example a bank to help finance new enterprises, an applied technological research institute to systematically learn new technologies and turn them into new products, a consulting company to help new firms start (a "factory factory"), an insurance company for members, and a polytechnic university.

Since the firms were cooperatives and, as a group, had the express goal of developing good jobs in the Basque country, the positive externality of fostering spin-offs and breakaways was "socialized" or internalized within the group (see Ellerman 1984). The original company did not have the option of "owning" a spin-off or preventing the spin-off if the mother company could not capture all the benefits. The new company would also be a cooperative that would have to "rest on its own bottom" or "walk on its own two feet"—within the group.[22] Thus the headquarters of the whole group encouraged groups within existing firms to coalesce around ideas to produce adjacent products in a spin-off. The potential managers and workers might be from a village or small region without much industrial development so by doing the spin-off near their homes they satisfied both economic and social goals. In a similar context, Jacobs noted that such "division would be a normal, untraumatic accompaniment of economic development itself, and of the increasing complexity of economic and social life" (Jacobs 1984, 215). Since the spin-off process was carried out in an organized and socially approved way, precautions could be taken so that it did not disrupt the original mother firm. It became part of how the group evolved.

CONCLUDING REMARKS

Our overall goal here is to call attention to Jane Jacobs's work not only as a writer about cities but as a writer about economies and development where cities have the central role as the main sites of development. Her emphasis on diversification is particularly relevant to today's debates about globalization. She is almost a one-person antithesis to orthodox economics which is professionally enamored with the logic of specialization, increased division of labor, and the theory that each country (or city region) should specialize in its comparative advantage.

According to comparative advantage theory, the North (industrialized countries) clearly has the comparative advantage in modern science, technology, and industrial production. The South (developing countries) should not indulge in the wasteful duplication of producing on its own (initially) crummy imitations of the industrial products produced so well in the North. The South should specialize in their comparative advantage, which is natural resources, agricultural products (which the North should buy more from the South to lock in that sterile pattern), and unskilled labor. Indeed, the South can in part function as a "bedroom community" for unskilled labor that becomes "transnational"—migrating back and forth to the North to take the jobs that northerners don't want.[23] Insofar as industrial products need to be produced in the South, this should be done by factories owned and operated by the multinational companies from the North which already have the comparative advantage in that sort of thing (which will tend to crowd out the development of that local capacity in a familiar colonial fashion). But it is "win-win" since the factories will use the cheaper local labor, one of the South's specialties. By thus urging the North and the South to each exploit their own comparative advantage, the development institutions that operate according to the "science" of economics—such as the World Bank (see Ellerman 2005) and the IMF—promote the goal of worldwide efficiency.[24]

But Jane Jacobs, being without the blessing of an intellectual formation in economics, spent a lifetime studying economies rather than economics, and she has arrived at a rather different viewpoint. Her perspective is productivist (or capabilities based) rather than consumptionist. Rather than starting with an artificial static conception of the economy and then perhaps later discovering that some cherished notions (e.g., static efficiency) might even cut against evolutionary dynamics,[25] she begins with a description of actual economies that is dynamic and evolutionary. In her ecological vision of economic life, she is a "diversitarian" in contrast to the "uniformitarian" tendencies of high modernism (e.g., Jacobs's bête noire in matters of "city planning," Le Corbusier) and often expressed in the idea "Why not do everything in the One Best Way?"[26]

> Lenin's design for the construction of the revolution was in many ways comparable to Le Corbusier's design for the construction of the modern city. Both were complex endeavors that had to be entrusted to the professionalism and scientific insight of a trained cadre with full power to see the plan through. And just as Le Corbusier and Lenin shared a broadly comparable high modernism,

> so Jane Jacobs's perspective was shared by Rosa Luxemburg and Aleksandra Kollontay, who opposed Lenin's politics. Jacobs doubted both the possibility and the desirability of the centrally planned city, and Luxemburg and Kollontay doubted the possibility and desirability of a revolution planned from above by the vanguard party. (Scott 1998, 147)

On the negative side, the Jacobs' Ladder theory provides a critique of the South's science fiction imports from the North that serve mainly to titillate the local elites and to forestall the slower development of those industrial capabilities in the South. Domestically, the Jacobs' Ladder theory shows the very minimal development impact ("sterility") of the one-way traffic of products and investments ("political factories") imported into poor regions, company towns, military bases, and other "mono-crop" enclaves that cannot "answer the challenge" by replacing and reexporting the imports in a self-sustaining process.

Finally, at the micro-level of the firm, her analysis of old work spawning new work revives an older theme of Pigou that each firm embodies a positive externality in the firm's "second product"—its organizational capacity to train people in technological and business capabilities. In the conventional firm where power comes from above, this potential for new job and enterprise creation goes largely untapped. What "king" ever voluntarily gave up his grip on part of the "kingdom" in the interests of diversified niche-filling development? The legal form of production serves as a constraint or fetter on economic development. There are two policy implications. One is that there may be policies that would help conventional firms to internalize the positive externality and thus to be less of a fetter on development (e.g., the examples of 3M and the Thermo Group). The other implication is that if firms are organized more with power coming from below, then the organizations will be more able to spawn new and diverse economic life. Rather than just specialize and expand old life with its attendant diseconomies of scale and scope, economic life would then better approximate the biological principle of plenitude that works to increase the mass and complexity of life primarily by spawning new life.

NOTES

1. In a book-length celebration of her ideas (Allen 1997), the appropriate chapter is labeled "Economies."
2. In retrospect, one might call attention to her last and unfortunately prophetic book, *Dark Age Ahead* (2004).
3. See Ellerman (2003) for Jacobs's treatment of migration issues.

4. See Sen (1999) for a recent capabilities-based notion of development and see List 1885 for an older productivist viewpoint.

5. "In economic life the amoebas do not always divide into more amoebas. Sometimes the people who manage to split off new organizations from an old one do not duplicate the older company where they got their start; instead, they combine their experience with a new idea. An example would be a purchasing agent for a restaurant chain who becomes dissatisfied with the scales he buys, has a better idea for their design and teams up with a machinist from a tool-and-die company and a designer of microprocessor controls to start a new enterprise manufacturing food wholesalers' scales. The new enterprise would be not a reproduction of the parent enterprise, but a mutant" (Jacobs 1980, 68).

6. See Arthur (2009) and Koppl et al. (2018).

7. See Peters and Waterman (1982) as well as Collins and Porras (1994) to update the story of 3M as the "Mutation Machine from Minnesota."

8. See Chapter 10 "Why Backward Cities Need One Another" in Jacobs (1984).

9. Even imported "factories" such as the BMW and Mercedes assembly plants in South Africa will largely serve only the purpose of gratifying the elites. Moreover, by soaking up much of the local demand for cars by those who can afford them, such plants will crowd out and foreclose on the possibility of there being a genuinely African car with all the technological ramifications that would follow from it.

10. Like Darwin, Wright thought it relevant to carefully observe artificial selection. Wright found that breeders do not keep all their animals together in one large interbreeding herd. They deliberately break the herd up into subherds, subpopulations, "races," or "demes" (as in demography). It is a question of balance. The subherds should be small enough so that the variety found in the subherd (through sampling error) or created through mutation, sexual reproduction, and genetic drift will be emphasized through inbreeding. But the subherd should not be so small that inbreeding leads to the quick fixation of ill-adapted genes and the deterioration or demise of the subherd. When a clearly superior example is produced in a subherd, then the seed is crossbred into the other subherds to give them the benefit of the innovation. But seeds could not be constantly crossbred between the subherds as that would defeat the benefits of their semi-isolation. Shifting balances were involved.

11. See Provine (1986) for more on Wright's work. On parallel experimentation schemes, see the chapter in this volume and the work of Charles Sabel and colleagues (such as, William H. Simon and Michael Dorf), for example, Dorf and Sabel (1998), in what might be called the Columbia school of legal pragmatism—itself the fruit of the joining across sectors of a politico-economic sociologist (Sabel) and legal scholars.

12. The problem of using new knowledge (either an innovation or new imported knowledge) to produce other products off the main line of business is related to what Norbert Wiener called the "inverse process of invention." Ordinarily we think of starting with a problem and then making an innovation or invention to solve the problem. But with the new "solution" in hand, we might then search for what other problems it might be able to solve. "It is just as truly a work of invention or discovery to find out what we are able to accomplish by the use of these new tools as it is

to search for the tools which will make possible a specific new device or method" (Wiener 1993, 91).

13. Or as Marx would put it, the mode of production puts fetters on the forces of production. And as recent history has confirmed, real-existing socialism put even greater fetters on the forces of production.

14. Jacobs gives an example from a service sector. "For one thing, restaurant chains keep splitting off new restaurants. Indeed, that is how they become chains in the first place—not by merely trying to add more tables, customers, cooks and cashiers into an ever bigger and bigger restaurant, but by multiplying into more restaurants. Besides that, restaurants give birth to independent progeny which are not branches or subsidiaries, but genuinely new enterprises" (Jacobs 1980, 67).

15. See http://www.thermo.com/; Peters (1992), and Bailey and Syre (1996).

16. There is no intrinsic reason why spin-offs should be restricted to new products. Even routine parts of the operation, such as copying (and printing), trucking, food preparation, secretarial services, cleaning services, and the like, could be spun out with long-term contracts to keep the original business with the mother firm (so the jobs are not "put to competition" for the old business). Then the spin-outs could fill many niches for similar work in the business environment which would expand the old work and perhaps diversify into new work—all of which would not happen while it remained a sterile captive of the internal division of labor in the mother firm.

17. In Taiwan, the spin-off entrepreneurs are said to prefer being the "head of a chicken than the tail of a horse." See Jacobs (1984, 99–102) on the Taiwanese experience.

18. Jacobs has noted the connection between top-down power and empire-building: "The biggest and most thoroughly centralized governments have always, finally, required the special environment of oppression to continue to maintain themselves. And some could never have attained their great size at all had they not grown in that environment" (Jacobs 1980, 77).

19. The virtues of small countries are more fully developed in the work of Leopold Kohr (1978).

20. In biological terms, the more that power is bottom-up in a firm, the more it is like an organism with reproductive cells under decentralized control throughout the organism rather than under central control in one specialized part.

21. For details, see the account by a preeminent American organizational theorist and his wife, Whyte and Whyte (1991).

22. In a democratic firm, where "corporate governance" is more than an oxymoronic phrase, the quality of the self-governance deteriorates as the firm gets larger so firms will tend to naturally subdivide anyway to keep the membership at workable levels. The upper limit might be between several hundred and a thousand members depending on the technologies involved.

23. See Ellerman (2003a) for more on this remarkable theory about migration. By this theory, just as a suburban bedroom community would not be considered "undeveloped" because the jobs were in a nearby city, so in today's globalized world, a country that accepted the "international division of labor" as a supplier of transnational labor would not be "undeveloped"—it is only a "bedroom community" vis-à-vis the developed world.

24. "Possibly because so many ambitious and expensive attempts to force or coax economic expansion have failed during the second half of the twentieth century, it has finally become permissible to say that the emperor has no clothes—that economic theory can't explain economic expansion" (Jacobs 2000, 158).

25. "A system—any system, economic or other—that at *every* point of time fully utilizes its possibilities to the best advantage may yet in the long run be inferior to a system that does so at *no* given point of time, because the latter's failure to do so may be a condition for the level or speed of long-run performance" (Schumpeter 1962, 83).

26. See Lovejoy (1960, 293–94) on "diversity itself as the essence of excellence" (quoted in Jacobs 1980, 114) and Kanigel (1997) on the "One Best Way."

Chapter 2

Two Institutional Logics

Exit versus Voice and Commitment

INTRODUCTION: THE TWO LOGICS

There are two logics, dual to one another, that run throughout mathematics and the sciences as well as throughout questions of institutional design. The underlying duality is series-parallel duality that is best known from electrical circuit theory.[1] The underlying model is the basic choice between multiple components connected in parallel or connected in series as in the two-terminal circuits in figure 2.1).

In a tree search model, there is the branching of a stem into parallel boxes and there is the series connection of boxes to make a long branch. In searching over a tree, there are two logics. If the answer is not found in box A (see figure 2.2), does one backtrack and *exit* the A branch and try a parallel branch (B or C), or does one stay *committed* to the A branch and try further boxes along it (A1 or A2)? If one chooses A1 and it is unsatisfactory ("doesn't have the answer"), then one has the choice to backtrack and exit the A1 branch and try A2 (or exit again to try B or C), or to stay committed to the A1 branch and try the further refinements A11 or A12.

The choice is between the parallel-oriented breadth-first strategy and the series-oriented depth-first strategy. "The ideas of breadth and depth are in competition throughout the whole history of combinatorial optimization" (Strang 1986, 609).

The main work on this topic in human affairs is Albert Hirschman's (1970) development of the contrast between the parallel-oriented logic of exit (exit the branch to try other branches) and the series-oriented logic of voice, loyalty, and commitment (stay loyal and committed to the given branch by searching further along it).[2]

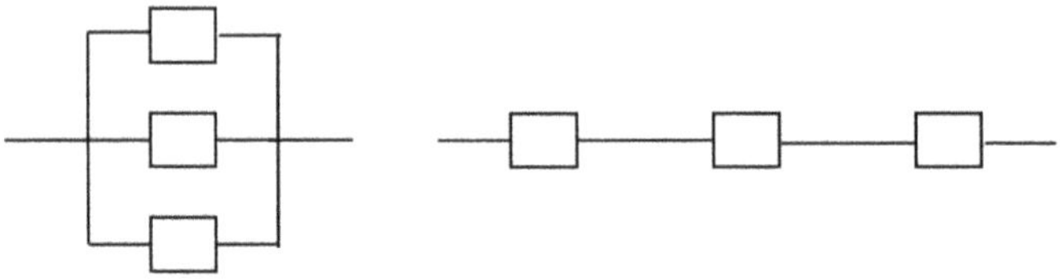

Figure 2.1 Parallel and Series Connections of Components.

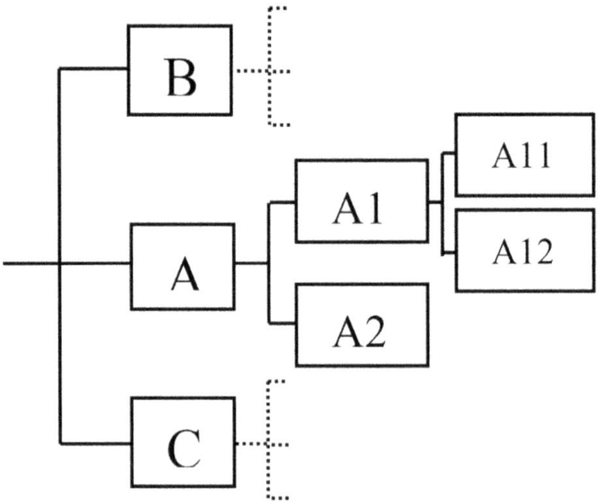

Figure 2.2 Breadth-First Search versus Depth-First Search.

As a variation on the tree model, we could think of options with characteristics. Suppose one has an option with unsatisfactory characteristics. Does one treat the characteristics as fixed and then seek improvement by exiting the option to find a better one? Or does one stick with the given option and try to change the characteristics for the better?[3] Hirschman referred to the change-the-characteristics strategy as *voice*: "Voice is here defined as any attempt at all to change, rather than to escape from, an objectionable state of affairs" (Hirschman 1970, 30). These two logics of exit or voice (commitment) are quite common in human affairs. Does the "unhappy camper" fold his tent and look for a better campsite or does he work to make the given campsite better? Every potential migrant faces the question: Exit to find a better home or commit to making home better?

Managers constantly face similar decisions. When a team of workers is not performing satisfactorily, the manager has two choices. One choice is to take the capabilities of the team members as fixed so that people need to be shuffled in and out of the team until the right team characteristics are obtained. Or a manager might proceed with more commitment to the team members and then try to work with them to better develop their capabilities until the team performed satisfactorily.

The two logics are quite ubiquitous. I will call the parallel-oriented approach in an organizational or institutional context, the *logic of exit*. Decline and dissatisfaction leads to exit and replacement. I will call the series-oriented approach using voice in an institutional context, the *logic of commitment*.[4] Decline and dissatisfaction leads to renewed commitment and the attempt to transform the characteristics (e.g., through the exercise of voice).

FIVE POINTS ON THE TWO LOGICS

My first point is simply the ubiquity of the two logics—as I hope will become clear in the course of the argument. I will focus on cases where the two system logics are incompatible rather than cases where they need to be blended to find the best system.

The second point is that sometimes there seems to be an awareness of only one logic, for example the belief that improvement can only come through exit and replacement. For a trivial example, young people might think that the only response to a dull razor blade is to throw it away and replace it with a new sharp blade. But in "the old days" there were straight razors; when the blade got dull, one would sharpen it. This is an example of the two logics as the replace versus repair strategies: buy cheap replaceable items and replace as necessary or buy more expensive quality items and repair as necessary.

The third point is that often the desired performance can be obtained by using a system based on either the logic of exit or the logic of commitment. Both ways are possible; the best system will depend on the particular circumstances.

The fourth point is that there are often interdependencies in a system based on one of the logics so that hybrids tend to be lethal rather than vigorous. If one tries to "mix and match" exit-based components with commitment-based components, then the system will most likely malfunction.[5]

For instance, in an exit-based system of conflictual labor relations, large inventories help to mitigate the holdup problem of workers going on strike. A just-in-time inventory system fits together with cooperative labor relations. But if a company with conflictual labor relations decides to try a just-in-time system to save on inventory costs, then any labor conflicts (e.g., truckers) will lead to costly holdups for the company.

Or in an exit-oriented system of arms-length finance, companies need low leverage and a large equity buffer since when the company hits some turbulence, their financiers may not be willing to extend or rollover their loans. But in a commitment-oriented system of relational finance, firms can have more leverage since their financiers are expected to stay committed in times of trouble.[6]

One of the (partial) explanations for the East Asian crisis in the late 1990s was that the globalization of finance tempted highly leveraged firms in countries that historically had relational finance (e.g., Korea) to "take advantage" of the cheap and easy finance available from international (arms-length) financiers. But then small shocks to the new "hybrid" system were soon amplified to a crisis when arms-length financiers did not rollover loans and firms had too much leverage to ride out the shocks. In such a system that got stuck halfway between the two system logics, there are two basic policy options. One option is to make a wholesale conversion to an exit-based system of arms-length finance. The other option is to curtail the impact of the exit-based features to maintain functionality in a modernized commitment-based system, for example, using capital controls to install "speed bumps" on the "hot money highway" of globalized arms-length finance.

The fifth point is that while one system logic may be appropriate in one case and the other logic in another case, there is however a "worst of both worlds" hybrid which combines the fixed characteristics of the one logic with the fixity of the option in the other logic. If both the option and the characteristics are fixed, then one has an unviable "lethal hybrid" that cannot change in the face of adversity and decline. Unfortunately, some attempts to create hybrids with the virtues of both logics may end up with the worst case that only combines their vices.[7] And some attempts to jump over the chasm by converting a system based on one logic into a system with the other logic may stall halfway across and fall into the chasm to get the "worst of both worlds."

I am focusing on cases where the two logics tend to be antagonistic or mutually exclusive (i.e., hybrids are more lethal than vigorous) so that the system needs to be based on one logic or the other. If the two logics are on the two axes, then we are interested in cases where the best solution is a corner solution.

There is a whole range of cases where the two logics are complementary rather than antagonistic. The logics appear as two "moments" that need to be optimally combined to have the best solution. Then the best case is not a corner solution but some convex combination of the two moments. For instance in complex adaptive systems, the parallel-oriented moment is called *exploration* (or variation) and the series-oriented moment is *exploitation* (or selection).[8] If the goal of the model is to reach a higher altitude on a rugged and cloudy "adaptive landscape," then exploitation means staying committed to the given hill and climbing higher on it, while exploration means jumping, traversing, or otherwise exiting to another hill that may be higher. In such a system, a corner solution would not work. A system with all exploration would jump in an agitated manner from hill to hill without settling down to climbing higher on any hill. A system with all exploitation would only climb the hill it is on so it would tend to get stuck on a low hill.[9]

TWO WAYS TO PUT EGGS IN BASKETS

One of my theses is that often there seems to an awareness of only one system logic to the exclusion of the other. This is probably nowhere truer than in neoclassical economics which is based on the exit-oriented logic of the market. But the one-sidedness also extends to basic questions of handling risks. One often finds the almost knee-jerk response to any risk problem; the solution is the parallel-oriented strategy of diversification. "Don't put all your eggs in one basket." Use one's resources to place many small bets rather than one or a few large bets. In terms of a tree search, this is the strategy of making an extensive parallel search of the first boxes on many different branches rather than an intensive search over the series of boxes along one branch.

The usual diversification recommendation to "spread your eggs between many baskets" makes the implicit assumption that the baskets have fixed characteristics (e.g., a fixed probability that the eggs in a basket will be broken by the basket tipping over or being dropped). But if the characteristics of some baskets can be significantly changed by a commitment of attention and control to one or a few baskets, then the dual risk reduction strategy emerges. Put all your eggs in one or a few baskets, watch them very carefully, and make sure the baskets are not tipped over or dropped.[10]

The logic of commitment enters through the door of flexible characteristics—in this case, the risk characteristics. The probabilities of a person having an accident might not be fixed independently of the person's activities but might depend on the precautions taken by the person. When the logic of exit (diversification) works *too* well, for example complete insurance against the consequences of accidents, then the insured will neglect taking precautions and hazards will increase, that is, moral hazard. To combat moral hazard, one has to move back a little way toward the logic of commitment by exposing the insured to some of the costs of accidents, for example deductibles and co-pay in medical insurance.

This foreshadows a basic theme. When the choice environment is parsed into a set of options each having certain characteristics, the choice of a commitment-oriented strategy or an exit-oriented strategy will in part depend, respectively, on the extent to which the characteristics are flexible or are fixed.

TWO BIOLOGICAL REPRODUCTIVE STRATEGIES

The choice of risk reduction strategy hinges on the question of whether or not a commitment of resources to one or a few options can significantly change the risk characteristics of those options. In biology, all organisms face the reproductive risk that their genes may not survive into the next generation.

Since organisms only have limited reproductive resources to address this risk problem, they tend to "choose" one or the other of the "corner solutions" to solving this risk reduction problem.

If organisms have little or no control over the risk characteristics faced by their offspring, then the organisms will tend to favor a diversification strategy called *r selection*. They spread their reproductive resources over many offspring as with most insects and fish, and then the offspring face the odds with little or no parental assistance. The emphasis is on the quantity rather than quality of offspring. However, if the parents can significantly control the risk characteristics faced by their offspring and if the offspring can be produced with a "quality" to improve their odds, then that species will tend to favor the commitment-oriented strategy called *K selection*. They invest their reproductive resources in a few "quality" offspring as with mammals and then they provide intensive parental care to the offspring.

TWO WAYS TO INCREASE RELIABILITY

Another example is from reliability theory in engineering. The risk is system failure when a component breaks down. The parallel-oriented approach to reducing that risk (increasing reliability) is redundancy. In the general parallel (exit-oriented) case, there may be two ways to explore parallel options, one at a time or, if possible, simultaneously. One form of exit-oriented behavior is to try one option, then another, and so forth. Another form of exit-oriented behavior is to try many options simultaneously as when eggs are spread between many baskets or when biological resources are spread over many offspring. These two forms of the parallel-oriented approach come out clearly in reliability theory.

The one-at-a-time approach to redundancy (parallelism) is called *standby redundancy*. The system uses one option or subsystem until it breaks down and then it switches to the standby system. An airplane might have a standby radio or navigational system; if the primary system breaks down, it can switch to the standby system. The simultaneous approach to parallelism is called *active-parallel redundancy*. For instance, an airplane with several engines is using active-parallel redundancy; if one engine breaks down, hopefully the others will suffice to land the plane safely. Otherwise, they may have to switch to the standby way of getting to the ground safely, parachutes.

Scarce resources are used to build reliability into a system. In some cases, using redundancy to increase reliability may not be technologically possible. The dual way to increase reliability is to use resources to improve the reliability characteristics of the components of the one system. Thus, the trade-off between the two logics in using resources to reduce risks and increase reliability is "redundancy versus improved elements" (Von Alven 1964, 240).

These examples illustrate the second point that there is another way to reduce risks than just distributing one's eggs between many baskets.

THE TWO WAYS TO GET FLEXIBILITY, PERFORMANCE, AND EFFICIENCY

Flexible Options or Flexible Characteristics in Given Option?

In the options and characteristics model, the two system logics differ by what is fixed and what is flexible. With the parallel- or exit-oriented logic, the characteristics of an option are taken as fixed, so flexibility is obtained by exiting one option and taking another. If workers do not have the desired skills for a new technology, then relocate or fire those workers and hire others with the desired characteristics. With the series- or commitment-oriented logic, the option is taken as fixed, so flexibility is obtained by changing the characteristics of the option. Workers with some commitment from the company for employment security would be more willing to learn new skills and retrain for new technologies since they would not be "working themselves out of a job." It is not a question of flexibility or not, but of achieving flexibility in one way in one system or in another way in the other system.

Exit versus commitment are the two logics that run through the design of institutions. The market is an institution that operates largely on the basis of the logic of exit. Economics developed first as the theory of markets and market behavior, so economics tends to see the world through an exit-oriented lens. "The economist tends naturally to think that his mechanism (exit) is far more efficient and is in fact the only one to be taken seriously" (Hirschman 1970, 16). For instance, under the exit-oriented logic all labor questions are "labor market" questions, while under the alternative commitment-oriented logic (e.g., in a Japanese-style firm), a labor question is a "human relations" or "human resources" question.[11]

Organizations (including political units or polities) would seem to be the natural setting for commitment-based strategies. If there are some costs or barriers to exit in the face of dissatisfaction, then the exercise of voice may be the better way to change things. Hence, one might expect to see organizations designed on the basis of the logic of commitment.

Allocative Efficiency or X-Efficiency?

More broadly, take an option to be a particular use of a resource and take the characteristic of the resource to be its productivity or effectiveness in that use. Then the two system logics give two ways to get improved performance and efficiency. The exit-oriented strategy is to move resources to higher-productivity uses (e.g., through the market) and the commitment-oriented strategy is to get higher productivity out of resources in the given use (e.g., in an organization). The exit-oriented notion of efficiency is *allocative efficiency* associated with markets. Resources in a certain use have fixed productivity so it is a question of the allocation of resources to the higher-valued uses. The commitment-oriented notion of efficiency is *X-efficiency* (Leibenstein 1966; 1984) where the principal variable productivity of a resource in a given use (e.g., in an organization) is human effort.[12]

If a skill is quite standardized and available on the market, then in that case the exit-oriented logic can work in a firm. The threat of dismissal calls forth more effort. The low-trust system is self-reinforcing in its system logic. Low trust leads to highly explicit contracts with competitive arms-length relationships with no need to invest in building trust or loyalty, and thus the low-trust environment is reproduced.

But the logic plays out differently when the jobs require more firm-specific skills and where the quality of effort is not only variable but largely hidden. If there was little mutual commitment between the staff and the management, then the staff would have little reason to put forth hidden effort and little incentive to invest time and effort in acquiring firm-specific skills. And management would have little incentive in upgrading staff skills that are not firm specific since the staff might then solicit and accept an offer from another firm that would not need to repeat the training. In firms where firm-specific "human capital" and quality effort are important, the human relations system will tend toward a commitment-based logic (see Blair 1995). A labor union can be a positive contributor to such a human relations strategy (see Freeman and Medoff 1984). High-trust relationships allow more incomplete relational contracts which require investment in building trust and loyalty so that the high-trust environment will be reproduced.

Since low-trust exit-oriented relationships and high-trust commitment-oriented relationships each tend to be self-reinforcing, there are two organizational equilibria. For instance, in Douglas McGregor's management theory (1960), the two equilibria based on the two logics are "Theory X" and "Theory Y."

There is also a motivational aspect to these two logics. The exit-oriented logic emphasized in economics goes along with extrinsic pecuniary motivation. But successful organizations sponsor another type of motivation where the individual "identifies" with the product and the organization, and also where the management shows that it "identifies" with the company staff (all of which might be seen as an "implicit contract" between management and the workers). That is motivational side of the internal commitment-oriented logic in the organization.

THE MODERN WIDELY HELD AMERICAN COMPANY

If the exit logic fits markets and the commitment logic fits organizations, then what would an organization look like if it was based on the logic of exit? This brings us to the "model" of the widely held American corporation. To apply the exit logic, there is one complication. Who's in and who's out? Who are the members of the organization?

There are actually "two companies": the company as a legal entity and the company as a working group of human beings.[13] The legal entity, the legal or de jure *firm*, has the shareholders as the members. But the members of the actual or de facto *firm* are the managers and workers who actually carry out the company's business. In a small closely held company, the de jure firm and the de facto firm are largely the same. But for the large modern publicly traded American company, there is very little overlap between the de jure firm (shareholders) and the de facto firm (employees including managers). Those who are actually inside the company (the staff) are from the legal viewpoint outside the firm and have only a market relationship (employment) with the firm. Those who are legally inside the company (the legal members of the company) are the far-flung shareholders who typically have no business relationship with the company aside from the share ownership and who typically have well-diversified portfolios of shares (figure 2.3).

The commitment-oriented logic of organizational design would be appropriate for a company, but the problem is that there are the two companies. The commitment-oriented design is applied, at best, to the de jure company. The shareholders are seen as the insiders, principals, members, and owners of the (de jure) company. When things are not going well, the shareholders are legally empowered to change "their company." And since the people who actually work in the company, the de facto company, are seen legally as

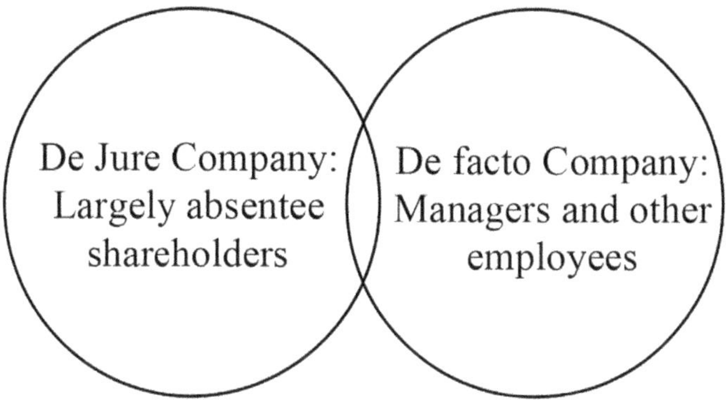

Figure 2.3 The Two Companies in a Publicly Traded American "Company."

having only a market relationship to the company (the employment relation), their role is modeled on an exit-based logic.

In the Anglo-American economies, starting from closely held firms (with little divergence between the de jure and de facto firms) the growth of the public market in equity shares has created these rather odd chimeras. And as the de jure firm ("ownership") has diverged more and more from the actual firm, the legal theory broke down. The transaction costs for dissatisfied far-flung shareholders to organize and actually change things were very high. And the returns from organizing enough shareholders would be shared by all shareholders, so there was also a strong collective action problem. Hence, shareholders used the "Wall Street Rule"; if you don't like the way things are going, exit by selling your shares.

Hence, the people legally empowered to implement a commitment-based strategy ("change things") use a de facto exit-based strategy (sell). And the managers and workers who are de facto in a position to implement a commitment-oriented strategy ("change things") are seen legally as being outsiders ("employees") on the other end of a market relationship with the company. They are not the principals or owners directly empowered by corporate law to change things—so in the eyes of the law, their only option is to quit ("exit") if they are dissatisfied (love it or leave it). Any attempt of workers to organize in unions to secure rights in the firm is seen as antithetical to the exit-based logic of competitive markets. The union is seen as the party on the other side of a contract with the company, not as a part of the internal governance structure of a company. Any attempt of the workers, the members of the de facto firm, to formalize powers to directly "change things" is seen as infringing on the "management rights" exercised by the supposed agents of the far-flung shareholders who are the legal members of the company.

Of course, this bizarre structure would not actually work. Some insiders gladly grabbed the levers of actual control dropped by the shareholders. Those insiders are the top managers, so we arrive at what Adolf Berle and Gardner Means called the "separation of ownership and control" (1932, 89) and at what is currently called the "corporate governance problem." The legal theory or "model" is shareholder capitalism; the underlying actuality is managerial capitalism. Since there is no legal legitimation for the actual system, the public relations machinery in the companies, in the business press, and in academia has broadcast the goal of "maximizing shareholder value" while the managers show their actual goals in their salaries, benefits, perquisites, (manipulated) stock options, and golden parachutes. But recently, the high corporate executive members of the Business Roundtable (2019) have shown that they are no longer willing to pretend being the hirelings of the shareholders. They prefer the role of being seen as the custodians of massive social resources to be managed in the interests of all the stakeholders, not just the shareholders. That is a much more prestigious cover story for the realities of managerial capitalism. And by being accountable to all stakeholders, they are not only in practice but in theory accountable to no group in particular.

And from the motivational viewpoint, the bizarre model structure would not work *unless* those who are legally outsiders on the other end of the employment contract—getting only the economic reward of salary or wage—were to a significant degree committed to and identified with the company. Although this is almost entirely ignored by conventional exit-oriented economics, Herbert Simon has emphasized the point:

> Organizations would be far less effective systems than they actually are if such (economic) rewards were the only means, or even the principal means, of motivation available. In fact, observation of behavior in organizations reveals other powerful motivations that induce employees to accept organizational goals and authority as bases for their actions. . . . (The) most important of these mechanisms (is): organizational identification. (Simon 1991, 34)

Hence, the members of the de facto company do in fact tend to identify with the company even though they are legally outside the company!

The large American firm is actually a rather odd and incoherent organization. Those who are legally inside the firm (shareholders) act as if they were outside, and those who are legally outside the firm (employees) act as if they were inside.

This mismatch between the model and reality leaves the analyst in a quandary. Should one analyze the rather mythical company model as it exists in the lawbooks and in the economics textbooks? That is the "American model" broadcast to the world by ivory tower academics who might think that American companies actually work that way. But since actual organizations need a healthy dose of commitment-oriented behavior to work well, the archetypical exit-oriented "American model" is a textbook model only. The actual large widely held American companies use a version of the logic of commitment. But the top managers who assume and exercise the legal rights of the insiders (owners) often try to treat all the *other* employees as outsiders on an exit-based model (e.g., in the labor relations system). Hence, the actual large widely held American firm ends up being something of a contested battleground between the two logics.

In any case, for analytical purposes we will juxtapose two rather pure models, a firm organized on an exit-based model and a firm organized on a commitment-based model.

THE MODERN JAPANESE COMPANY

In their introduction to a book of essays by Japanese authors about the Japanese-style firm, Ronald Dore and Hugh Whittaker echo Herbert Simon at least about the Japanese case: "Most of the authors would agree that if you want to understand what goes on in Japanese boardrooms, you can throw most of the writings that go under the rubric 'agency theory' out of the window" (1994, 3).

In the postwar era, the large Japanese firms have perhaps gone the furthest to develop the organizational logic of commitment and to contrast it with the logic of exit. For instance, to one trained to think in terms of the logic of exit, any immobilities, rigidities, or barriers to exit would just seem inefficient and irrational. But Japanese economists have evoked the example of useful barriers to exit as in the practice of a captain being expected to go down with his ship.

> The way in which underpayment of wages in the early years of service and the acquisition of firm-specific skills create barriers to exit is obvious. These exit barriers perform several important functions for the firm as an organizational entity. The first is the incentive function whereby the interests of the firm and the interests of the individual are linked. Unable easily to exit, people can only protect their interests by working to ensure that the firm prospers. . . . The interlinking of interests means that when crisis looms, efforts are redoubled. The option of leaving the sinking ship is not freely available, either to the crew or the captain. (Kagono and Kobayashi 1994, 94)

Barriers to exit can enhance identification and thus X-efficiency.[14] During the last quarter century, the township-village enterprises (TVEs) have been a driving part in the remarkable Chinese transition. But their success has been something of a mystery to the orthodox economic viewpoint—lack of conventional ownership and lack of labor market flexibility. The TVEs exemplified the logic of commitment. The management identified with the staff since they had to provide jobs and related services to the people of the township or village, and the workers identified with the firm since that was their one chance for a good job (the Chinese government tried to prevent free mobility). The loss in allocative efficiency due to factor immobility seems to have been more than counterbalanced by the increase in X-efficiency since the Chinese growth episode over the last quarter century is the largest in recorded history.

A simple cooperative action game (of the prisoner's dilemma variety) can be used to illustrate the difference between a company based on low trust with individual optimization and a company based on high trust, identification with the firm, and a cooperative corporate culture (see Leibenstein 1984 for the best treatment of this approach to the Japanese firm). The players A and B could be thought of as managers and workers (or as any two groups in the firm) who need to cooperate together to increase the X-efficiency of the firm (table 2.1).

If each player chooses the individualistic not-cooperate action, then they receive the noncooperative payoff of $A and $B. If they cooperate, then the total result increases by (say) 2 which we assume is evenly split to arrive at the cooperative payoffs of $A+1 and $B+1. But if one party opportunistically chooses the individualistic noncooperative option when the other party acts cooperatively, then the total result remains the same (no increase without cooperation of parties) and two units are shifted to the opportunistic party. The strategy pair (Not Cooperate, Not Cooperate) is the dominant equilibrium solution. No matter which strategy one player chooses, it will always pay the other player to take the noncooperative action. But that noncooperative outcome ($A, $B) is dominated by the cooperative outcome ($A+1, $B+1) which is better for both parties.

This prisoner's dilemma-type game is a generic representation of the countless cooperative action situations that occur continuously and at every level in the complex multiperson productive operation of a firm. In each given situation, effective monitoring and enforcement might be applied at a certain cost to change the payoffs and thus assure the cooperative outcome. But this "external" neoclassical solution is hardly feasible over the countless cooperative action situations that occur in a complex team operation.

> The question is not whether free riders exist—much less employees who exert something less than their maximum—but why there is anything *besides* free-riding. Why do many workers, perhaps most, exert more than minimally enforceable effort? Why do employees identity with organizational goals at all? (Simon 1991, 34)

That question is left unanswered in the exit-based American-style model. The Japanese-style company uses the alternative "internal" solution of developing a corporate culture of mutual commitment and cooperation that leads to

Table 2.1 Typical Cooperative Action Game

		Payoff to	*Player B*
	Payoff to Player A, B	Cooperate	Not Cooperate
Payoff to	Cooperate	$A+1, $B+1	$A–2, $B+2
Player A	Not Cooperate	$A+2, $B–2	$A, $B

Source: Author.

a virtuous circle or high-level self-reinforcing equilibrium. This cooperative culture is feasible because the managers and workers see themselves as the members of a commitment-based community and will reap the joint fruits of their cooperative efforts.

One logic or the other ramifies through all the aspects and structures of a firm. Sometimes a firm organized on the logic of exit is stereotyped as the "American firm" and a firm organized on the logic of commitment is the "Japanese firm" or "J-firm" (Aoki 1988). But without promoting stereotypes, we can still summarize and compare in table 2.2 some of the ways that the two logics affect firm structure.[15]

OWNERSHIP FOR LIQUIDITY OR FOR ENTERPRISE?

Perhaps the last line of table 2.2 requires some explanation. We can distill this wisdom from the academic scribblings of the defunct economist, John Maynard Keynes. Keynes was much concerned with the adverse effects of the stock exchange on real investment and enterprise. Investment in productive enterprise is largely irrevocable, and the management of enterprise requires a long-term commitment and the application of "intelligence to defeat the forces of time and ignorance of the future" (Keynes 1936, 157).[16] In short, it is based on the logic of loyalty and commitment. But when investment is securitized as a marketable asset on the stock exchange, then it "is as though a farmer, having tapped his barometer after breakfast, could decide to remove his capital from the farming business between 10 and 11 in the morning and reconsider whether he should return to it later in the week" (Keynes 1936, 151). The stock exchange panders to the "fetish of liquidity" and thus continually undermines the bonds of long-term commitment that are so important to problem-solving and productive enterprise. Keynes, of course, wrote this long before today's problems with stock options and short-termism. Today's practice of the captain's exit facilitated by a golden parachute is the opposite of the practice of the captain going down with the ship.

In addition to this continual erosive effect, the stock exchange also absorbs otherwise productive capital in the function of speculation—which Keynes defined as "the activity of forecasting the psychology of the market" (Ibid., 158). Keynes saw no problem when speculation was but a bubble on the stream of enterprise, but it was quite another matter "when enterprise becomes a bubble on a whirlpool of speculation. When the capital development of a country becomes a by-product of the activities of a casino, the job is likely to be ill-done" (Ibid. 159). This is even more true when the casino is global rather than national.

Table 2.2 Two Firms

	Firm Based on Logic of Exit	*Firm Based on Logic of Commitment*
Efficiency	Allocative efficiency: moving resources to the use with the best return (high mobility).	X-efficiency: getting the best return from resources in the given uses (low mobility).
Change strategy	Replace what you have with something better. Problem is to improve choice among options with fixed characteristics.	Transform what you have into something better. Problem is the transformation of given option to improve its characteristics.
Source of flexibility and change	Exit (change takes place through entry and exit from the organization). Rather flight than fight. Error leads to replacement.	Voice (change takes place by transformation within organization). Rather fight than flight. Error leads to learning.
Labor mobility	High mobility so changes take place primarily by hiring workers embodying new knowledge.	Low mobility so changes take place primarily by workers learning new knowledge and skills.
Contractual relationships	Arms-length.	Relational.
Role of management	Agents of shareholders.	Senior leaders of community.
Role of company board	Representatives of shareholders.	Council of community elders with representatives of major related organizations (e.g., main bank).
Role of shareholders	Absentee investors.	One of stakeholder groups along with suppliers and customers.
Shareholder interest	Maximization of company profit (assumption that shareholders are normally unrelated to company).	Shareholding often representative of business relationships, the latter being the primary economic interest. Little attention to unrelated floating shareholders.
Transactions with related shareholders	To be controlled by independent directors or forbidden by "firewall" regulations.	Normal part of relational contracting where shareholding is symbolic of business relationship (called "cronyism" by critics).
Model of supplier relationships	Competition between standardized producers with feedback through the market.	Cooperation with a small number of suppliers to continuously improve product through nonmarket feedback.

(*Continued*)

Table 2.2 Two Firms *(Continued)*

	Firm Based on Logic of Exit	*Firm Based on Logic of Commitment*
Relations to suppliers and customers	Auction market contracting based on assumption of mobility and exit leading to greater allocative efficiency.	Relational contracting based on assumption of immobility and voice leading to greater X-efficiency.
Stability in relationships	Low-trust relationships ⇒ highly explicit contracts with competitive arms-length exit-oriented relationships so no need to invest in building trust ⇒ low-trust relationships.	High-trust relationships ⇒ incomplete relational contracts with voice-oriented relationships requiring investment in building trust ⇒ high-trust relationships.
Style of interpersonal relationships	Standardized, professionalized behavior as a means of coordinating people. Low interpersonal knowledge associated with high turnover.	Familiarity, intimacy in long-term relationships as means of coordinating people. High interpersonal knowledge associated with low turnover.
Labor training	Responsibility of worker as it increases value on labor market.	Responsibility of company since immobility allows company to benefit.
Job definition	Extensively specified job definition to limit opportunism since there is little commitment.	Job flexibility and low monitoring based on worker commitment to company.
Wage determination	Rate for job determined by market. Payment attached to job. Equal pay for equal work.	Rate determined by seniority and assessed merit. Payment attached to person. Undergoing rate at beginning and over it at end as an incentive to stay.
Worker motivation	Individual pecuniary self-interest (noncooperative strategy).	Members expected to identify with firm and shared interest (cooperative strategy).
Organized worker representation	Trade union (adversary relation based on workers versus company)—my jam or your jam.	Enterprise union (oppositional relation loyal to company)—our jam today or our jam tomorrow.
Response to decline	Reduce employment and other direct costs to maintain profits.	Maintain employment, reduce hours, and retrain workers for new product lines.
Business ownership	Stock market liquidity. Firm as "investment."	Illiquidity of closely held business. Firm as enterprise.

Source: Author.

Today, Keynes's "stock exchange" must be updated to the global market for bonds, stocks, and currencies. The dangers to investment in enterprise that Keynes highlighted during his day are even greater in our own. Yet Keynes recognized that there is no simple answer in making investment illiquid as "this might seriously impede new investment." Few will enter if the door locks behind them. "This is the dilemma" (Ibid. 160). But since investors on today's public capital markets are not enterprisers, the solution lies in the direction of converting equity shares into variable income debt-like instruments that are still liquid.

MARKETS AND ORGANIZATIONS: NOT ONLY MARKETS

Consider the application of the logic of exit versus the logic of commitment in an organization. The exit logic looks at an individual as a market participant—even inside an organization. The individual's actions within the organization are evaluated according to how the actions affect the person's market opportunities, for example in acquiring more marketable skills, increasing bargaining power, and the like.

In contrast, the logic of commitment looks at the individual as a member of an organization so that a different set of factors come into play such as trust, voice, firm-specific skills, cooperation, voice, and identification with the organization. It is this whole logic of commitment and the conception of an organization other than just a nexus of market contracts that is missing in the vision of conventional neoclassical economics. Thus, all the investment climate reasoning concerned with building productive organizations tends to be ignored unless it can be reduced back to market behavior.

HERBERT SIMON'S VISION OF THE ORGANIZATIONAL ECONOMY

One person who spanned the disciplines of economics and organizational theory and who spent a lifetime investigating both markets and organizations was economics Nobel-laureate Herbert Simon. Economists tend to have a cognitive map of the world (like Saul Steinberg's famous *New Yorker* cover) where markets dominate the landscape except for small market failures (small "lumps in a pail of buttermilk") known as "organizations" off in the distance. Having studied both organizations and markets throughout his career, Simon found that the reality in the advanced economies was almost the opposite.

Instead of thick markets connecting small organizational dots, Simon saw a world of organizations with thin markets connecting them. Indeed, he objected to the very phrase "market economy."

> The economies of modern industrialized society can more appropriately be labeled organizational economies than market economies. Thus, even market-driven capitalist economies need a theory of organizations as much as they need a theory of markets. The attempts of the new institutional economics to explain organizational behavior solely in terms of agency, asymmetric information, transaction costs, opportunism, and other concepts drawn from neo-classical economics ignore key organizational mechanisms like authority, identification, and coordination, and hence are seriously incomplete. (Simon 1991, 42)

The economic theory of contracts and agency imagines a world where causal chains are well defined, where consequences can be imputed, at least probabilistically, to specific agents, where contracts can be clearly drafted, where performance criteria can be explicitly specified and they measure the right variables, and where fulfillment of the criteria or lack thereof can be objectively verified. It is a world where "complexity, uncertainty, instability, uniqueness, and value conflicts" (Schön 1983, 14) or, again, "uncertainty, complexity, and value conflict" (Hirschman and Lindblom 1971) can be somehow controlled or ignored. In such an imagined world, much of human activity could be carried out under performance-based contracts.

> But such (performance-based) reward systems are effective only to the extent that success can be attributed accurately to individual behaviors. If the indices used to measure outcomes are inappropriate, either because they do not measure the right variables, or because they do not properly identify individual contributions, then reward systems can be grossly inefficient or even counterproductive. (Simon 1991, 33)

Simon went on to note that these considerations are not nit-picking; they cut to the core of the rationale for organizations rather than markets.

> In general, the greater the interdependence among various members of the organization, the more difficult it is to measure separate contributions to the achievement of the organizational goals. But of course, intense interdependence is precisely what makes it advantageous to organize people (i.e., in organizations) instead of depending wholly on market transactions. The measurement difficulties associated with tying rewards to contributions are not superficial but arise from the very nature and rationale of organization. (Simon 1991, 33)

THE PERIODIC "(RE-)DISCOVERY" OF PERFORMANCE-BASED CONTRACTS

One area where these issues are periodically played out is that of output-based or performance-based contracts. From time to time, private sector management "discovers" the idea of paying for performance (not just for time put in), of paying for outputs (not just inputs), and of management by objectives accomplished (not just intentions). It all sounds so obvious and so sensible that one must ask, "Why didn't people think of this before?" The answer is that they did. And they discovered that it doesn't work too well—aside from fairly rude forms of labor. In areas of human effort where effort, commitment, and the application of intelligence are important, the carrots and sticks of external motivation are insufficient for sustained performance (see, for example, Chapter 11 on "Inducements" in Stone 1997). Beyond simple and specific products, the determinants of quality are rarely susceptible to external monitoring.

One area where these issues periodically play out is in education. In the United States today, parents and local politicians are "discovering" the idea of paying teachers for performance. One would hope that the substantive goal of schoolteachers is to awaken and foster a self-starting learning capacity in the students—but that goal is difficult for a third party to objectively certify. Hence, the measurable proxy goal of passing standard tests is used, and then teachers are pushed by educational administrators to fulfill the "performance-based" requirements by drilling students to pass the standard tests. In this way, the shoe-horning of education into the procrustean bed of performance-based contracts would probably do more harm than good to the original substantive goals of education.

What sort of activities can or cannot be farmed out to arms-length market-based private provisioners under performance-based contracts? Even in a country with highly developed markets such as the United States, there is considerable controversy about maximal private provisioning (e.g., public schools, public safety, social welfare services, public health services, prisons, and so forth). It is even more controversial in Europe. When this philosophy is mired in controversy in developed market economies, then it is very difficult to understand how private provisioning with output-based contracts could be done well in the developing countries with their much less developed markets.

EXTRINSIC AND INTRINSIC MOTIVATION

But let us assume away the problems of identifying and measuring the relevant variables and let us heroically assume away the "uncertainty, complexity, and value conflict" that afflicts human activities. Could we *then* replace governmental and private organizations with virtual nexuses of performance-based contracts? This brings us to the question of motivation. The economic theory of agency contracts is based on "economic" motivation, the "carrots" of monetary compensation, and the "sticks" of contractual penalties or termination of contracts. But this approach to motivation is based only the extrinsic motivation that can be used by the "principal" to control the behavior of the "agent." Yet it seems that extrinsic motivation works as a long-term motivator for only a rather narrow band of rudimentary activities ("ditch-digging" and piecework are classic examples). More often the intrinsic motivators of craftsmanship, workmanship, professionalism, pride, self-esteem, and a sense of vocation, calling, and organizational identification are prominent, and the extrinsic motivators of "carrots and sticks"—while still important—are more in the motivational background.

Piece rates and pay-for-performance schemes are examples of carrots in the foreground trying to get people's attention and guide their actions. An equitable salary more geared to experience and seniority would be an example of keeping the carrot of pay in the motivational background so that other more intrinsic motives might emerge in the foreground to guide action. The tight coupling of pay with performance, as implied by agency theory, is beside the point when the pay is in the background.

These considerations are quite clear in the quality-based (e.g., "Japanese") management methods that take organization seriously. For instance, Edward Deming's "New Economics" recommends to "abolish incentive pay and pay based on performance" (1994, 28), for example to pay salespeople by salary rather than by commission. Deming recommends replacing a system based on close monitoring and quality bonuses with a system using (for the most part) trust based on self-esteem and pride in the quality of one's work. This approach to quality relies not on cleverly constructed pay-for-performance schedules but on switching over to a quality system driven largely by intrinsic motivators such as self-esteem and pride in one's work—in short, quality as a calling. Simon came to similar conclusions about organizations in general. He identifies pride in work and organizational identification as some of the most important motivators. These intrinsic motivators are not controlled by the purse strings of managers. Other influential management theorists make the same point.

> "Intrinsic" rewards . . . are inherent in the activity itself; the reward is the achievement. They cannot be *directly* controlled externally, although characteristics of the environment can enhance or limit the individual's opportunities to obtain them. Thus, achievement of knowledge or skill, of autonomy, of self-respect, of solutions to problems are examples. (McGregor 1966, 203–04)

Paying someone to "identify" with the organization is like trying to "buy love." The means corrupts and falsifies the end.

ANOTHER LOOK AT CORPORATIONS

Since the American "model" is essentially only a textbook and lawbook model, to what extent is it really a possible option? In the American model, the employees have the legal role as the outside suppliers of an input—but in fact they are the firm as an organization of people. This leads to a remarkable schizophrenia of the "two companies." There is the firm in the eyes of the law whose members are the shareholders scattered far and wide, and who typically trade into the stock simply as an investment without any intent or capacity to play a human role in the firm. This is the firm that has a "meeting" once a year. In contrast to this de jure firm, there is the de facto firm consisting of the people who work in the firm—who have a meeting every working day to actual produce the product and conduct the business of the firm.

The large widely held American company actually *works* because most of those who are legally inside realize that they are really outside and act like it (absentee shareholders using logic of exit), and most of those who are legally outside the company act like they are inside it (employees identifying with the company). Thus, the actual American-style company is torn between the two logics and tends to work well only when it ignores the exit-oriented design logic and uses the logic of commitment.

In figure 2.3, the two companies were presented as a Venn diagram of two overlapping circles. There are four areas, the two parts in one circle but not the other, the overlap, and the area outside both circles. These four areas can also be represented in 2 x 2 table 2.3 of the parties in or out of the legal (de jure) firm and in or out of the de facto firm.

Ordinary consciousness often reflects the de facto company. The employees are often thought of as the members of the organization. Consider the following from a perfectly standard managerial accounting textbook:

> An organization can be defined as a group of people united together for some common purpose. A bank providing financial services is an organization, as is a university providing educational services, and the General Electric Company producing appliances and other products. An organization consists of *people*, not physical assets. Thus, a bank building is not an organization; rather, the organization consists of the people who work in the bank and who are bound together for the common purpose of providing financial services to a community. (Garrison 1979, 2)

Table 2.3 Who's In and Who's Out of the Two Companies

	Inside De Facto Company	*Outside De Facto Company*
Inside legal company	Shareholder members working in company	Absentee "members" (shareholders) of company
Outside legal company	Employees of company	Suppliers of things to company

Source: Author.

Garrison is talking entirely about the de facto company, not the company as it exists in law. Look at the books on the business shelves in your local bookstore. Find a book that uses some expression like "members" of the company. Chances are that the author, like Garrison above, is referring to the employees (including managers) of the firm, not the far-flung shareholders who are the legal "members."

As Anglo-American stock markets have spread shares far and wide, the idea that the stockholders are in any real sense the "owners" or "members" of a publicly traded company has become a sheer fantasy. There are several groups invested in keeping the fantasy alive. Many economists and lawyers have acquired their professional competence in mastering the legal model and the economic logic of exit behind it. Anything else falls short of the One Best Model. And there are the top managers who have mightily profited from the eclipse of the shareholders. They have every interest in keeping the fantasy of "shareholder capitalism" alive as the cover story for the reality of managerial capitalism—much as the nomenklatura of the Communist Party had every interest in keeping the fantasy of "People's Democracy" alive.

What Berle and Means described as the "separation of ownership and control," John Maynard Keynes described as the "euthanasia of the rentier, of the functionless investor" (Keynes 1936, 376) caused by the public equity markets. This separation of ownership and control along with the unaccountability of managers and the resulting abuses has created the "corporate governance problem." Who is to be the new legitimate members of the company? While a few wistfully hope for the resurrection of "responsible private owners" in the form of massive institutional investors run by portfolio-managing bureaucrats, others search the horizon for various "stakeholders" who together with the regulatory agencies and law courts might create a "new accountability." But they are searching for legitimacy in all the wrong places.

There already is a class of members who make up the firm, the de facto firm consisting of the people who work in it. In a company designed on the basis of the logic of commitment, they would be the legal members of the company. That would extend the virtues of the family firm and the family farm (both having de facto firm = de jure firm) to the large corporation.

Many parties have their interests affected by a company, and better judicial and regulatory oversight is needed to protect those legitimate outside interests. But since the staff of a company are the de facto firm, they are the ones who could actually monitor the management of their company to address the corporate governance problem directly. "The only cohesive, workable, and effective constituency within view is the corporation's work force" (Flynn 1973, 106).

The British conservative Lord Eustice Percy put the matter well sixty years ago:

> Here is the most urgent challenge to political invention ever offered to the jurist and the statesman. The human association which in fact produces and distributes wealth, the association of workmen, managers, technicians and directors, is not an association recognised by the law. The association which the law does recognise—the association of shareholders, creditors and directors—is incapable of production and is not expected by the law to perform these functions. We have to give law to the real association and withdraw meaningless privilege from the imaginary one. (Percy 1944, 38; quoted in Goyder 1961, 57)

To conclude, we cannot do better than quote the visionary corporate leader, Owen D. Young (1874–1962), founder of RCA, president and chairman of General Electric, and *Time* magazine Man of the Year for 1929:

> Perhaps someday we may be able to organize the human beings engaged in a particular undertaking so that they truly will be the employer buying capital as a commodity in the market at the lowest price . . . . If that is realized, the human beings will then be entitled to all the profits over the cost of capital. I hope the day may come when these great business organizations will truly belong to the men who are giving their lives and their efforts to them, I care not in what capacity. Then they will use capital truly as a tool and they will be all interested in working it to the highest economic advantage. . . . Then we shall dispose, once and for all, of the charge that in industry organizations are autocratic and not democratic. . . . Then, in a word, men will be as free in cooperative undertakings and subject only to the same limitations and chances as men in individual businesses. Then we shall have no hired men. (Young 1927, 392)

Yes, then we shall have no more rented[17] people.

NOTES

1. The duality that is more familiar in economics is convex duality (Rockafellar 1970). The dualities are related; convex duality is the integral or anti-derivative of series-parallel duality (see "Parallel Addition, Series-Parallel Duality, and Financial Mathematics," chapter 12 in Ellerman 1995).

2. Jane Jacobs (1992) develops a variation of the theme with the contrast between the exit-oriented commercial syndrome and the commitment-oriented guardian syndrome.

3. In the correspondence between the tree search model and the options-characteristics model, the breadth-first strategy corresponds to treating characteristics as

fixed so as to favor exit (from A to B or C), and the depth-first model corresponds to sticking with an option but trying to change its characteristics (from A to A1 or A2).

4. The expressions "logic of exit" and "logic of commitment" are used by Kagono and Kobayashi (1994), who develop the two logics of organizational design by contrasting the American-style firm and the Japanese-style firm (see the section below on "The Modern Japanese Company").

5. See Jacobs's analysis (1992) of corruption resulting from a "monstrous hybrid" between the commercial and guardian syndromes.

6. See Goldberg (1980) for the contrast between relational and arms-length contracts.

7. For instance, many Panglossian treatments of migration and development see people using the "exit to find a better home" logic but then either returning from a "temporary" migration with needed skills or at least sending back remittances to fuel local development so that the virtue of "committing to make home better" will also be realized. But, as the saying goes, "there is nothing more permanent than 'temporary' migration" and the remittances are spent largely for consumption purposes; see Jacobs (1984, 122) on remittances; and overall, see Ellerman (2003a). In this case, the desire to take the exit logic but still get the virtues of the other logic has largely proved to be a vain hope.

8. See, for example, Pagels (1988) or Axelrod and Cohen (1999).

9. Economists often assume a simplified "one hill" model where hill-climbing mechanisms (local optimization) will suffice.

10. Hence, probability theory neglects the dual risk reduction strategy when it takes the probability distribution as being independent of the "bets" made on each outcome.

11. For instance, the advice of the World Bank to developing countries about labor is in the "labor markets" topic area; there is no "human resources" topic area. But for its own staff within the World Bank, there is a Human Resources vice president but no "Labor Market Vice President." Thus, the Bank staff looks outward for clients through an exit-oriented lens and inward for themselves through a commitment-oriented lens.

12. Notice that the exercise of voice now appears as the exercise or calling forth of effort broadly interpreted. Although the terminology of X-efficiency came later, Hirschman has emphasized the importance of the alternative notion of efficiency in economic development: "development depends not so much on finding optimal combinations for given resources and factors of production as on calling forth and enlisting for development purposes resources and abilities that are hidden, scattered, or badly utilized" (1958, 5).

13. For instance, in the management literature this is closely related to W. Richard Scott's (1998) distinction between a corporation as a "rational system" and as a "natural system."

14. A perfect labor market is similar to perfect insurance in that it gives workers no incentive to put forth effort (i.e., improve their effort characteristics) since, if caught shirking, they can exit and costlessly find the equivalent job elsewhere. The efficiency wage hypothesis is that firms will introduce imperfections by paying more than the

supply price for a standard type of work so that workers will have something to lose if found to be shirking. See Akerlof and Yellen (1986).

15. See Clark (1979) or Dore (1987) for similar tables.

16. In the same vein, Hirschman refers to "that 'long confrontation between man and a situation' (Camus) so fruitful for the achievement of genuine progress in problem-solving" (Hirschman 1973, 240).

17. The reference to the employment relationship as the *renting* of persons is unusual but technically correct and not a point of controversy; it is fully acknowledged in conventional economics itself. As Paul Samuelson (1915–2009), the first American Economics Nobel prize winner, put it in his economics textbook: "Since slavery was abolished, human earning power is forbidden by law to be capitalized. A man is not even free to sell himself: he must *rent* himself at a wage" (Samuelson 1976, 52 [his italics]).

Chapter 3

Parallel Experimentation

INTRODUCTION

In the late nineteenth and early twentieth centuries, evolutionary analogies smacked of the cut-throat, survival-of-the-fittest, and red-in-tooth-and-claw imagery of social Darwinism and free-market economics. Today this has much changed due in part to revolutions in biology itself and in part to the modeling of "biological" processes using very different substrata in the literature on artificial life and complex adaptive systems. We are freed to use biological metaphors in many different fields. Dynamic processes first discovered in biology might be abstractly formulated and be found to have applications in quite different fields (e.g., genetic algorithms or predator-prey dynamics). It could also work in reverse. We might first isolate fundamental processes at work in other areas and then look to see if the "blind watchmaker" (Dawkins 1986) of evolution had, perhaps, found similar mechanisms long ago.

My topic in this chapter is the process of *parallel experimentation*, which I take to be a process of multiple experiments running concurrently with some form of common goal, with benchmarking comparisons made between the experiments, and with the migration of discoveries between experiments wherever possible to ratchet up the performance of the group. The thesis is that this is a fundamental scheme to enhance variation, innovation, and learning in contexts of genuine uncertainty.

> The use of a parallel-path strategy for the solution of difficult development problems is standard practice in several of our outstanding industrial laboratories. It is extremely common in agricultural and medical research. And in the

> atomic-bomb project, one of the most spectacularly successful military projects the United States has ever undertaken, the parallel-path strategy was employed. (Nelson 1961, 353)

This set of ideas about innovation and learning keeps popping up in different fields including evolutionary theory, so my aim here is to try to draw out the analogies and triangulate on the ideas.

The theme of parallelism has received renewed attention in the modern complexity sciences, for example the brain-inspired theories of neural networks and parallel distributed processing.

> [The] theme under the aegis of complexity is *the emphasis on parallel (network) rather than serial (hierarchical) systems*. . . . The distinction between serial and parallel systems is quite general. The serial system can be generalized to a hierarchical system like the pyramidical organization chart for a corporation, the church, or the military. Hierarchical systems are such that there are a "top" and a "bottom" at every level. . . . Parallel systems generalize to what I will call a "network." A network has no "top" or "bottom." Rather it has a plurality of connections that increase the possible interactions between components of the network. Most real system are mixtures of hierarchies and networks. (Pagels 1988, 50)

It will be useful, however, not to cast our net too widely. As considered here, parallel experimentation assumes enough of a common goal—a cooperative aspect—so that benchmarking between experiments is meaningful and discoveries could be usefully communicated between experiments to ratchet up the whole group.[1] Perhaps the borderline case is the common experimental design to concurrently test a number of already-delineated treatments on random samples of individuals to decide which is best. Ronald A. Fisher's F-test provides a type of benchmarking between the treatment groups to see if the variance between groups is significantly different from the variance of individuals within groups.

SEWALL WRIGHT'S SHIFTING BALANCE THEORY OF EVOLUTION

Sewall Wright (1889–1988) together with the same Ronald A. Fisher and J. B. S. Haldane were the three progenitors of one of the revolutions in modern biology, the mathematical theory of population genetics (see Provine 1971). In the recent complexity science literature, Wright is more often mentioned as the inventor of the "fitness landscape" to represent optimization on a very rugged and cloudy landscape. Yet the fitness landscape was only a tool Wright used to expound his shifting balance theory of evolution.[2]

Natural selection is a mechanism to push a population up a fitness hill—but it may be a very low hill. "The problem of evolution as I see it is that of a mechanism by which the species may continually find its way from lower to higher peaks in such a field" (Wright 1932; reprinted in Wright 1986, 163–64). How does evolution ever get the population back down a hill and across a valley of low fitness to climb a much higher hill? If selection operates to cut down variety to the survival of the fittest, what is the mechanism to increase variety in order to find a path from low to higher hills? Many biologists, Fisher and Haldane among them, don't think any special theory is required. They have faith that the variety introduced in the whole population by mutation, sexual reproduction, genetic drift, and changes in the environment will suffice. Sewall Wright was not satisfied with that explanation.

Like Darwin, Wright thought it relevant to carefully observe artificial selection. Wright found that breeders do not keep all their animals together in one interbreeding herd. They deliberately break the herd up into subherds, subpopulations, "races," or "demes" (as in demography). It is a question of balance. The subherds should be small enough so that the variety found in the subherd (through sampling error) or created through mutation, sexual reproduction, and genetic drift will be emphasized through inbreeding. But the subherd should not be so small that inbreeding leads to the quick fixation of ill-adapted genes and the deterioration or demise of the subherd. When a clearly superior example is produced in a subherd, then the seed is crossbred into the other subherds to give them the benefit of the innovation. But seeds could not be constantly crossbred between the subherds as that would defeat the benefits of their semi-isolation. Shifting balances were involved. How small to make the subherds and how much crossbreeding between the subherds?

Seeing these processes at work in artificial breeding and selection, Wright reasoned that Nature might have found some version of parallel "experimentation" with naturally forming subpopulations and cross-fertilization by migration.

> Judging from animal breeding, (Wright) thought that natural populations must be subdivided into small-enough partially isolated subgroups to cause random drifting of genes but large-enough subgroups to keep random drifting from leading directly to fixation of genes, for this was the road to degeneration and extinction. Mass selection within subgroups was followed by selective diffusion from subgroups with successful genetic combinations. The final step was the transformation of all subgroups by the immigration of organisms with a superior genotype and subsequent crossbreeding. (Provine 1986, 236)

Using the terminology of the field, a text in population genetics describes the theory as follows:

> In the shifting balance theory, a large population that is subdivided into a set of small, semi-isolated subpopulations (demes) has the best chance for the subpopulations to explore the full range of the adaptive topography and to find the highest fitness peak on a convoluted adaptive surface. If the subpopulations are sufficiently small, and the migration rate between them is sufficiently small, then the subpopulations are susceptible to random genetic drift of allele frequencies, which allows them to explore their adaptive topography more or less independently. In any subpopulation, random genetic drift can result in a temporary reduction in fitness that would be prevented by selection in a larger population, and so a subpopulation can pass through a "valley" of reduced fitness and possibly end up "climbing" a peak of fitness higher than the original. Any lucky subpopulation that reaches a higher adaptive peak on the fitness surface increases in size and sends out more migrants to nearby subpopulations, and the favorable gene combinations are gradually spread throughout the entire set of subpopulations by means of interdeme selection. (Hartl and Clark 1997, 259)

The point is that by dividing the population into demes or races, there is more variation and exploration. Since the results can be reaped by the whole population through crossbreeding, the overall rate of advance is increased.

> The average adaptiveness of the species thus advances under intergroup selection, an enormously more effective process than intragroup selection. The conclusion is that subdivision of a species into local races provides the most effective mechanism for trial and error in the field of gene combinations. (Wright 1932; reprinted in Wright 1986, 168)

The implicit rivalry or competition between demes is not to be confused with the competition between individuals within each deme and within the main population. The "parallelism" in the shifting balance theory is the parallel experimentation of the different demes or subpopulations.[3]

The "Wright stuff" is periodically reinvented even within biology, for example in Manfred Eigen's (1992) "quasi-species" theory of evolution for molecular or viral evolution. The observed rates of molecular evolution are measurably faster than are predicted by simple hill-climbing models of evolution. The molecules or viruses do not evolve single file (i.e., serially); they spread out over the value landscape in groups of variants. There could be a spectrum of related mutant groups one of which might make it to a higher peak.

> It is precisely in the mountainous regions that further selectively superior mutants can be expected. As soon as one of these turns up on the periphery of a

> mutation spectrum the established ensemble collapses. A new ensemble builds up around the superior mutant, which thus takes over the role of the wild type (the main variety). (Eigen 1992, 25; quoted in Dennett 1995, 192)

Daniel Dennett notes that Eigen's theory is not as revolutionary as he claims: "Sewall Wright himself, in his 'shifting balance theory,' tried to explain how multiple peaks and shifting landscapes would be traversable not by individual 'wild-type' exemplars, but by various-sized populations of variants" (Dennett 1995, 193).

The analogy between this evolutionary scheme and parallel experimentation to generate and share good ideas is not lost on biologists. Richard Dawkins illustrates evolution with a computerized model of spiders evolving with fitness determined by the fly-catching properties of their various webs.[4] The spiders are divided into "three 'demes' evolving in parallel."

> These were thought of as evolving independently in three different geographical areas. But—here's the point—not *completely* independently. There is a trickle of genes, meaning that an individual occasionally migrates, from one local population to another. The way I put it was that these migrant genes were a kind of injection of fresh "ideas" from another population: "almost as though a successful sub-population sends out genes that 'suggest' to a less successful population a better way to solve the problem of building a web." (Dawkins 1996, 136)

The smallness of the subpopulations plays a role in promoting greater variety in the experiments. This boils down to the mathematical fact that the smaller the number of independent random variables added together, the greater the "random walk" in the sum of the variables. This fact has a marvelous illustration.

> An intuitive explanation can be given for this size effect: it is the spontaneous random perturbations of the system's micro-units that serve to push it out of the neighbourhood of one potential minimum (or maximum in our case) and beyond the point of instability, whence it can move towards the other point of locally minimum (maximum) potential. In a larger population it is a lower-probability event that enough independently distributed random perturbations will be positively correlated to produce such a "shock." This is the same principle that prevents a large herd of horses that are tethered together from moving any great distance in a finite time, whereas, as any cowboy knew, a small band of horses tied together for the night could easily be out of sight by sunrise. (David and Foray 1994, 72)

Of course, the outcomes of human experiments are not just random variables, but a similar principle seems to hold, namely that there is more creativity in small than large groups. Thus, systems will show more out-of-sight creativity and dynamic development with coordinated parallel experiments carried out by small groups (with systematic diffusion of successes between the groups ratcheting up the whole group) than with experimentation in one large group.

PARALLEL AND SERIES EXPERIMENTATION

From the biological example, we might try to abstract the characteristics of a parallel experimentation scheme ("the Wright stuff") and compare it to the dual form of series experimentation.

Parallel is dual to series.[5] Parallel experimentation is taking place when there are a number of experiments taking place simultaneously all roughly with some common goal. In a scheme for series experimentation, all the resources to be used currently would be expended on the one best prospect or most promising experiment to be performed. If it did not resolve the problem, then all the resources in the next round or phase would again be put into what the experts or authorities consider the best experiment taking into account the previous results.

We immediately see one criterion for choosing between the two types of experimental schemes. If enough is known about a domain that it can be reliably determined what is the One Best Way (see Kanigel 1997), then there is a prima facie case for putting one's limited resources there. By the same token, parallel experimentation arises out of the lack of such definitive knowledge. When one knows that one doesn't know the best experiment with any certitude, then there is a case for dividing one's resources between a number of promising approaches.

One might imagine a "series advocate" and a "parallel advocate" giving arguments for and against each methodology. For the series proponent, a multiplicity of experiments is wasteful duplication. Isn't it rational to put one's resources on the best option? The experts will tell us what is the best experiment or approach; otherwise we would not give them the recognition and rewards appropriate to experts. Then it is safer to put one's resources on their knowledgeable choice rather than waste anything on what the authorities do not support. Scattering our resources among less-promising options will detract from our best chance of getting the breakthrough by putting all our resources on the most promising option. In any case, arguing that "we really don't know what is best with enough certainty" only makes the experts and the organization look bad in public—as if they don't know their business or can't make up their minds. Why would anyone want to support a methodology that makes the organization (and its experts) look bad?[6]

Our sophisticated series advocate is, of course, aware of the "rule" not to put all our eggs in one basket. But that rule is based on the assumption that the probabilities (e.g., of tipping over or dropping a basket of eggs) do not change with the number of eggs in the basket. Horses do not run faster if more money is bet on them. But if one's resources for keeping a watch on egg baskets are rather limited and one can better control a basket by applying more resources (time and energy) to watching it, then the best way to reduce risk may be not to spread your eggs over a number of baskets but to "put all your eggs in one basket and watch it very carefully." Note the similarity between the case where one "knows" that one can protect and control only one basket if it is watched closely enough and the case where one "knows" that the answer lies along a certain path if only one puts in enough resources to find it. In both cases, one would put all the resources on that option. Why take unnecessary risks by scattering one's eggs in different baskets if risk is best reduced by focusing on one basket?[7]

Parallel experimentation is based on the opposite knowledge, the Socratic knowledge that one does not know—acknowledged ignorance. There is an old distinction between risk, where rough probabilities are known, and genuine uncertainty, where the probabilities are unknown and where one has only conflicting hunches. Parallel experimentation is based on genuine uncertainty.

A sober reading of the history of science and engineering shows that experts are often rather myopic. They see a few steps ahead. But the disruptive paradigm-shifting discoveries tend to come "out of left field"—from outside the conventional framework that is the stock in trade of the experts. This sort of known ignorance pushes for the "waste and duplication" of a parallel approach.

> Development work is a messy, time-, and energy-consuming business of trial, error and failure. The only certainties in it are trial and error. . . . Indeed, development work is inherently so chancy that by the law of averages, chances of success are greatly improved if there is much duplication of effort. . . . Just so, when Pasteur, that wise old man, begged for enlarged support of the biological sciences, he begged for multiplication of laboratories. (Jacobs 1969, 90–91)

EVALUATION: SERIES OR PARALLEL

Each type of experimentation has a corresponding type of evaluation. In series experimentation, evaluations have to compare the results of the experiments to previous results where the experts might also be helpful in establishing the standards and in interpreting and evaluating the results. In most any case, the sequential experiments would lead to improvements over previous results so an organization's evaluation can point with pride at the outcomes: "My portfolio increased in value over last year"; "Our performance is an improvement over last year"; "Without the new Action Plan, our performance would have been much worse than last year." For a forward-looking organization, an evaluation might also focus on what further improvements might have been expected or might be possible. It is all a safe and sane procedure for organizations to secure steady progress toward their goals.

In parallel experimentation, a quite different type of evaluation is possible, namely the sideways benchmarking comparisons with the outcomes of the other parallel experiments—as is common in designed experiments. It is perhaps serendipity that the parallel scheme has this built-in type of evaluation since parallel experimentation would tend to be used precisely when there is a dearth of experts or prior experience to decide on the "best treatment." It is a "bootstrapping" type of evaluation.

EXPLORATION AND EXPLOITATION

We have argued that series and parallel experimentation schemes can be seen as polar opposites. In reality, the best methodology for search in a given case will usually be a judicious mixture of these two extremes. The two extremes can be thought of as two different basis vectors, each other vector is a combination of them.

These two "vectors" or "moments" or "strategies" occur in many other guises. When optimizing in a multipeaked but cloudy landscape, there is the series-oriented strategy of climbing the hill you are on (fight rather than switch), and there is the parallel-oriented strategy of trying to investigate another hill that might be the true peak since, due to the clouds, we know we do not know that this is the true peak (switch rather than fight). Simulated annealing is a mathematical version of the blacksmith heating iron to jar the looser atoms into new configurations and then quickly cooling it so they will settle into new lower energy configurations (thus strengthening and hardening the iron). In evolution (including its mathematical versions in genetic algorithms), there is the process of selection which, as it were, starts with the commitment to the existing set of genetic possibilities and then exploiting or refining them to determine the fittest, or there is the process of variation (e.g., mutation, sexual reproduction, and genetic drift) which works to exit the given hill on the fitness landscape and explore other possibilities. Sewall Wright's parallel experimentation theory addressed the need to better explain how that exploration might take place.

The trade-off between exploration and exploitation is ubiquitous.

> In general, investments in options and possibilities associated with "exploration" frequently come at the expense of obtaining returns on what has already been learned, "exploitation." The two possibilities form a fundamental trade-off. An early and striking exposition of the trade-off occurred in the context of the "two-armed bandit problem," in which a player with a fixed supply of coins play two slot machines that have unknown and potentially different rates of payoff. (Axelrod and Cohen 1999, 44)

Serial experimentation with the machine that had the highest initial payoffs would increase short-run gains but parallel experimentation would help long-run gains by reducing the error in determining which machine is in fact better.[8] In other words, exploitation will get one a little higher on the given hill, but exploration will be needed to help to determine if one is climbing the right hill in the first place. And switching to a higher hill is rendered more difficult by giving up the "sunk costs" expended in climbing the given hill.

In a search tree of possible paths, the two strategies become the strategies of breadth-first versus depth-first search.[9] Is it best to commit to a branch and exploit it in depth (since the experts think the answer is along that branch) or should one emphasize breadth by exploring many branches but thus with less depth (since this may be a topic about which there are no "experts")? Does a detective spend more time following up on a given suspect or searching for more suspects? Every arborist faces the choice of allowing the tree's energy to go into making more branches or of pruning off branches to force the growth along what I take to be the main branch. Branch or prune? Albert Hirschman (1970) explored the dynamics of the two strategies as exit (exploration: looking for other options) and voice (exploitation; commitment to given option). For instance, the basic choice in migration is "exit to find a better home" or "commit to making home better." Explore more options or exploit given options? Variation (finding more possibilities) or selection (choosing best among given possibilities), as in table 3.1?

EXAMPLES OF INSTITUTIONS FOR PARALLEL EXPERIMENTATION

Rivalrous Firms in the Market

Perhaps the first example is that of a competitive market. But the relevant notion of competition is not the atomistic perfect competition of consumers or producers that must take price as given. It is the rivalry of medium-to-large firms that threaten to take away market share from each other.[10] Benchmarking between firms provides the best real-time measure of how a firm is doing. A firm can depend on some rivals to innovate so, like the Red Queen, it has to

Table 3.1 The Two Strategies

	Selection	*Variation*
Evolution	Selection of fittest among given possibilities	Variation to generate more possibilities
Optimization on rugged cloudy landscape	Climbing the hill you are on (fight rather than switch)	Jumping to other hills (switch rather than fight)
Genetic algorithms	Exploit	Explore
Experimentation	Series experiments, each putting most resources into the One Best Way	Parallel experiments putting some resources on a number of promising ways
Evaluation	Compare to previous results in sequential experiments	Compare to current results in simultaneous experiments
Simulated annealing	Cooling (to settle into nearby low energy configurations)	Heating (to generate a new set of possible configurations)
Searching a tree	Depth-first search	Breadth-first search
Growing a tree	Pruning	Branching
Hirschmanian dynamics	Voice: commit to making the given option better	Exit: exit to find a better option

Source: Author

innovate as well just to keep up. When innovations are made, then the rivals have to figure out how to license, work around, or otherwise assimilate the new ideas. This "crossbreeding of a new gene" back into the other "subherds" to lift the performance of all is limited by the degree and nature of intellectual property protection.

"Scientific socialism" used series-oriented reasoning to provide a rational alternative to the irrational duplication and waste of the market. Engineers and consumer experts could agree on the current best product for a certain use. Then the returns to scale of modern manufacturing could be fully exploited to mass produce that product. In the meantime, researchers would be devising and testing ways to make still further improvements so that the One Best Product would get even better.

The Communities of Science

Perhaps the purest example of parallel experimentation as a scheme for collective innovation and learning is provided by the communities of scientific researchers working in a field. They also work in small semi-independent groups who constantly face the same shifting balance decisions about working in bigger or smaller groups, or closely following what others are doing versus striking off in new directions. Innovations are quickly transmitted via the scientific literature to the other groups for intersubjective verification and cross-learning. The knowledge available to all the groups is ratcheted up.

The series advocate would again like to use "what we know" to cut down on the wasteful exploration of discredited or untested ideas. The experts should be able to broadly agree on the best path of research and then centrally controlled resources should allocated along that path. Perhaps the most famous example in recent history in the life sciences was the Soviet experts' decision that Lysenkoism represented the path for Soviet genetics to take. The other branches on the tree could be pruned away.

Common Law

Parallel experimentation arrangements involve both competition and cooperation in varying degrees. The market is competition within the cooperative agreement to abide by certain rules of the game. Science is cooperation with a judicious mixture of competition. Both are examples of what Michael Polanyi called a "spontaneous order" (1951)—a scheme of horizontal cooperation and competition without central direction (although there may be centrally enforced rules).

Polanyi considered a system of common law as another example. Judges face adjudicative situations and have to apply the evolving body of common law or, where precedent fails, the judges use their small measure of independence to innovate and add to that body of law. A system of common law can be seen as an evolving problem-solving system that accumulates a body of knowledge and guidelines. The body of the law grows out of the results of the parallel coordinated adjudications and are not dictated from a central authority.[11]

Parallel Exploration of Ideas

It is extraordinarily difficult to hold two or more competing ideas or theories in suspension while at the same time caring which one is true or would be best for the case at hand. In *The Crack-up*, F. Scott Fitzgerald famously noted that the "test of a first-rate intelligence is the ability to hold two opposed ideas in the mind at the same time, and still retain the ability to function" (Fitzgerald 1945, 68). John Dewey emphasized that scientific inquiry involves

> willingness to hold belief in suspense, ability to doubt until evidence is obtained; willingness to go where evidence points instead of putting first a personally preferred conclusion; ability to hold ideas in solution and use them as hypotheses to be tested instead of as dogmas to be asserted; and (possibly the most distinctive of all) enjoyment of new fields of inquiry and of new problems. (Dewey 1939, 145)

Carl Sagan recommends parallel exploration not only for science but for anyone who wishes to think critically and skeptically; it is part of the "fine art of baloney detection."

> Spin more than one hypothesis. If there's something to be explained, think of all the different ways in which it could be explained. Then think of tests by which you might systematically disprove each of the alternatives. What survives, the hypothesis that resists disproof in this Darwinian selection among "multiple working hypotheses," has a much better chance of being the right answer than if you had simply run with the first idea that caught your fancy. (Sagan 1996, 210)

The rush to judgment based on prejudice (premature convergence in a search) is the sin for which the parallel exploration of idea or theories is the penitence. "Baconian idols of the tribe, the cave, the theater, and den have caused men to rush to conclusions, and then to use all their powers to defend from criticism and change the conclusions arrived at" (Dewey 1939, 146). This is such a strong tendency that various institutional innovations try to address the problem. The basic idea of the parallel exploration of ideas is usually expressed as competition in the marketplace for ideas[12]—"the proposition that truth naturally overcomes falsehood when they are allowed to compete. . . . The belief that competing voices produce superior conclusions (is) . . . implicit in scientific reasoning, the practice of trial by jury, and the process of legislative debate" (Smith 1988, 31).

Within organizations, the idea might be implemented with some form of organized legitimate opposition or devil's advocacy—which is considered in the chapter on contestation and devil's advocacy.

Series and Parallel Project Selection

Series and parallel experimentation appear in a slightly different guise in the contrast between series and parallel project selection.[13] With series selection, a project has to jump over a series of hurdles. Rejection by any one of the evaluators means rejection of the project. But in parallel selection, a project can be submitted to a number of evaluators. The project is selected if it passes any one of them. If it fails to be selected by one party, the project can be resubmitted for a second chance with another party.

Parallel selection is essentially parallel experimentation from the viewpoint of a project or an idea. If multiple parties are carrying out experiments, then we could think of a project or idea going from party to party to try to be accepted or "discovered." But with series experimentation, the project or idea only has one chance to eventually emerge as being accepted or discovered as the series of experiments go on.

Let us now suppose two kinds of projects or ideas, good and bad, where good projects should be accepted and bad ones rejected. But the characteristics are hidden. Then there are two types of error: type I error of rejecting a good project (false positive) and type II error of accepting a bad project (false negative). Assume the evaluators (strung in series in the one case and spread out in parallel in the other) have a certain probability of accepting a good project and a probability of rejecting a bad project. "Two results immediately emerge: *polyarchical organizations* (parallel selection) *accept more bad projects . . .; while hierarchical organizations* (series selection) *reject more good projects*" (Sah and Stiglitz 1985, 293). Of course, it is best to avoid both types of error but eventually the design of a selection mechanism will have to trade off one error for another. Series selection tends to commit type I error, rejecting some good projects but rarely letting a bad project pass. Parallel selection favors the opposite sin of type II error, accepting some bad projects but rarely rejecting a good project. Although individual decision-making centers might reject a good project, the overall system of having many second chances would make it very rare for a good project to be rejected overall.

The losses and gains will depend on the nature of the projects. If a bad project would release into the air a biological pathogen that would cause great damage, then one would prefer a decision-making mechanism that would error on the side of caution, that is, avoid type II errors ("like the plague") and be more tolerant of type I errors. This is the reasoning behind the "precautionary principle" advocated by some environmentalists. For these situations, the popular wisdom is "Better safe than sorry" or "The better part of valor is discretion." This could be implemented by having series project selection, a single channel with multiple stages each of which would have to accept the project in order for it to pass.

But the projects faced by economic enterprises are usually of a different sort; when a bad project is selected, then only some time, energy, and economic resources are wasted. Failure is not fatal; indeed, some economic institutions such as the limited liability company and social safety nets are designed to take some of the "sting" out of the death of a project. In these situations, the popular wisdom is "Nothing ventured, nothing gained" or "Better to have tried and failed than not to have tried at all." Richard Tawney indicated a preference for type II errors when he asserted that "rashness is a more agreeable failing than cowardice" (1954, 235). This would be implemented by the dual arrangement of parallel project selection, multiple decision centers where acceptance by any one is sufficient for the project to pass.

> In the end, the best way for managers to keep indirect selection systems from spiraling out of control may be to operate several of them in competition, even if some inconsistencies result. This contrasts with the example of many capital

> budgeting systems, which suffer from the "abominable no-man" syndrome: one thumbs-down verdict anywhere along the approval chain can terminate a project proposal. Better is the approach of companies such as Ore-Ida, the potato processor, which has given many different people, designated "Ore-Ida fellows," the ability to seed innovations with grants. In this way, different vicarious selection systems run in parallel, providing more than one means for variations to propagate. (Anderson 1999, 139)

Now contrast a society with parallel experimentation such as Renaissance Europe, which had competing centers of power, and centralized China at the same time (Ming Dynasty). Take the viewpoint of a project, such as Columbus's project. The political fragmentation of Europe gave it more of a chance than the centralized structure of China. Columbus was turned down by the King of Portugal and two Spanish dukes before submitting his proposal to Ferdinand and Isabella, who finally accepted it in 1492. In China, Columbus would not have had a second chance.[14] Indeed, after the spectacular voyages of the Chinese fleet under Zheng He to Africa in the early 1400s, the Ming Dynasty had by Columbus's time made a centralized decision to give up sea expeditions and stop producing seagoing vessels.

With centralized or monopoly project selection, there is no fear that a rejected innovation will be adopted by a competitor while an accepted innovation might have an uncertain effect on the monopoly. Thus, hierarchical centralization has been a recipe for uniform and essentially static societies from Ancient Egypt to the Soviet Union characterized by more "discretion" or "cowardice" (type I error). By the same token, in a market economy, the multiplicity of parallel decision-making centers means more "rashness" (type II error).

> Western economies authorize a large number of enterprises, as well as individuals who might form new enterprises, to make decisions to accept or reject proposals for innovation, their own or others'. The rejection of a meritorious proposal by a half-dozen decision-making centers is presumably less probable than its rejection by only one. The system is thus biased toward the acceptance of proposals. (Rosenberg and Birdzell 1986, 258)

Developing and transitional countries are weighted down with the inertia of the past. Political, religious, and customary authorities may see any real change as the potential release of a "pathogen," so they tilt toward type I error and stasis. The prospects of development push for a tilt toward parallel experimentation with multiple competing decision-making centers that favor type II error—the "rashness" of innovation and entrepreneurship—over type I error—the "discretion" and conservativism of "better safe than sorry."

Series experimentation tends to be the rule where there is a central authority that seeks to improve its position but will not tolerate disruptions from other parallel experiments. Only the center experiments; the periphery implements. Otherwise, the center would be giving up power to the periphery to find a different future.

> Initially, the West's achievement of autonomy stemmed from a relaxation, or a weakening, of political and religious controls, giving other departments of social life the opportunity to experiment with change. Growth is, of course, a form of change, and growth is impossible when change is not permitted. And *successful* change requires a large measure of freedom to experiment. A grant of that kind of freedom costs a society's rulers their feeling of control, as if they were conceding to others the power to determine the society's future. The great majority of societies, past and present, have not allowed it. Nor have they escaped from poverty. (Rosenberg and Birdzell 1986, 34)

In one context after another, it is the resistance of those in power to make a "grant of that kind of freedom" that impedes the more frequent use of parallel experimentation.

PARALLEL EXPERIMENTATION IN VARIOUS THINKERS

Hayek, Polanyi, and Lindblom on Spontaneous Orders and Mutual Adjustment

Friedrich Hayek (see "Competition as a Discovery Procedure" in 1984), Michael Polanyi (1951; 1966), and Charles Lindblom (1965; 1990) have all emphasized some of the similarities between markets, science, and democratic pluralism as spontaneous orders showing various degrees of mutual adjustment without central direction. All have criticized the hubris of "synoptic" knowledge that often lies behind centralized series experimentation. Parallel experimentation schemes are often supported by the acknowledged ignorance of that type of knowledge. And all three have emphasized the multitude of parallel agents who coordinate with and learn from each other without central direction.

These conceptions of a spontaneous orders are, however, somewhat broader than the sharper notion of parallel experimentation. In terms of the biological root metaphor, the parallel experimenting subpopulations are of the same species. Thus, the competitive rivalry of firms in the same business would be a parallel experimentation scheme while all the interactions of producers and consumers are subsumed into the broader notion of the market as a spontaneous order. In science, it is rivalry and cooperation of groups working on the same general problem—a "society of explorers" (Polanyi 1966)—that is parallel experimentation while the conception of "science" as a spontaneous order might be much broader. Within a multiparty system, the parties might compete to present solutions to common problems to the voters. Within a federation of states, the states might function as political laboratories to each try to find solutions to common vexing problems. The states might be more inclined to crossbreed solutions than parties, but in both cases there would be some implicit or explicit cross-learning from the parallel efforts. But, again, the idea of the political system as a system of mutual adjustment is much broader. Thus, I only wish to record the idea of parallel experimentation as a part of their broader conceptions of the market, science, and a "self-guiding society" (Lindblom 1990).

Burton Klein's Vision of Technology Development and Dynamic Economics

Albert Hirschman shared with Charles Lindblom the skepticism about the synoptic or comprehensive knowledge assumed by state planners. Hirschman (1958) used to criticize the idea of a state-coordinated "big push" toward balanced growth in a developing country. Hirschman proposed an alternative approach which he called "unbalanced growth." The idea was to work with and try to catalyze the endogenous economic and political pressures that arise from both bottlenecks and sudden openings to galvanize scattered energies to make structural changes.

The similarities between Hirschman and Lindblom led to them writing a joint paper (1971) that also discussed the work of Burton Klein. In an early work on technology development, Burton Klein writing together with William Meckling (1958) contrasted dynamic technology development strategies with the usual Olympian or "synoptic" approach of operations research. In the usual approach, the analyst, Mr. Optimizer, would gather the best current views, perhaps a consensus of the experts, as to what was the best option and then plans would be drawn to rationally allocate resources to develop that option—much like a development program based on the Official Views determined by the consensus of experts at elite development agencies. This is the strategy of series experimentation.

Klein and Meckling proposed an alternative approach of Mr. Skeptic, parallel experimental development of several main options with early prototyping to "see what works" and then let later allocation decisions be guided by the results of these experiments.

> They (Klein and Meckling) allege that development is both less costly and more speedy when marked by duplication, "confusion," and lack of communication among people working along parallel lines. Perhaps more fundamentally, they

> are against too strenuous attempts at integrating various subsystems into a well-articulated, harmonious, general system; they rather advocate the full exploitation of fruitful ideas regardless of the "fit" to some preconceived pattern of specifications. (Hirschman and Lindblom 1971, 66–67)

Note the critique of the overplanning according to initial preconceptions. Klein and Meckling see the problem as "*not* one of choosing among specific end-product alternatives, but rather a problem of choosing a course of action initially consistent with a wide range of such alternatives; and of narrowing the choice as development proceeds" (1958, 352). This is a recurring theme in the parallel experimentation literature.

> If . . . the innovation involves major uncertainties, for example, the creation of some never-before-seen item of hardware, then it is very easy to "overplan" the project and thereby decrease or even destroy the effectiveness of the work . . . . Like fundamental research, radical innovation is inherently a learning process. The best initial design concepts often turn out to be wrong—dead, hopelessly wrong—simply because not enough is yet known about how the job can (and cannot) be done. There is also what can be called a "false summit" effect. When one climbs a mountain, one sees ahead what appears to be the top of the mountain, but over and over again it is not the summit, but rather a shoulder on the trail that blocks the view of the real summit. (Kline and Rosenberg 1986, 297)

In his later work, Burton Klein developed his earlier analysis of parallel technology development projects in the presence of genuine uncertainty into a full-fledged vision of dynamic economics (1977; 1984). Klein, like many others wanted to develop Schumpeter's vision of a truly dynamic economy driven by entrepreneurial energies to continuously innovate and to create a perennial gale of creative destruction. Klein focused on rivalry between firms threatening each other's market shares as the driving force of dynamics. Klein specifically saw rivalry as promoting innovative effort, for example the X-efficiency (Leibenstein 1966) of galvanizing scattered energies and played down the static notion of allocative efficiency. Klein noted that Louis Brandeis had used a similar argument in favor of rivalrous competition in spite of the wastes or duplication that might be involved. In 1912, when economists were still perfecting the notion of allocative efficiency, Brandeis gave an "X-efficiency argument" in favor of the "wastes" of rivalrous competition in contrast to the static efficiency of big combines and trusts.

> Incentive and development which are incident to the freer system of business result in so much greater achievement that the waste is relatively insignificant. The margin between that which men naturally do, and that which they can do, is so great that a system which urges men on to action and develops individual

enterprise and initiative is preferable, in spite of the wastes that necessarily attend the process. (Brandeis quoted in: Mason 1946, 382)

In planning new growth in a forest, static efficiency would suggest planting trees in openings for best access to sunlight; diminishing returns would set in as trees began to shade one another. Immanuel Kant recognized that the "means which nature employs to bring about the development of innate capacities is that of antagonism within society," and he represented the insight with the analogy of trees competing in a forest:

> In the same way, trees in a forest, by seeking to deprive each other of air and sunlight, compel each other to find these by upward growth, so that they grow beautiful and straight—whereas those which put out branches at will, in freedom and in isolation from others, grow stunted, bent and twisted. All the culture and art which adorn mankind and the finest social order man creates are fruits of his unsociability. (Kant 1991 (orig. 1784), 46)

Starting with Alfred Marshall's metaphor of the various firms in an industry as being like young, middle-aged, and old trees in a forest (1961, 315), Klein found, perhaps unknowingly, Kant's metaphor to illustrate dynamic efficiency. "And to put my proposition in terms of (Marshall's) analogy: when business firms compete by imposing risk upon each other they contribute not only to their own success but to the growth of the forest. One the other hand, when they fail to compete in deeds and seek the help of the government in exempting them from risk-taking, a few old trees can jeopardize the growth of an entire forest" (Klein 1977, 233–34). Static allocative efficiency is often evoked to criticize "wasteful" competition and "duplicative" parallel experiments but the rivalry that promotes X-efficiency tends to counteract that static inefficiency.

Another recurring theme in the parallel experimentation literature is the deemphasis on static efficiency in favor of a dynamic efficiency characterized by continuing problem-solving and innovation. In a dynamic setting, variation- and innovation-related characteristics such as flexibility, versatility, diversification, and resilience gain in importance; perfect adaptation to the old environment may turn out to be premature convergence and overadaptation.[15]

> When one firm might operate in text-book fashion by carefully optimizing its products for the market at particular points in time, another might never engage in such a seemingly rational strategy, yet, in five or ten years time will completely outdistance the first firm. . . . In all disciplines, dynamic considerations were brought into play by trying to understand phenomena which did not agree with a static paradigm. Biologists, for example, found that characteristics which permitted species to adapt to a given environment were by no means the same as those required for survival in a rapidly changing environment. (Klein 1984, 199)

Returning to the biological root metaphor, the de-emphasis on static efficiency is also seen in the idea of semi-isolation from the fitness pressures "in a larger population" in order to "pass through a 'valley' of reduced fitness" to then climb a higher peak elsewhere. Similarly within large firms, they can better break free of past routines and innovate if they establish "breakout" (Downs 1967, 160) units or "entities separate from current operations" in order to "incubate new projects" (Teece 1998, 153), for example limited autonomy internal units such as "skunkworks" operations.[16] A similar means can be used to combat premature convergence in neural networks.

> Selection and retention overwhelm variation because positive feedback loops reinforce the first set of successful connections that emerge, tending to lock the pattern in. A set of neural networks performs best when, early in their training, communication between the networks is limited. Each network is given time to build its own interpretation before being exposed to the conclusions of others, so some solutions are allowed to emerge that do not initially seem as successful as others. (Anderson 1999, 123)

The shifting balance theory is also about the semi-isolation of parallel subpopulations that can develop their own "ideas" without being overwhelmed by the selective pressures of the main population.[17] Philip Anderson goes on to note that this "insight helps explain why savvy managers often isolate innovation teams from the rest of the organization during the formative, exploratory learning period" (1999, 123).

The same basic idea is expressed by Burton Klein in his dynamic analysis of technology development decisions in contrast to the conventional "economizing" decisions to maximize the use of existing resources.

> He . . . advocates looseness in goal-setting and gradual, oblique, or multiple approaches to the goal. . . . In addition, he argues that it is rather secondary interest to the developer to achieve an efficient combination of inputs. His main interest is achieving a breakthrough to a new product or to radically improved performance characteristics. (Hirschman and Lindblom 1971, 69)

By having only a secondary interest in the static hill-climbing pressure for an "efficient combination of inputs," the development effort might cross a low-static-efficiency valley to a higher peak on the other side, that is, find "radically improved performance characteristics." In a similar manner, the semi-isolation of Sewall Wright's subpopulations together with their greater variation might allow them to escape the current hill on the fitness landscape and to cross through a valley of reduced fitness to climb a higher peak elsewhere.

Jane Jacobs's Vision of Development through Volatile Intercity Trade

Although working well outside the confines of the "professional" study of economies known as "Economics," Jane Jacobs's voraciously eclectic work (1969; 1984) contributes to the tradition emphasizing the virtues of open-ended multiple approaches and the limitations of centralized urban planning.

She arrives at a parallel experimentation process between cities by focusing first on how old work leads to new diversified work within cities and then on the volatile trade between cities. To become more ramified and complex, an economic settlement should have different uses for imports to produce diversified and multistaged products with a significant part for local use. Each specialization of old work to achieve efficiency will soon lead to new work as the diversification of outputs into various product niches, to backward integration to produce previously imported inputs, and perhaps to unexpected "matings" with nearby processes and products to produce novel offspring. This is the sort of innovation that tends to happen when diverse people with various skills and complementary knowledge jostle together in companies, and companies jostle together in cities. "This process in which one sort of work leads to another must have happened millions of times in the whole history of human economic development" (Jacobs 1969, 53).

In a parallel experimentation model, each city could be seen as an experimenter. Given these processes of old work leading to new work within cities, the cities can grow through a process of dynamic interaction with each other by direct or indirect rivalry. To play in the "game," a city must produce something which it can export—perhaps based on its natural endowment. This is its "message" and "challenge" to other cities. The export earnings can then buy imports from other cities that were not produced in the given city. But if the other cities were not too advanced, then the import will present a plausible challenge to be replaced through learning and improvisation and perhaps improved upon within the city. Thus, the products traded between cities are the "ideas" or "discoveries" transmitted from one city to another.

In the meantime, the other cities might be replacing the original exports of a city; its temporary advantage might be competed away. Now the domestic and perhaps improved version of the originally imported products can then be reexported perhaps to the other cities that are less developed or have different specializations. The new export earnings will then purchase other more challenging imports, and the process can repeat itself ratcheted up at a higher level.

In this matter, a diversified group of innovative cities can through trade learn from each other and are ratcheting up or "developing on one another's shoulders" (Jacobs 1984, 144). This could well be called the "Jacobs'

Ladder" mechanism of development through volatile intercity trade (see the chapter on Jane Jacobs).

Jacobs also develops her version of Hirschman's vision of the innovative developmental process of problem-solving leading to more problems and pressures which in turn calls forth more problem-solving and so on. Instead of a vision of integrated rational planning based on a comprehensive overview, Jacobs and Hirschman as well as Lindblom and Klein all envisage a process driven by endogenous pressures that call forth innovative problem-solving from multiple agents which, in turn, creates beneficial cross-learning and rivalrous counterstrategies—moves and countermoves—ratcheting forward through seesaw advances.

Donald Schön and Everett Rogers on Decentralized Social Learning

The default theory of social learning is that the center makes policy innovations—series experimentation—which are then transmitted to the periphery.

> (The standard approach) treats government as center, the rest of society as periphery. Central has responsibility for the formation of new policy and for its imposition on localities at the periphery. Central attempts to "train" agencies at the periphery. In spite of the language of experimentation, government-initiated learning tends to be confined to efforts to induce localities to behave in conformity with central policy. (Schön 1971, 177)

But social learning can take place in a decentralized bottom-up manner with centralized coordination. In large multiplant companies, innovation may take the form of new ways of socially organizing and structuring productive processes, for example quality circles or self-managed work teams. Separate plants might perform pilot experiments to find out "what works and what doesn't." The headquarters office frames the experiments, detects the successes, and plays the knowledge-broker to help other plants cross-learn from the successful ones. In the Japanese system of just-in-time inventories, there is local problem-solving by teams, benchmarking between teams, and continuous improvement ratcheting up the performance of the teams.[18]

Schön described a similar process involving the government and the periphery of local units trying to carry out a certain social reform.

> Government cannot play the role of "experimenter for the nation," seeking first to identify the correct solution, then to train society at large in its adaptation. The opportunity for learning is primarily in discovered systems at the periphery, not in the nexus of official policies at the center. Central's role is to detect

> significant shifts at the periphery, to pay explicit attention to the emergence of ideas in good currency, and to derive themes of policy by induction. The movement of learning is as much from periphery to periphery, or periphery to center, as from center to periphery. Central comes to function as facilitator of society's learning, rather than as society's trainer. (Schön 1971, 177–78)

Decentralized parallel experimentation with centrally sponsored framing and benchmarking followed by peer-to-peer cross-learning in the periphery (like deme-to-deme cross-learning in Wright's theory) is a more appropriate model than research at a central facility followed by the teaching-dissemination of the results.

In Everett Rogers's early work on the diffusion of innovations, he focused on the classical hub-and-spokes or center-periphery model of diffusion. "In this classical diffusion model, an innovation originates from some expert source (often an R&D organization). This source then diffuses the innovation as a uniform package to potential adopters who accept or reject the innovation. The role of the adopter of the innovation is that of a passive accepter" (Rogers 1983, 333).

Spurred on by Schön's work (1971), he became aware of decentralized diffusion systems with horizontal diffusion between peers (which might involve partial reinvention of the model) rather than vertical transmission from experts to adopters.

> During the late 1970s I gradually became aware of diffusion systems that did not operate at all like the relatively centralized diffusion systems that I had described in my previous books. Instead of coming out of formal R&D systems, innovations often bubbled up from the operational levels of a system, with the inventing done by certain users. Then the new ideas spread horizontally via peer networks, with a high degree of re-invention occurring as the innovations are modified by users to fit their particular conditions. . . .
>
> Gradually, I began to realize that the centralized diffusion model was not the only wheel in town. (Rogers 1983, 334)

Perhaps the best example of a parallel system of decentralized innovation and diffusion in a developing country is in China over the last quarter of a century. The Chinese recognized local reform models which could be in a region, county, commune, or even brigade, and could be in any sector or area such as administration, health, education, or industry. The center would recognize a "model" which could then be visited by groups from all over China that want to make a similar reform in their locality.

> The diffusion of innovations in China is distinctive in that it is (1) more horizontal in nature, (2) less dependent upon scientific and technical expertise,

> and (3) more flexible in allowing re-invention of the innovation as it is implemented by local units. These aspects of decentralized diffusion are facilitated by China's use of such diffusion strategies as models and on-the-spot conferences. The "learning from others" approach to decentralized diffusion in China was adopted officially as a national policy in the national constitution in 1978. (Rogers 1983, 340–41)

The same period marks the beginning of China's historic record of growth and development at the end of the twentieth century.

Stuart Kauffman's Theory of Parallel Patch Development

The recent work in the complexity sciences (e.g., Gell-Mann 1994; Kauffman 1995) has produced an explosion of evolution- and-biology-inspired model building. Stuart Kauffman's theory of patches (1995, Chapter 11) is an example of a model that captures some of the themes of parallel experimentation. Imagine a large, say, 120 x 120, sheet or lattice of cells. Each cell contains a 0 or 1. The "fitness" of a cell depends not only the value in it but the value in some set of neighboring cells according to some given interconnections. The goal is maximizing the total fitness of the lattice. Flipping the value in one cell will not only change the fitness for that cell but the fitness of the given values in the connected neighbors. A flip could increase fitness in a cell but so worsen the fitness in the neighbors that the net change in fitness is negative.

The first decision criterion is to flip a cell if the net change for the whole sheet is positive. This will soon lead to a local maximum where any further change is blocked by the side effects on the fitness of other cells. This is like Sewall Wright's problem of the whole population being stuck on a local maximum of fitness. Kauffman asks the same question as Wright: "The next question is how to escape." Kauffman's solution is somewhat similar to Wright's; divide the population of cells into patches that are semi-isolated in the sense that they can innovate without considering the spillover effects outside the patch. The interconnections are still there, but the decision rule allows a cell to be flipped if it increases the fitness of the patch (regardless of the spillover effects on neighboring patches).

When all the cells are in one big patch, Kauffman called that the "Stalinist limit" since an individual is only allowed to change if it helps the whole collectivity. Breaking the sheet into, say 5 x 5, patches creates some decentralized freedom for variation; the individual can change if it helps the local patch. The breaking up of the whole population into subpopulations or patches will in general allow enough variation for the system to move to a higher peak on the fitness landscape.

Then the question is the "tuning" of the size of the patch (the number of affected neighbors can also be changed). Too large a patch would lead to the Stalinist rigidity of some low-level local maximum. The limit on smallness of patches is individual cells which Kauffman calls the "Leftist Italian" limit of chaos (e.g., one-person political parties). Somewhere in between, there is the "sweet spot" of a patch size that will give "order on the edge of chaos"; the variation that will allow the system to find an excellent maximum while avoiding the rigidity of being stuck at a low maximum and the chaos of ceaseless activity toing and froing.

Sewall Wright had a similar problem of shifting the balance to find the sweet spot for the best adaptive advance:

> The most general conclusion is that evolution depends on a certain balance among its factors. There must be gene mutation, but an excessive rate gives an array of freaks, not evolution; there must be selection, but too severe a process destroys the field of variability, and thus the basis for further advance; prevalence of local inbreeding within a species has extremely important evolutionary consequences, but too close inbreeding leads merely to extinction. A certain amount of crossbreeding is favorable but not too much. (Wright 1932; reprinted in Wright 1986, 170)

While Kauffman's language of "order on the edge of chaos" is recent, the idea of finding the most adaptive order in the right balance between order and disorder goes back at least to Sewall Wright's shifting balance theory of evolution expounded in the early 1930s.

When Kauffman explained the patch theory to Robert Axelrod, then Axelrod noted that

> a federal system with partitioning into local semiautonomous regions could be thought of as a mechanism that allowed "experimentation" such that novel solutions might be invented "locally," and then copied elsewhere. Oregon innovates; the rest of the country imitates. (Kauffman 1995, 271)

Axelrod described a parallel experimentation scheme. This also shows that the patch theory is not quite the same since each patch faces its own problems (like an unhappy family in Tolstoy's *Anna Karenina*). A good solution for one patch cannot be crossbred to the other patches since each patch and its cells have, in general, a different set of underlying interconnections. In biological terms, the patches are different coevolving species, not subpopulations of the same species. But with that difference aside, I can concur with Kauffman when he muses "that analogues of patches, systems having various kinds of local autonomy, may be a fundamental mechanism underlying adaptive evolution in ecosystems, economic systems, and cultural systems" (1995, 264).

POLICY INNOVATION CONTESTS AS PARALLEL EXPERIMENTATION

Our theme is that when a central agency does not know the answer (almost always the case in questions of development), then its best strategy is to sponsor a program of parallel decentralized experiments with discussion, benchmarking, and horizontal learning between the experimenters—all of which will tend to ratchet up the performance of the whole group.

Charles Sabel and Sanjay Reddy have proposed just such a mechanism of parallel experimentation for social learning for development:

> From these general considerations, it is possible to sketch the kernel of a two-level economic-development framework that encourages constraint-relaxing learning—offered only as an example. At the "top," a benchmarking committee of the relevant government entities and qualified private actors collaborates with potential users to establish the initial substantive and procedural criteria for participation and defines the initial metrics by which applications are to be ranked. At the "bottom," project groups—whose members can be public or private entities or partnerships of both—compete to present projects that score highly under the emergent criteria. "Top" and "bottom" are in quotation marks because the relation between them is cyclical, not hierarchical: one entity proposes a framework for action, the other revises the proposal in enacting it, the first responds to the revisions, and so on. Lead actors dominate early project rounds; weaker actors come to the fore in later ones. After each round, the selection criteria, benchmarks, and institutional arrangements are adjusted to reflect improved measures of performance and a richer operational understanding of success. There is thus public learning as well as learning by private agents. Because the implicit theory of economic development—expressed in the operationally applied selection criteria—is revised in light of the means chosen to pursue them—the pooled experience of actual projects—we can call these arrangements "experimentalist." (Sabel and Reddy 2007, 85)

Start with a persistent social problem in a developing or transitional country, for example how to do bankruptcies and industrial restructuring, how to promote small private firms in a corrupt environment, how to fight endemic corruption, how to provide public services, and so forth. The agency (e.g., some appropriately local development agency) proposes a competition (e.g., between national regions, states and cities) for the best approach to addressing the problem. To qualify, an entrant must make public the "theory" or ideas behind their approach. Moreover, they must agree to be judged by certain public benchmarking criteria (which they might themselves propose).

Based on the proposals, some of which could describe already existing programs, the agency will select a certain number of winners and will provide material assistance in some form, for example a block grant. The assistance will always require a substantial matching contribution (which could be as prior investment) from the entrants to assure that they want to solve the problem and are not just in it to get the assistance. In any case, the aid provided by the agency is the least important part of the parallel experimentation scheme. The more the aid, the more a central agency will be emboldened to start dictating "answers"; so, the aid should be unobtrusively small so as not to interfere with the primary motivation of the public hunt for solutions to address a pressing problem.

The others in the contest will learn the winning theories as to how the problem can be addressed and they may choose to adapt their own mode of operation. After a certain time period, the results are assessed according to the previously agreed-upon benchmarks to see who the real winners were. There might be a second round of assistance where aid would go to those who did well in the first round (whether they previously received assistance or not). The point is to encourage horizontal or cross-learning between those who did well and those who didn't. Project funds might also be used to sponsor visits or secondments so that the laggards could learn directly from the emerging success stories. The modes of operation may be adjusted from one's own experiment and from the experience of others. The public benchmarking establishes a rolling standard that will ratchet up as social learning improves performance (continuous improvement). Matters of local pride and prestige will play a role.

The public benchmarking between parallel experiments and ratcheting up of standards of performance are the heart of a real-time notion of parallel evaluation that stands in sharp contrast to the traditional notion of evaluation. Conventionally, the experts decide on the One Best Way which was duly implemented. Then after a number of years, an evaluation is performed to learn from the results. Leaving aside all the huge problems in the objectivity of evaluations and the resistance of bureaucracies to learning (due to the implication of prior error), the idea is that experts will take the "learnings" to heart to give still better redesigned recommendations the next time. But under conditions of knowing that you do not know the One Best Way, the best approach seems to be parallel experimentation and the real-time evaluation of benchmarking and communication of ideas between the experiments.

NOTES

1. For example, in the parallel foraging of the social insects (e.g., bees or ants), the common goal is food and successes are communicated to the larger group.
2. The main papers from the 1930s are collected together in Wright (1986).

3. Fisher and Wright had a correct but rather cool professional relationship. Fisher never supported the shifting balance theory even though it could be seen as Nature's tinkering way of developing and carrying out different treatments on samples drawn from a large population and then determining the treatment with the best results, that is, the sort of thing that Fisher famously considered in artificial experimental design and statistical analysis of variance.

4. See Tanese (1989) for an early use of Sewall Wright's idea of subpopulations in computerized genetic algorithms.

5. See chapter 12, "Parallel Addition, Series-Parallel Duality, and Financial Mathematics," in Ellerman (1995).

6. Note how the series advocate mixes theoretical and organizational arguments. That is, indeed, how these issues arise in practice.

7. These two strategies for reducing risks correspond to the two basic reproductive strategies designed to reduce the risk that parents will leave no offspring to reproduce again. Where parents have little or no control over the chances of the offspring to survive, then they use their energy to produce a large number of offspring like many insects or fish—"they distribute their eggs into many baskets"—which is called the "r selection" strategy. If parents can control their environment well, then they can concentrate their energies in a few offspring as with mammals—"put their eggs in a few baskets and watch them very carefully"—which is called the "K selection" strategy.

8. The original statement of the problem (Thompson 1933) was even closer to our topic, the choice among different ways of treating an illness in a population. The greater use of one technique would tell more about its chances of effecting a cure, but the use of various techniques would give more comparative information about which might be the best technique.

9. "The ideas of breadth and depth are in competition throughout the whole history of combinatorial optimization" (Strang 1986, 609).

10. There is perhaps an analogy here in evolutionary theory. Often the competition in evolution is only pictured at the atomistic level of individuals but Wright focused on the competition and selection between the subpopulations or demes. In a small but not too small inbreeding population, an innovation would have a better chance to be developed, reinforced, and tested. An innovation in a large population would have a greater chance of being lost before it is really developed and tested.

11. The development of the Linux operating system (see Axelrod and Cohen 1999) by the coordinated effort of thousands of programmers provides a modern example of what can be produced in a spontaneous order or "bazaar" rather than a "cathedral" (see Raymond 2001).

12. John Milton (1957a) expressed the idea in his defense of intellectual freedom in *Areopagitica*. "And though all the winds of doctrine were let loose to play upon the earth, so Truth be in the field, we do injuriously, by licensing and prohibiting, to misdoubt her strength. Let her and Falsehood grapple; who ever knew Truth put to the worse, in a free and open encounter?"

13. See the work of Raaj Sah and Joseph Stiglitz (1985) summarized in Stiglitz (1994)

14. "European-style wars between internal political units became rare in China after 960 A.D. The absence of political competition did not mean that technological progress could not take place, but it did mean that one decision maker could deal it a mortal blow" (Mokyr 1990, 231).

15. Premature convergence (going too far along the wrong branch) is the "dual" error to the wasteful consideration of too many parallel options (too much branching away from the right branch).

16. See also Chapter 7, "Autonomy and Entrepreneurship," in Peters and Waterman (1982). The name "skunkworks" derives from Al Capp's L'il Abner comic strip where "Kickapoo joy juice" was brewed in a semi-isolated still with an occasional dead skunk thrown in for flavor.

17. After a preliminary acquaintance with a new field of intellectual endeavor and its problems, suppose that an idea occurs to one about one of the problems. It is important to follow out the idea on one's own—deliberately refraining from reading what the experts have to say on the matter. Only later when one has acquired some footing of one's own through this active learning should one open up again and establish contact with the received wisdom in the field. By such a "naïve" and "wasteful" procedure (a self-imposed "skunkworks"), one can avoid getting stuck in the deep ruts cut by those who have gone before (premature convergence), ruts which might have prevented them from solving the problem. For an individual or organization already with formed views, the path to innovation may well lie in the "discrediting" (Weick 1979, 215) of "what we know."

18. This example with the parallel experimentation of teams plays a major role in Charles Sabel's theory of learning by monitoring (1994).

Chapter 4

Contestation and Devil's Advocacy

DEVIL'S ADVOCACY AND COUNTERVAILANCE

How can a large bureaucratic agency advance from a church-like model toward an open learning model? One way is for the agency to foster some competition within the agency.[1] For instance, the defendant's right to an attorney in an American courtroom takes away from the prosecutor the monopoly right to present evidence and arguments. A judge may not go to the jury before both sides of the arguments have been heard, and a patient should not go to surgery before getting a second opinion. Even the Roman Catholic Church get beyond the "Church model" when considering someone for sainthood; it has a "devil's advocate" (*Advocatus Diaboli*) to state the other side of the story. A development agency should not pretend to greater authority or infallibility when it canonizes a good practice success story as the One Best Way. Thus, devil's advocacy might not only be tolerated but fostered in a development agency functioning as an open learning organization.[2]

This idea of the constructive role of public criticism goes back at least to the role of Socrates in Athens as a gadfly:

> For if you kill me you will not easily find a successor to me, who, if I may use such a ludicrous figure of speech, am a sort of gadfly, attached to the state by God; and the state is a great and noble horse who is rather sluggish owing to his very size, and requires to be stirred into life. I am that gadfly which God has attached to the state, and all day long and in all places am always fastening upon you, arousing and persuading and reproaching you. (Plato *Apology*, 30–31)

The penchant for competition seems to be one of the key features of Athenian Greece[3] that distinguished it from other societies of antiquity, and Socrates represented the use of dialogue and contestation as the road to improving knowledge. "The form Socrates' teaching took—intellectual dueling before a sportive audience—looks much odder to us than it did to Athenians, whose whole culture was based on the contest (*agōn*), formal and informal, physical, intellectual, and legal" (Wills 1994, 163). This also relates to the broader theme of democracy as being based on government by discussion.

> The traditional theory of the contest and interplay of group interests was not so much a scientific description as a normative injunction; in fact it contained the moral basis of liberal democracy. In order for the truth to be known, this theory argued, speech must be free; in order for wise decisions to be made, all the interests must be in the field and all the values articulated. The ancestry of this liberal pluralism might well be traced, beyond Mill and Madison and Montesquieu, all the way to the dialectical principle of Socrates: the method of verbal contest or discussion grounded on the faith that there was indeed a truth to be reached, through mutual deliberation, on which reasonable men could agree. (Matson 1966, 107)

Immanuel Kant recognized that the "means which nature employs to bring about the development of innate capacities is that of antagonism within society," and he represented the insight with the analogy of trees competing in a forest:

> In the same way, trees in a forest, by seeking to deprive each other of air and sunlight, compel each other to find these by upward growth, so that they grow beautiful and straight—whereas those which put out branches at will, in freedom and in isolation from others, grow stunted, bent and twisted. All the culture and art which adorn mankind and the finest social order man creates are fruits of his unsociability. (Kant 1991 (orig. 1784), 46)

Similarly, there is the oft-quoted line:

> In Italy, for thirty years under the Borgias, they had warfare, terror, murder and bloodshed, but they produced Michelangelo, Leonardo da Vinci, and the Renaissance. In Switzerland they had brotherly love, they had five hundred years of democracy and peace, and what did they produce? The cuckoo clock. (Orson Welles in *The Third Man* 1949)

Of course, not all antagonism or unsociability is helpful so Hirschman (1995) has investigated which forms of social conflict are beneficial (see also Coser 1956), a question that also goes back to the contrast between Socrates's provocative dialogues to improve knowledge and the Sophists's eristic methods to simply defeat an opponent.

But, for our purposes, the focus is on the difference between an organization that incorporates (hopefully beneficial) antagonism and one that aims at a nonantagonistic idea of agreement, cooperation, and "playing with the team"—a small society like that dryly satirized by Kant as the Arcadian ideal where men would be "as good-natured as the sheep they tended" (1991, 45). Some modern research (Lloyd 1996) have used this contrast to address the question of why, after such a promising beginning in ancient China, science developed strongly in ancient Greece but not in China. The key feature in ancient China was the intermixing of power with questions of empirical truth—a feature shared with the role of the church in the Middle Ages or with Lysenkoism (and the role of the party in general) in the Soviet Union. The Emperor's Mandate of Heaven was based on a view of the world that pictured the Emperor in the central role of maintaining the harmony between Heaven and Earth. The views of philosophers and scientists needed to accommodate that basic scheme. In contrast, the Greek intellectual life exhibited "radical revisability" (Lloyd 1996, 216) where the masters would offer theories completely at odds with those of their rivals—a practice that would not be allowed where the Mandate of Heaven was seen as being based on the Official Theory. Chinese intellectual life put the emphasis on accommodation and harmony while the Greeks thrived on antagonism and adversariality. The differences extended throughout social and legal affairs.

> Differences between individuals or groups that might well have been the subject of appeal to litigation in Greece were generally settled (in China) by discussion, by arbitration, or by the decision of the responsible officials. The Chinese had, to be sure, no experience that remotely resembled that of the Greek dicasts (large public juries), nor, come to that, that of Greek public participation in open debate of political issues in the Assemblies. (Lloyd 1996, 109)

Given the rather clear historical verdict of the mixing of power and knowledge in ancient China, the Medieval Church, and the more-recent Communist Party, there seems to be little reasoned basis for a development agency dedicated to promoting development knowledge to adopt "Official Views" on some of the most complex and subtle questions facing humankind.

Indeed, the arguments for not taking official institutional views seem so clear that perhaps one should try to explain why the leaders of the major development agencies stick with the old "Official Views" policy. But this is to ask why someone in a position of power would oppose a regulation that would weaken that power for fear that it might be abused. While the power-holder might abstractly agree with a regulation for others who might abuse the power, it is not needed right now (while they are in power). Paraphrasing Augustine's description about his preconversion self: "Give me chastity and self-control, but not just yet" (Augustine 2006, 177), power-holder's reply is perhaps: "Yes, the policy should be changed—but not just yet."

Aside from not licensing Official Views, how might an agency promote internal adversariality? Devil's advocacy is one practice that might be fostered in a development agency functioning as an open learning organization. The political scientist Alfred De Grazia recommends such a countervailance system as a part of any large bureaucracy. "The countervailors would be a corps of professional critics of all aspects of bureaucracy who would be assigned by the representative council of an institution to specialize as critic of all the subinstitutions" (1975, 168). The devil's advocacy concept can also be applied to written documents. When Jefferson complained about the one-sided press, James Madison half-seriously asked: "Could it be so arranged that every newspaper when printed on one side, should be handed over to the press of an adversary, to be printed on the other, thus presenting to every reader both sides of every question, (so) truth would always have a fair chance" (quoted in Smith 1988, 41). Perhaps the op-ed page in a newspaper could be seen in this light. Although all development agencies have various newsletters and bulletins from management to communicate to staff, I am unaware of any which allow independent "op-eds" to be published in it by staff or outsiders.

Another example is the systematic inclusion of dissenting opinions in higher court decisions made by a panel of judges. The concept could be applied widely to written reports recommending a specific policy or course of action. A well-constructed options paper will not just argue the virtues of the preferred option but will present the best alternatives—or better yet, have those alternatives presented by their advocates. Conference volumes often present the main papers along with written comments and criticism by the discussants. Some journals (e.g., *The Behavioral and Brain Sciences* and *The Journal of Economic Perspectives*) are organized in the powerful and rewarding format of invited papers followed by criticism, commentary, and counter-articles all in the same issue. The *Opposing Viewpoints Series* of Greenhaven Press is an excellent example of a book series that focuses on giving point and counterpoint on the major issues (e.g., Rohr 1989). The preface in each volume cites John Stuart Mill in *On Liberty*:

> The only way in which a human being can make some approach to knowing the whole of a subject, is by hearing what can be said about it by persons of every variety of opinion, and studying all modes in which it can be looked at by every character of mind. No wise man ever acquired his wisdom in any mode but this. (Quoted in preface to Rohr 1989, 10)

Such a format of point and counterpoint would seem quite appropriate for institutions that want to foster intellectual inquiry and knowledge development. Yet development agencies operating on a de facto church model want to bombard the client with one-sided arguments leading to uniform advice and do not want to "confuse" or "distract" the client with conflicting ideas (particularly when coming from within the agency). Instead of functioning as a "Church" enunciating a canonical view, an institution could allow multiple viewpoints, each argued passionately by its advocates while adopting none as its official viewpoint. The client would have to decide and take responsibility for that decision.

THE GENERAL CASE FOR DEVIL'S ADVOCACY

The general case for a more systematic devil's advocate or countervailance role in an organization is much the same as the case for genuine debate and open discussion. The classical statements for that argument[4] are in John Milton's *Areopagitica* (1644), Thomas Jefferson's *Bill for Establishing Religious Freedom* (1779), Tunis Wortman's *A Treatise Concerning Political Enquiry* (1800), John Stuart Mill's *On Liberty* (1859), and John Morley's *On Compromise* (1877). If little is known on a question, then real debate and the "clash of adverse opinions" are some of the best engines of discovery. Since "each rooster likes to crow on top of his own dungheap," the dungheaps are more likely to be objectively appraised if there are many other roosters in the barnyard. If "partial truths" are known, then it is better to allow the half-truths to collide since intercourse should produce an offspring closer to a whole truth. Mill argued that even in cases of settled opinions, debate and discussion serve to disturb the "deep slumber of a decided opinion" so that it might be held more as a rational conviction rather than as an article of faith. "So essential is this discipline to a real understanding of moral and human subjects, that if opponents of all-important truths do not exist, it is indispensable to imagine them, and supply them with the strongest arguments which the most skillful devil's advocate can conjure up" (Mill 1977, 245).

Intellectual liberty and tolerance are fundamental to the heritage of the Reformation and Enlightenment. Rather than a "Church" to protect "Truth" and suppress "Error," free discussion and debate fueled by the collision of opposing opinions are the best security against error.

These principles of philosophical liberalism were first hammered out in the battle for religious freedom. Jefferson asked that his tombstone record only three deeds. In addition to the Declaration of Independence, he was the author of the Virginia's 1779 "A Bill for Establishing Religious Freedom," which argued in part that truth "is the proper and sufficient antagonist to error, and has nothing to fear from the conflict unless by human interposition disarmed of her natural weapons, free argument and debate; errors ceasing to be dangerous when it is permitted freely to contradict them."[5] The toleration for dissent and debate is fundamental to the spirit of a university, not to the spirit of a church. The third deed was being founder of the University of Virginia.

PROBLEMS IN IMPLEMENTING DEVIL'S ADVOCACY

What can go wrong in trying to implement a devil's advocate role? One problem is the domestication of the devil's advocate. A "domesticated" devil's advocate maintains a role in the councils of power by keeping dissent well within the bounds of certain spoken or unspoken assumptions (which are often part of the problem) and by not getting "carried away" by going public or appealing to the opposition (see Janis 1972, 120). The devil's advocacy function can become ineffective by being ritualized, taken for granted, or restricted to minor approved variations on the "groupthink" status quo.

Intimidation is a related problem. Arguing against the conventional or received wisdom is more akin to a battle than a tea party.

> Recognition of dynamic conservatism [i.e., self-reinforcing nature of status quo (DE)] explodes the rational myth of intervention pervasive in official rhetoric, which envisages social change as a process made up of analysis of objectives, examination of alternatives, and selection of the most promising routes of change. . . . The rational myth assumes implicitly that transformation occurs in a vacuum rather than in the plenum of self-reinforcing systems . . . (or) that rational plans will implement themselves, or they leave the question of implementation to a mysterious process of sales, persuasion, or politics.
>
> Actual patterns of transformation center around crisis and reveal variations of invasion and insurgency. (Schön 1971, 59)

The devil's advocacy role should be a protected part of "programmed conflict" role-playing to improve decision-making and should not be attributed to the personal "perversity" of the individual in that role. This brings within an organization the role of and the protections for opposition political parties.

The devil's advocate functions as an intellectual ombudsman, shop steward, or public defender for alternative viewpoints. Those who oppose a strategy may be too prudent or vulnerable to individually speak out, and the difficulties of collective action may hinder coordinated opposition. An institutionalized devil's advocate role can serve as a lightning rod to collect and aggregate opposing views and thus resolve the collective action problem.

Rotation of the devil's advocate function can help to prevent domestication and intimidation. To implement the rotating DA function, temporary teams can be assigned to prepare the cases for the alternative policies. Individuals identified with one position can be asked to present the case for the opposition (just as authors at some academic conferences are asked to give each other's papers). Rotation also helps to keep a specific individual from being sidelined or dismissed for being only a naysayer, for not being a team player, or even for being "disloyal."

And finally, there is the problem that if there is an "official" devil's advocate, then this may be seen as relieving other staff members from exercising their critical reason in public so that they can take the path of least organizational resistance with a clear conscience. It isn't "their job" to publicly argue against the vanities and inanities of the high officials in the organization. But a well-implemented devil's advocacy role would be part of a general democratization of the organizational culture which would change the usual penalties attached to the public exercise of critical reason.

DEVIL'S ADVOCACY AS THE QUALITATIVE VERSION OF THE OPPORTUNITY COST DOCTRINE

In economics, the opportunity cost doctrine evaluates an option or good by comparing its value to the value of best alternative. If plan B is the best alternative to plan A (and the plans are mutually exclusive), then the opportunity cost of choosing plan A is the value foregone by not choosing plan B. Plan A is preferable if its value exceeds its opportunity cost. The application of the opportunity cost doctrine requires the analysis and evaluation of the best alternative—and that is the more general role of devil's advocacy even when quantitative values cannot be assigned to the alternatives. By eliciting plan B, devil's advocacy generalizes the opportunity cost doctrine from cost-benefit analysis to general policy analysis. In a rivalrous market, competition provides the B plans so that organizational devil's advocacy could be seen as an attempt to provide the benefits of benchmark competition *within* an organization.

One pseudoscientific method of evaluation is to see if the benefits of expending resources on plan A exceed the benefits of the "untreated" or "control" plan B (namely, doing nothing). But a genuine evaluation of plan A would compare its benefits to the benefits of expending the same resources on the best alternative plan B (not an untreated control sample of doing nothing). The design of the best alternative plan B is usually devilishly difficult. But it is the job of the devil's advocate in the sense of constructive criticism since it is usually beyond the inclinations of the sponsors of plan A.

EVALUATION = RETROSPECTIVE DEVIL'S ADVOCACY

Evaluation should be seen as the retrospective devil's advocate role.[6] It is this role of considering the best alternative use of the resources which is so often overlooked when organizations congratulate themselves for projects that "have a positive impact" and "succeed in fulfilling their objectives." There are enormous "groupthink" pressures of conformity to be a team player by "celebrating our successes" rather than "dwelling on hypothetical counterfactuals" (about what might have been done with the resources). Economists often seem to be as allergic as anyone to "dwelling on what might have been" even though that is the underlying logic of the opportunity cost doctrine. Without the backward-looking devil's advocate, the most informative negative feedback and learning may be lost, and the organization is condemned to repeat its "glorious" past.

VARIATIONS: ADVERSARIAL LEGAL PROCESS, THE LOYAL OPPOSITION, SEPARATION OF POWERS, AND CIVIL SOCIETY

The general devil's advocacy role has been incorporated into various institutions. The state requires significant prima facie evidence to charge a person with a crime. In spite of that evidence, the adversarial system gives the defendant the right of legal representation to have access to the evidence, to call witnesses, and to contest the charges in an open court before the judge and jury. For an individual viewpoint, this could be seen as a matter of individual rights, but from a social viewpoint the adversarial system of legal proceedings seems to increase the quality of social decision-making on the important questions of guilt or innocence.

In a multiple-party democracy, the main party out of power forms the institutionalized "loyal or legitimate opposition" that plays the political devil's advocate role (see Ionescu and de Madariaga 1972). The loyal opposition forms an independent power base of those who seek to express opinions and policies at variance with the party in power. Without such a protected role, those out of power can be isolated, atomized, and silenced, and the iron law of oligarchy will hold full sway (see Michels 1962; Ellerman 1988).

The separation of powers within a government or an organization is intended to diminish or prevent the problems that arise from the exercise of unified and unopposed power.

> This policy of supplying, by opposite and rival interests, the defect of better motives, might be traced through the whole system of human affairs, private

> as well as public. We see it particularly displayed in all the subordinate distributions of power, where the constant aim is to divide and arrange the several offices in such a manner as that each may be a check on the other—that the private interest of every individual may be a sentinel over the public rights. (Madison, *Federalist Paper No. 51*)

Centralized power can be abused in private and public bureaucracies as well as in democratic government. The general idea of separation of powers, with one interest checking the overextension of another interest, has a broader applicability in organizations.

Public evaluation of government policies and actions requires a protected public space for ideas to be discussed, for views to be aired, and for opposing opinions to collide. This requires a free press, access to the electronic media, and a tradition of tolerance for open discussion in spite of adverse impact on vested interests. Courageous and outspoken individuals are not enough; it takes a multitude of vigorous nongovernmental organizations (NGOs) and associations to sustain the sphere of civil society. Thus, in the broadest sense, civil society and the traditions of public discussion that undergird it support the devil's advocacy function in liberal democratic countries.

NOTES

1. This is expressed in the "marketplace of ideas concept—the proposition that truth naturally overcomes falsehood when they are allowed to compete. . . . The belief that competing voices produce superior conclusions (is) . . . implicit in scientific reasoning, the practice of trial by jury, and the process of legislative debate" (Smith 1988, 31).

2. Devil's advocacy (see Schwenk 1984) is interpreted broadly to include a number of related techniques to better elicit the main policy alternatives. A *Cassandra's advocate* (Janis 1972, 217) is a person who emphasizes alternative interpretations of data and focuses on all the things that can go wrong ("Murphy's Lawyer"). The *Rashomon* effect (see Schön 1971, 210) illustrates that the same set of circumstances and events can be interpreted very differently by different people. Discussion organized as a debate between the proposed policy and the best alternative has been called the *dialectical method* (see Schwenk 1989; or Tung and Heminger 1993). *Multiple advocacy* (Haas 1990, 210), equivocality (Weick 1979, 174), and double visioning (see Schön 1983, 281) refer to the practice of not only allowing but fostering the presentation of two or more policy options.

3. The locus classicus for this emphasis on contestation in Greek civilization is Burckhardt (1998).

4. See Levy (1985) and Smith (1988).

5. Jefferson echoes John Milton's defense of intellectual freedom in *Areopagitica* (1957a). "And though all the winds of doctrine were let loose to play upon the earth,

so Truth be in the field, we do injuriously, by licensing and prohibiting, to misdoubt her strength. Let her and Falsehood grapple; who ever knew Truth put to the worse, in a free and open encounter?"

6. When other possibilities are being realized simultaneously with the given project—as in parallel experimentation—then evaluation can be based on direct comparison and benchmarking between the parallel experiments (see the chapter 3 on parallel experimentation).

Chapter 5

The Indirect Approach

INTRODUCTION

The sort of "direct approach" criticized in this chapter is the sort of direct control often attempted by some central authority through introducing and manipulating of external or economic incentives ("carrots and sticks"). Critiques of centralized allocation mechanisms are usually based on informational difficulties (Hayek). Here we focus on how centralized mechanisms override and undercut autonomy. Indirect methods focus on being more autonomy compatible. Three very different examples of an "indirect approach" will serve to introduce the variety and importance of the idea:

- the indirect approach in matters of strategy in military as well as broader human affairs,
- the indirect approach to learning about the higher animals (in comparison with, say, insects), and
- the indirect approach as a class of social policies that operate by enabling private and collective actors instead of trying to directly control their actions.

THE INDIRECT APPROACH IN STRATEGY

Liddell Hart's (1895–1970) classic book *Strategy* (1967) evolved from a 1941 book entitled *The Strategy of Indirect Approach.* Hart saw that the indirect approach that he recommended in military strategy was in fact part of a much broader indirect approach that could be applied elsewhere in human affairs:

> With deepening reflection . . . I began to realize that the indirect approach had a much wider application—that it was a law of life in all spheres: a truth of philosophy. . . .
>
> This idea of the indirect approach is closely related to all problems of the influence of mind upon mind-the most influential factor in human history. (Hart 1941, x)

THE INDIRECT APPROACH IN BIOLOGICAL LEARNING MECHANISMS

A very different area where the "indirect approach" is prominent is in the comparative biology of learning mechanisms. Here are two very different ways in which teaching and learning can take place. Both ways occur biologically if we view what is transmitted through the genetic mechanism from an organism to its offspring as the biological version of what is transmitted from the teacher to the learner. For many organisms, insects being a good example, the specific behaviors (that are fitted to certain stable environments) are transmitted by the genes from parents to offspring. The individual organism does not engage in learning from the environment as the appropriate behaviors are already determined by the structure of the organism that was transmitted through the genes. Thus, any learning takes place only at the species level, not at the individual level. Norbert Wiener calls this "phylogenetic learning" as opposed to "ontogenetic learning" (1961, 169). For instance, insects have only phylogenetic learning, whereas the mammals ("higher animals") have both phylogenetic learning and ontogenetic learning.

> (The) very physical development of the insect conditions it to be an essentially stupid and unlearning individual, cast in a mold which cannot be modified to any great extent. . . . On the other hand . . . the human individual (is) capable of vast learning and study . . . (and) is physically equipped, as the ant is not, for this capacity. Variety and possibility are inherent in the human sensorium-and are indeed the key to man's most noble flights-because variety and possibility belong to the very structure of the human organism. (Wiener 1954, 51–52)

In animals capable of ontogenetic learning, the genes do not transmit the specific behaviors that might be fitted to certain environment; instead, the genes transmit the learning mechanisms to the offspring. The animal then interacts with, adapts to, and learns from the environment. In this manner, the animal can learn much more complex activities in a wide variety of environments than could possibly be transmitted directly by the genes. Indeed, the adjectives "direct" and "indirect" can be used to describe these two approaches to learning.

> The gene-pattern, as a store or channel for variety, has limited capacity. Survival goes especially to those species that use the capacity efficiently. It can be used directly or indirectly.
>
> The direct use occurs when the gene-pattern is used directly to specify the regulator. The regulator is made (in the embryo) and the organism passes its life responding to each disturbance as the gene-pattern has determined. . . .
>
> The indirect use occurs when the gene-pattern builds a regulator (R_1) whose action is to build the main regulator (R_2), especially if this process is raised through several orders or levels. By achieving the ultimate regulation through stages, the possibility of large-scale supplementation occurs, and thus the possibility of an ultimate regulation far greater than could be achieved by the gene-pattern directly. (Ashby 1963, 270–71)

In the indirect case, the first regulator transmitted by the genes is the learning mechanism, and the second main regulator is the whole set of activities learned by the animal through interaction with the environment.

> (The learning mechanism's) peculiarity is that the gene-pattern delegates part of its control over the organism to the environment. Thus, it does not specify in detail how a kitten shall catch a mouse, but provides a learning mechanism and a tendency to play, so that it is the mouse which teaches the kitten the finer points of how to catch mice.
>
> This is regulation, or adaptation, by the indirect method. The gene-pattern does not, as it were, dictate, but puts the kitten into the way of being able to form its own adaptation, guided in detail by the environment. (Ashby 1960, 234)

The direct method (where genes transmit behaviors) and the indirect method (where the genes transmit a learning capacity) are essentially the genetic versions of two basic pedagogies. In the direct method, the teacher transmits knowledge to the passive student who absorbs and uses the knowledge as needed. In the indirect method, the teacher fosters and awakens an intrinsic desire for learning on the part of the learner who then takes the active role in (re)discovering and appropriating knowledge. In the indirect method, the teacher does not transmit knowledge, but "puts the (learner) into the way of being able to form (the learner's) own adaptation, guided in detail by the environment." Jose Ortega y Gasset uses a metaphor similar to Ashby's:

> He who wishes to teach us a truth should not tell it to us, but simply suggest it with a brief gesture, a gesture which starts an ideal trajectory in the air along which we glide until we find ourselves at the feet of the new truth. . . . He who

> wants to teach a truth should place us in the position to discover it ourselves. (Ortega 1961, 67)

These two methods are also described in the old Chinese story that giving a man a fish only feeds him for a day while teaching him how to fish feeds him for a lifetime. Ashby develops a similar story. Suppose that a father only had ten minutes to teach his child the meanings of English words. Using the direct method, the father would teach the child the meaning of a small number of words.

> The indirect method is for the father to spend the ten minutes showing the child how to use a dictionary. At the end of the ten minutes the child is, in one sense, not better off; for not a single word has been added to his vocabulary. Nevertheless, the second method has a fundamental advantage; for in the future the number of words that the child can understand is no longer bounded by the limit imposed by the ten minutes. The reason is that if the information about meanings has to come through the father directly, it is limited to ten-minutes' worth; in the indirect method the information comes partly through the father and partly through another channel (the dictionary) that the father's ten-minute act has made available.
>
> In the same way the gene-pattern, when it determines the growth of a learning animal, expends part of its resources in forming a brain that is adapted not only by details in the gene-pattern but also by details in the environment. The environment acts like the dictionary. While the hunting wasp, as it attacks its prey, is guided in detail by its genetic inheritance, the kitten is taught how to catch mice by the mice themselves. Thus, in the learning organism the information that comes to it by the gene-pattern is much *supplemented* by information supplied by the environment; so the total adaptation possible, after learning, can exceed the quantity transmitted directly through the gene-pattern. (Ashby 1960, 236–37)

THE INDIRECT APPROACH IN SOCIAL POLICIES

For examples of an indirect approach in social policies, we might consider a survey of global trends in economic and social development commissioned by the United Nations Centre for Human Settlements (UNCHS) (Habitat) and carried out by the CERFE group in Rome. The report painstakingly analyzed fifty-eight urban policies.

Generally speaking, the overwhelming majority of urban policies enacted or encouraged by governments, local entities, and international organizations appear to be based on what we might term an *indirect approach*, which is characterized by the following:

- the tendency of public subjects to avoid direct intervention to resolve problems or provide services, thus leaving greater room for action by other private and collective subjects;
- the tendency of public actors to be structured in an effectively decentralized manner;
- the growing tendency to resort to a variety of sources of financing, especially local sources (CERFE 1995, Chapter 1.8).

Thus, governments have been turning away from the more customary direct approach, the report of which is characterized by:

- exclusive recourse to public entities for the provision of services and infrastructure;
- centralized decision-making authority; near exclusive recourse to public funding for the supply of services and the construction and maintenance of infrastructure (CERFE 1995, Chapter 1.8).

My purpose here is to try to pull together from antiquity to modem times a wide variety of strategies and theories that promote an indirect approach to learning, management, developing critical reason, spiritual progress, and broader social and institutional change. What are the basic limitations on direct approaches such as the economic theory of agency, and what are the underlying reasons for the efficacy of an indirect approach?

TOWARD A CRITIQUE OF AGENCY THEORY

This emphasis on indirect approaches grows in part out of misgivings with the economic theory of agency.[1] Agency theory focuses on the common situation wherein one person or group, called the "principal," desires to obtain certain behavior from another person or group called the "agent." The principal-agent language is borrowed from the legal relationship of agency and is used in economics in a broader context. Douglas McGregor writing in 1948 before the principal-agent language was established in the economics and management literature refers to the principal and agent, respectively, as "*A*" and "*B*": "*A* always refers to the individual (or group) who is attempting to induce a behavior change, and *B* always refers to the individual (or group) whose behavior is affected" (1948; reprinted in 1966, 155).

Agency theory is based on *homo economicus,* or in McGregor's terms, on the Theory X view of people (1960; 1966; 1967). Positive and negative economic incentives ("carrots and sticks") must be supplied by the principal to induce the appropriate behavior by the agents. Left to their own devices, agents cannot be trusted to act in the manner desired by the principal so an incentive structure must be applied to redirect the agents in the desired manner. Agency theory is a sophisticated direct approach. McGregor's alternative Theory Y is an indirect approach.

Many of the modem management strategies that have grown out of McGregor's classic formulation of Theory Y will thus have a significant indirect component. Our purpose is to dig into the intellectual background to indirect approaches, which at the same time can be seen as showing limitations on the strictly economic approach to "agency" relationships.

The direct approach of Theory X and the indirect approach of Theory Y cannot simply be applied at the same time (although managers often seem to try). The approaches are more substitutes than complements but it is not simply a matter of choosing one or the other. It is a question of foreground and background. The case in favor of a Theory Y approach is not a case against any carrots or sticks per se, but a case that the carrots and sticks should be kept in the background as motivational backstops. It is a question of who is in the driver's seat, not who is in the car.

Piece rates and pay-for-performance schemes are examples of carrots in the foreground trying to get people's attention and guide their actions. An equitable salary more geared to experience and seniority would be an example of keeping the carrot of pay in the background so that other more intrinsic motives might emerge in the foreground to guide action. The tight coupling of pay with performance, as implied whenever possible by agency theory, is beside the point when the pay is in the background. For instance, Deming's "New Economics" recommends to "abolish incentive pay and pay based on performance" (1994, 28), for example, to pay salespeople by salary rather than by commission. Deming recommends replacing a system based on monitoring and quality bonuses with a system using (for the most part) trust based on self-esteem and pride in the quality of one's work. In short, this approach to quality relies not on cleverly constructed pay-for-performance schedules but on switching over to a quality system driven largely by intrinsic motivators (see below) such as self-esteem and pride in one's work—in short, quality as a calling.

THE HELPER-DOER RELATIONSHIP

The focus will be on the relationship where some party A tries to induce a change in the behavior or beliefs of another party B. Sometimes the first party might be called the "principal" and the second the "agent" in keeping with the idea of exploring Theory Y or indirect approaches to the agency relationship. But the agency terminology is freighted with connotations from economics and the law that are sometimes inappropriate, so I will also use the terminology of A being the "helper" and B the "doer," or "doers." Then the Theory Y and indirect approaches fall in line as ways for "helpers" to help others to help themselves to "do" something, while the Theory X and direct approaches are ways of influencing others to do something, but not ways of helping others to become more autonomous. Theory X does not take the autonomy of the agents or doers as a constraint, not to mention as a goal.

How can helpers provide assistance that is compatible with the autonomy of the doers? This is the quintessential problem of autonomy-compatible assistance; how to "help others to help themselves." The task is not to "help others"; it is the quite different task of "helping others help themselves." The notion of an autonomy-compatible assistance has a whiff of paradox since it is an external intervention that somehow does not override or undercut the other person's internal locus of causality. For instance, if the helper has a significant impact, then to what extent are the others really "helping themselves," or if they are really helping themselves, then what is the role of the would-be "helpers"?[2]

There is a similar "learning paradox" in pedagogy (that we will explore); if the teacher "gives" the knowledge to the student, then the student probably has little understanding or "ownership" of the knowledge, but if the student actively rediscovers and appropriates the knowledge as their own, then the knowledge does not "come from" the teacher. The various answers to the problem of autonomy-compatible assistance are all approaches that could be termed "indirect"—and thus our focus.

At various points, I must ask the basic question: "Why an indirect approach; why not a direct approach?" What exactly is the problem with a more direct approach? There are many ways or at least answers—in many terminologies. In the language of autonomy, the problems with the direct approaches are immediate; they cut across the autonomy of the agents or doers. In a direct approach (carrots and sticks), the agent is controlled and acted upon; the relationship does not enable the agent to become more self-acting or autonomous. Only an indirect approach is compatible with maintaining, if not increasing, the doer's autonomy.

INTRINSIC AND EXTRINSIC MOTIVATION

The concepts of extrinsic and intrinsic motivation can be useful in making these distinctions. An intrinsically motivated activity is an activity carried out by individuals for its own sake. The activity is an end in itself, not an instrumental means to some other end (such as satisfying biological needs or "tissue deficits"). The factors that determine the meaning of "for its own sake" are usually based on the self-identity of the person or persons carrying out the activity. An intrinsically motivated activity might be accompanied by extrinsic motivators if the latter are not controlling, that is, if they do not take over the locus of control.[3] For instance, professors typically pursue their professional work for its own sake even though there is a salary and other emoluments in the background. Indeed, much of the story is concerned with the question of the locus of control for an activity. Autonomous activity has an internal locus of control. A bribe or threat to get one to do what one would not ordinarily do establishes an external locus of control.

The economic theory of agency works with extrinsic variables such as monetary rewards or penalties to the agent that the principal can affect and change since the goal of the theory is to design incentive structures to elicit the desired results from the agent. By following the incentives provided by the "incentive-compatible" reward scheme, the agent will be led to achieve the results desired by the principal. From the agent's viewpoint, such an incentive structure represents extrinsic or external motivation. Money is the most obvious (extrinsic motivator), but promotion, praise, recognition, criticism, social acceptance and rejection, and "fringe benefits" are other examples.

> "Intrinsic" rewards, on the other hand, are inherent in the activity itself; the reward is the achievement. They cannot be *directly* controlled externally, although characteristics of the environment can enhance or limit the individual's opportunities to obtain them. Thus, achievement of knowledge or skill, of autonomy, of self-respect, of solutions to problems are examples. (McGregor 1966, 20.3–4)

There is now a considerable body of literature in psychology, sociology, and organizational behavior on intrinsic and extrinsic motivation as well as the closely related notions of autonomy, self-determination, and internal locus of control.[4] Although considerations of intrinsic motivation have figured prominently in the romantic critique[5] of classical economics, the topic has until recently only received sporadic treatment in economics literature.[6] Bruno Frey's *Not Just for the Money* (1997) was the first book-length treatment of the topic of intrinsic motivation in the economics literature.

Again, the question can be asked: "Why an indirect approach; why not a direct approach?" Motive is part of action. If an action has an intrinsic motive, then it cannot be induced by extrinsic motivation. This is the old "can't buy love" argument in the terminology of intrinsic- extrinsic motivation. One can buy "loving behavior" but not love. The extrinsic motivation is inconsistent with the condition of being in love. Any action which involved an intrinsic motive could not be induced by extrinsic motivations, only a similar behavior.[7] "Bought love" is a motivationally inconsistent state: if it is love, then it is not "bought" (although money may be involved incidentally in the background), and if it is bought, then it is only loving behavior.

This "not for sale" argument applies to all nonpecuniary motives, not just to intrinsic motivations. McGregor mentions praise and recognition as extrinsic motivators. Yet "bought praise" or "bought recognition" would be counterfeit since money payments are not genuine grounds for giving someone else praise or recognition. In contrast, there is no contradiction in paying someone to "prostitute" themselves in certain ways or to undertake a mercenary endeavor as that motivation is quite consistent with the proposed action.

Thus, one must always match tools to tasks. The direct approach utilizes certain tools such as the "carrots and sticks" of agency theory, and yet those tools may be inconsistent with the motives of the desired actions. A carrot cannot motivate a noncarrot-driven action. Such actions require an indirect approach.

BY-PRODUCTS RATHER THAN PRODUCTS OF CHOICE

Jon Elster has considered a large class of mental and social "by-product" states that cannot be brought about by deliberate choice (I 983, Chapter II: "States that are Essentially By-Products"). One cannot "produce" a state that is *essentially* a by-product, just as one cannot machine-produce a handmade artifact. One can only machine-produce counterfeit "handmade" artifacts.

Imposed "autonomy" and bought "love" are among the examples of motive-inconsistent states. The principal cannot pay or threaten the agent to have such states as the motive contradicts the grounds for such states. The problems arise for cognitive states as well as for volitional states. Belief in some statement P, for example, would be grounded in some reason that could qualify as grounds for belief. Getting paid to believe P or believing P for instrumental reasons such as to attract another person or to be a member of a belief-based organization (church[8]) are not among those grounds,[9] although they may well be reasons for some "believing behavior." A "bought belief" is the cognitive version of the inconsistency involved in a "bought nonpecuniary motive" such as "bought love."

Here again, the answer is clear to the question: "Why an indirect approach; why not a direct approach?" A direct approach may be self-defeating like shining a flashlight to get a better look at "darkness"; the approach dispels the goal.[10] A by-product is at best the product of "indirect means" (Elster 1983, 56). Mental states and conditions have their antecedents or grounds. A direct approach using an instrument that did not fulfill those antecedents or grounds would only produce a counterfeit state or condition (like a "bought belief"). Only an indirect approach that tried to foster or to be a midwife to the right conditions or grounds would have a chance of success.

MCGREGOR'S THEORY Y: A PROTOTYPE INDIRECT APPROACH

It is quite instructive to look at the genesis of McGregor's indirect Theory Y. He did not start with the traditional manager-subordinate relationship but with the relationship between a staff expert (e.g., in human relations, accounting, finance, and engineering) who is to help a line manager with a particular problem. It is perhaps because the line manager is not subordinate to the staff expert that McGregor has to explore indirect approaches: "The function of the staff expert in human relations is necessarily indirect."[11] This is the topic in McGregor's 1946 article "The Staff Function in Human Relations" which even precedes the "Theory X" and "Theory Y" terminology. At the end of the article, he muses that this approach might be applied by "the line manager to his own subordinates" (1948; reprinted in 1966, 170). McGregor did just that in his classic presentation of Theory Y in *The Human Side of Enterprise* (1960).

McGregor describes Theory Y as being based on the principle of integration and self-control[12] where "integration" refers to the situation where an individual "can achieve his own goals *best* by directing his efforts toward the objectives of the enterprise" (1960, 61). Management's task is not to provide incentives; the "task is to provide an appropriate environment—one that will permit and encourage employees to seek intrinsic rewards *at work*" (1967, 14). The contrasting Theory X is based on the principle or philosophy of direction and control using the type of incentives that management can provide, that is, extrinsic incentives.

I will outline Theory Y in a broader principal-agent setting where the "principal" or "helper" is trying to help the "agent" or "doer" to accomplish certain tasks. The general purpose is for the helper to help the doer or doers to help themselves. In an organizational setting, the principal (helper) would have a managerial role, the agent (doer) would be a subordinate (or another manager as in McGregor's staff-line example), and the tasks would be in furtherance of organizational goals.

Step 1: Starting from the Doer's Problem

The helper starts from the doer's engagement with an organizational problem, a problem that the helper is to help the doer solve. The helper is not to start with what the helper as expert thinks is "the problem."

Step 2: Seeing the Problem through the Doer's Eyes

The helper explores with the doer the problem as perceived by the doer. How does the doer perceive and conceptualize the difficulty? If the helper sees the situation differently, then this should be explained clearly without trying to manipulate the doer's perceptions or impose the helper's view of the problem.

Step 3: Helping the Doer Pursue Own Ends to Best Solve the Organizational Problem

This is the core of the indirectness of the approach. Starting with the doer's problem within the organization and seeing the problem through the doer's eyes, the helper can then offer knowledge and experience to help the doer find the best way to further the doer's own intrinsic ends while addressing the organizational problem. The helper is not to "teach" the doer what the helper considers the best solution.[13] This is particularly difficult for engineers and economists who "know" the "one best (or optimal) way" to solve the problem. The helper is to create a learning situation so that the doer can arrive at what the doer considers to be the best solution to the problem in view of his own ends and capabilities.[14]

> *A's* [DE: Helper's] objective is to utilize his skill to create a situation in which *B* (doer) can learn, and to make his knowledge available so that *B* may utilize it to augment his own need satisfaction in ways consistent with the achievement of organizational objectives. (McGregor 1966, 163)
>
> Fundamentally the staff man . . . must create a situation in which members of management can learn, rather than one in which they are taught. (Ibid., 161)

As the arrived-at solution is the fruits of the doer's own labor, the doer has a natural ownership of it which leads to much more effective implementation (e.g., more effective than the typical partial, half-hearted, and sullen implementation of the expert's imposed "solution").

If the helper's favored approach or solution is sound, then a learning situation should be feasible wherein the doer can arrive at it or something close to it. As may be more likely the case, the helper's favored solution may be incomplete or require adaptation to local circumstances so "perhaps the greatest challenge in the methods outlined above (is that) they offer to (helper and doer) alike a valuable opportunity to learn" (McGregor 1966, 168).

Step 4: Helping Doer to Implement, Test, and Refine the Doer's Solution

Having worked with the doer to arrive at what the doer considers the best solution, the helper needs to assist the doer in testing it, refining it, and gaining the skill and self-confidence for full implementation of the refined solution. This at the same time builds trust on the part of the helper that the doer will take responsibility for the problem-solving.

Step 5: Helping Doer Gain Autonomy and Take Responsibility for Solution

In this final stage, the helper's goal is to assist the doer to achieve independence ("leave the nest") and to take full responsibility for the solution and its implementation—as well as for finding own solutions to similar problems that might arise in the future. There are two sides to this "separation" or "leaving the nest" problem: getting the doer to avoid dependency and assume responsibility and getting the helper to have the trust to "let go" and to avoid trying to take responsibility.[15]

The helper must avoid the benevolent "giving" of a solution to a grateful doer as that develops dependency and the doer does not learn to help himself. Just as the doer needs to take responsibility, the helper needs to avoid trying to "take responsibility." This is particularly difficult since helpers have their own bosses or principals, so the helper naturally wants to take ownership of the solution. "If [the helper's] own need for power is too strong, he will not be able to create or maintain an effective relationship with *B* (the doer). If he is overanxious for recognition, he is likely to destroy the results of his work with B by seeking credit for *B's* accomplishments" (1966, 167).

This is the classic ownership problem. If the helper takes ownership of the solution in the eyes of the organization, then we are back in the case where the doers are called upon to implement someone else's plan with the aforementioned lack of effectiveness. The helper is never more successful than when the doer finds the *doer's* solution.[16]

INDIRECT APPROACHES: INTELLECTUAL BACKGROUND IN ANTIQUITY

Indirect approaches in the agent-principal relationship or the helper-doer relationship will be explored by looking at the history of these diverse but interrelated ideas.

Taoist Antecedents

Direct approaches usually express a controlling and engineering mentality (stereotypically masculine) often associated with the West, while indirect approaches motivated by organic nurturing and enabling attitudes (feminine) are associated with the East. Eastern religions, particularly Taoism, have some clear early arguments against a direct controlling approach to human affairs.

> For those who would like to take control of the world and act on it—
> I see that with this they simply will not succeed. (Lao-Tze 1989, Chapter 29)

In contrast, Taoism has the central concept of *wu-wei*, which is variously translated by "action by inaction" or "effortless action." Perhaps *wu-wei* can be best understood as a general metaphor for the *indirect* approach. Certainly the "inaction" implies refraining from direct controlling actions that, as noted earlier, may defeat their purpose. A proper indirect approach by the helper will enable and enlist the intrinsic motivation and best energies of the doers so that matters will progress effortlessly on their initiative. A clear example is in learning. Learning externally imposed lessons requires quite an effort, but "when I study a subject which I love—no matter how many years it takes me to learn it—I never feel that I am making any effort" (Smullyan 1977, 161). When the teacher refrains from "teaching" a topic (in the sense of "pumping" knowledge into the pupil) and instead awakens the learner's interest in the topic so that learning becomes self-motivated, then that is the *wu-wei* of the indirect approach on the part of the teacher-helper.

Applied to government, an interfering and overbearing government will stifle and crowd out the initiative and self-activity of the people.

> The more prohibitions there are, the poorer the people become.
>
> . . .
>
> I deal in no business and the people grow rich by themselves.
>
> I have no desires and the people are simple and honest by themselves. (Lin 1948, Chapter 57 of the *Te-Tao Ching*)

Thus, the best *wu-wei* of the government is that which best enables the people to help themselves (which is not necessarily laissez-faire).

The Socratic Method

In the West, we may start the history of the indirect approach with Socrates (469–399 BC). Socrates did not teach, but those who engaged him in dialogue were engaged in learning. He had no writings, and the systemic doctrines expressed in the Platonic dialogues seem to be more attributable to Plato. Socrates was the quintessential helper whose aim was to help others, the doers, to learn to think for themselves. Most people think rather passively reflecting external opinions and values. Socrates exemplified critical reason that could take up the common opinions and values and critically examine them. But he did so in an indirect way by asking questions which would spur the learners to reexamine their own thoughts.

As in McGregor's initial steps, the helper should not "preach the Truth" but should start where the doer is, see the situation through the doer's eyes, and activate the doer's own energies in addressing the problem.

> If education is understood in the Socratic way, as an eliciting of the soul's own activity, it is natural to conclude, as Socrates concludes, that education must be very personal. It must be concerned with the actual situation of the pupil, with the current state of the pupil's knowledge and beliefs, with the obstacles between the pupil and the attainment of self-scrutiny and intellectual freedom. (Nussbaum 1997, 32)

It is important to understand that Socrates's direct goal was not the transmission of truth; otherwise, Sophists's lectures or sermons might have been the chosen pedagogical device rather than dialogue. Socrates's goal was not to instill a specific set of doctrines in his pupils (a temptation Plato could not resist) but to enable them to employ their critical reason so that after critically reexamining themselves during the dialogue and thereafter, the pupils would have "ownership" of the results. By living the examined life of reason, the learners would come to know themselves and to be autonomous.

As Socrates's goal was not to transmit specific doctrines, he (unlike the Sophists) always professed what is now known as "Socratic ignorance." Since he did not "know,"[17] he would have to constantly ask questions to better elucidate the topic.[18] The purpose of the questions was not for Socrates to find answers for himself but to get the pupils to think for themselves. Thus, Socratic questioning is an indirect method, a method designed not to better control and instruct the student, but a method designed to self-activate the learner during the dialogue and perhaps thereafter. Socrates aimed not to be the "Father of Truth" but the midwife of critical reason.

The Socratic teacher is described not only as a coach, a catalyst, or a midwife but as a "brooder" both in the sense of one who meditates about questions but as a hen brooding over her eggs and chicks. Scott Buchanan, the Socratic architect of the renowned learning program at St. John's College (Annapolis, MD), describes the Socratic teacher as

> knowing more than the pupil does, yet in some sense not conveying it but seeing that it is made available to the pupil. The great use of superior knowledge is to understand what the pupil is learning as it is learned. It takes great wisdom to be able to follow a learning pupil sensitively enough to know what the next step is for him, and you don't press the next step. You watch it happen. If it sticks, you help it a bit, but it's not a transmission or an imposition or a filling of a vessel of any of those things. Those are all bad images of the real teaching function: the real one is this penetration of the intelligence, of one intelligence into another. (Buchanan 1970, 51)

This view of the Socratic role of the teacher also follows from the constructivist pedagogy of Jean Piaget's genetic epistemology (e.g., Piaget 1955; 1970).

> To summarize what Piaget said about active methods, he pointed out that the criterion of what makes an "active" method active is not the external actions of the learner. He said, for example, that Socrates used an active method with language and that the characteristic of the Socratic method was to engage the learner in actively constructing his own knowledge. The task of the teacher is to figure out what the learner already knows and how he reasons in order to ask the right question at the right time so that the learner can build his own knowledge. (Kamii 1973, 203)

The Path of Stoicism

Many paths diverged from Socrates and Plato: Aristotle and his school, the Skeptics, the Epicureans, and the Stoics. For the purposes of understanding indirect approaches, the golden thread runs through the Greek and Roman Stoicism of Chrysippus, Cleanthes, Zeno, Seneca, Epictetus, and Marcus Aurelius (although the thread of Neoplatonism will be picked up later).

In this example of the helper-doer relationship, Socrates is replaced by the Stoic teacher who functions as a physician for the soul of his interlocutors, the doers who seek to follow this path. Again, the teacher must start with the particular situation of the doer and see the situation through the doer's eyes in order to be more helpful. "Just as it is appropriate for the (physician) of the body to be "inside" as they say, the affections . . . that befall the body and the therapeutic treatment that is proper to each, so it is the task of the physician of the soul to be "inside" both of these, in the best possible way" (Chrysippus, quoted in Nussbaum 1994, 328–29).

In order to better engage the self-activity of the student, the teacher focuses on practical problems, not abstract philosophical themes.[19] The use of concrete examples and stories serve the same end.

Yet a problem did arise in the transition from Socrates to the Stoics, a problem that has and perhaps will always tend to undermine the strengths of the indirect approach. Epigrams, sayings, and writings accumulated from the sages of the past. Instead of developing their own critical facilities or the autonomy of their wills, students could now memorize the "lessons" of Socrates and the previous Stoic philosophers and then regurgitate them with flourish and skill to become "sages" themselves. For this modus operandi, no indirect pedagogy was needed; the direct approach of indoctrination in the "lessons" and "great books" of the past would suffice. Thus, one finds Epictetus (AD 55–135) going to great lengths verbally lambasting his students for these pretensions. Seneca (AD 1–65) likewise chides his correspondent Lucilius on the desire to accumulate sayings.

> It is disgraceful that a man who is old or in sight of old age should have a wisdom deriving solely from his notebooks. "Zeno said this." And what have you

> said? "Cleanthes said that." What have you said? How much longer are you going to serve under others' orders? . . .
>
> To remember is to safeguard something entrusted to your memory, whereas to know, by contrast, is actually to make each item your own, and not to be dependent on some original and be constantly looking to see what the master said. (Seneca 1969, Letter 33)

In the same spirit, Martha Nussbaum today chides those who would erect "The Great Books" as authorities to be learned, revered, and deferred to, and suggests a "more Senecan title, such as 'Some useful and nourishing books that are likely to help you think for yourself'" (1997, 35).

The goal of the indirect method is the self-transformation of the learner, not to make the learner into "an instrument for what others have to say" (Seneca, Letter 33). But the written word (or remembered spoken word) always provides the temptation to revert to the easier direct method of teaching so that the pupils might at least display some of the outward behavior that might accompany self-transformation.[20]

Learning in Neoplatonism

There is a stream of thought supporting indirect methods that comes from Plato more than Socrates. Plato argued that, as is seen most clearly in mathematics, concepts do not come from experience but arise within the mind itself. The Platonic ideas or forms are innate in the mind and arise in consciousness through a process of recollection or reminiscence perhaps prompted by our sense experience. The theme of innate mental structures and mechanisms triggered—but not controlled—by experience has percolated down through Western thought (e.g., Plotinus, Augustine, the Cambridge Platonists, Descartes, Leibniz, Kant, and Humboldt) to find its most sophisticated modern expression in the school of generative linguistics (e.g., Chomsky 1966).

For our purposes, it is sufficient to see how the theory of the mind as an active generative organ supports the indirect approach, while the opposing theory of the mind as a passive *tabula rasa* or wax block supports the direct approach. Plato has some passive images of the mind as a wax block (*Theaetetus* 191-5) or a mirror or reflector (*Timaeus* 71). But Socrates (*Symposium* 175d) noted that wisdom was not the sort of thing that could flow as through pipes "from the one that was full to the one that was empty." In a direct statement about education, Plato uses the cave allegory where the soul turns away from the shadows to see the forms:

> If this is true, then, we must conclude that education is not what it is said to be by some, who profess to put knowledge into a soul which does not possess it, as

> if they could put sight into blind eyes. On the contrary, our own account signifies that the soul of every man does possess the power of learning the truth and the organ to see it with; and that, just as one might have to turn the whole body round in order that the eye should see light instead of darkness, so the entire soul must be turned away from this changing world, until its eye can bear to contemplate reality and that supreme splendour which we have called the Good. (*Republic* 518)

In Plotinus, the Platonic process of recollection becomes an explicitly active process represented by metaphors such as an overflowing fountain or a radiating light.

> In discussing the human perception of the divine overflow, Plotinus explicitly rejected the concept of sensations as "imprints" or "seal-impressions" made on a passive mind, and substituted the view of the mind as an act and a power which "gives a radiance out of its own store" to the objects of sense. (Abrams 1953, 59)

The opposing metaphors of the mind as a passive mirror or as an active lamp correlate with two opposite pedagogies. One pedagogy sees the student as being essentially passive: a wax tablet on which knowledge is stamped, a mirror or reflector for knowledge (Plato, Locke), a vessel or cistern into which knowledge is poured (Cudworth,[21] Coleridge, Dewey), a phonographic record onto which knowledge is recorded (Dewey, Gramsci, Ryle), and so forth. The teacher supplies the knowledge that is imprinted into the student, crammed into the student as into a bag (Maritain), forced into the student through a "funnel" (Buber), drilled into the student as into hard and resisting rock (Dewey), or forced into the student using a "grease gun" (McGregor).

The other pedagogy sees the student's mind as taking a more active role represented by metaphors such as lamp, fountain, or projector—or often by organic metaphors of a growing plant. The teacher then has a more subtle indirect role of a guide, coach, or midwife to foster and nurture the student's active search for and appropriation of knowledge. Some of the subtlety of the teacher's indirect role can be expressed using the metaphor of the internal fountain. External pressure can obscure or block the flow of the fountain (like turning off a faucet or hose). External help can then unblock the fountain or open the faucet, but the subtle point is that external help cannot directly supply the pressure to make the fountain flow. That pressure has to come from within.[22]

The Learning Paradox and Augustine

The insights of a philosophical tradition are sometimes expressed in a deliberately provocative slogan, epigram, or paradox. One of the striking epigrams of Neoplatonism is the thesis that "no man ever does or can teach another anything" (Burnyeat 1987, 1). This epigram is a variation on Meno's Paradox or the Learning Paradox. In the *Meno* dialogue, Socrates attempts to indirectly "teach" a slave boy some truths of geometry. Socrates claims that people cannot be directly taught such truths, they must recollect them. One interpretation of Meno's Paradox is that a priori truths such as the truths of geometry must be recollected since no amount of empirical investigation can verify the truths of mathematics. But that is a paltry interpretation; Augustine (who "Christianized" Neoplatonism) and others gave a stronger interpretation to the claim that "no man ever does or can teach another anything."

In *De Magistro* (The Teacher), Augustine developed an argument (in the form of a dialogue with his son Adeodatus) that as teachers teach, it is only the student's internal appropriation of what is taught that gives understanding and knowledge:

> Then those who are called pupils consider within themselves whether what has been explained has been said truly; looking of course to that interior truth, according to the measure of which each is able. Thus, they learn . . . . But men are mistaken, so that they call those teachers who are not, merely because for the most part there is no delay between the time of speaking and the time of cognition. And since after the speaker has reminded them, the pupils quickly learn within, they think that they have been taught outwardly by him who prompts them. (*De Magistro*, Chapter XIV)

The basic point is the active role of the mind in *generating* understanding. This is clear even at the simple level of understanding spoken words. We hear the "auditory sense data" of words in a completely strange language as well as the words in our native language. But the strange words "bounce off" our minds with no resultant understanding while the words in a familiar language prompt an internal process of generating a meaning so that we understand the words.

> Nothing can be present in the mind (Seele) that has not originated from one's own activity. Moreover understanding and speaking are but different effects of the selfsame power of speech. Speaking is never comparable to the transmission of mere matter (Stoff). In the person comprehending as well as in the speaker, the subject matter must be developed by the individual's own innate power. What the listener receives is merely the harmonious vocal stimulus. (Humboldt 1997, 102)

There are many variations on this theme of the active mind in understanding. John Dewey made a point about ideas that is similar to the Learning Paradox, a point that supported Dewey's active learning pedagogy.

> It is that no thought, no idea, can possibly be conveyed as an idea from one person to another. When it is told, it is, to the one to whom it is told, another given fact, not an idea. The communication may stimulate the other person to realize the question for himself and to think out a like idea, or it may smother his intellectual interest and suppress his dawning effort at thought. (Dewey 1916, 159)

The common element in the various interpretations of the general learning paradox, "no man ever does or can teach another anything," is that the external transmission from the speaker-teacher to the listener-learner does not itself account for the active role of the mind in generating an understanding of what was received. The external transmission prompts and guides the internal process; the internal processing appropriates what is received and makes it our own.

The "Augustinian point" is that what is often taken as a "direct process" (e.g., transmitting or disseminating knowledge) is actually a more indirect process. Today, "knowledge processes" in organizations are constantly designed using "transmission" images of direct methods when in fact a more subtle understanding and implementation of indirect methods would yield a better chance of success.

MODERN VARIATIONS ON THE INDIRECT APPROACH

Rousseau's Copernican Revolution in Pedagogy

Ortega y Gasset (1883–1955) asks what has been the "great historic advance in pedagogy," and he answers that it was the turning inspired by "Rousseau, Pestalozzi, Froebel, and German idealism." Earlier pedagogy had focused on the teacher and on the subject matter, but with Rousseau the themes known today as self-direction, autonomy, active learning, and learner-centered education came to the forefront. "The innovation of Rousseau and his successors was simply to shift the center of gravity of the science from knowledge and the teacher to the learner, recognizing that it is the learner and his characteristics which alone can guide us in our effort to make something organic of education" (Ortega 1966, 46).

The helper's assistance is often incompatible with the autonomy of the doers because the help is undertaken in the spirit and conception of social engineering. The success of the natural sciences from Galileo and Newton through the Enlightenment to understand and control Nature inspired attempts in the developing psychological, social, political, and economic sciences to similarly "engineer" social outcomes. Although ancient civilizations had their "social engineers," the new aspect was "that the engineering paradigm now becomes a highly conscious, central paradigm. There is the growing conviction that the only *real* problems of men are precisely those amenable to an engineering approach" (Schwartz 1978, 194). The "romantic" reaction to this technocratic strand of Enlightenment thought can be traced to Rousseau.

Here again we see the two theories of the mind represented by the two metaphors of the mirror and the lamp (Abrams 1953). Locke saw the mind as beginning with a *tabula rasa* receiving and mirroring elementary sensations that were with experience and education associated into more complex mental structures. This "mirror" approach lent itself easily to social engineering as seen, for example, in the later development of behaviorism. Descartes, following the Platonic tradition, saw the mind as a lamp endowed with innate structures that unfold and mature under the impact of experience and through the stimulus of action. Rousseau developed a version of the "lamp" theory, although he was more given to organic metaphors of natural growth assisted by appropriate care.

Learning is an active growth, not the accretion of layers as in the "growth" of a pearl. Pedagogy based explicitly or implicitly on the engineering approach sees the teacher as actively depositing new layers of knowledge rather than seeing the learner as taking the active role growing new layers of understanding. A teacher might take pride at explaining everything thoroughly for the student, but that crowds out an active role for the student.

> Talent at instruction consists in making the disciple enjoy the instruction. But in order for him to enjoy it, his mind must not remain so passive at everything you tell him that he has absolutely nothing to do in order to understand you. The master's *amour-propre* must always leave some hold for the disciple's; he must be able to say to himself, "I conceive, I discern, I act, I learn." (Rousseau 1979, 248)

This problem is repeated manifold when administrations in schools want their staff (teachers or task managers) to "show results" which in turn leads to those helpers taking an instrumental or engineering approach in their assistance to the ultimate doers (see McClintock 1982). The end result is that the doers' *amour-propre*, pride, and ownership is crowded out and overridden so they cannot say, "I conceive, I discern, I act, I learn."

Ortega also mentions Pestalozzi (1746–1827) and Froebel (1782–1852) as continuing to emphasize a learner-centered pedagogy in Rousseau's tradition. Indeed, Pestalozzi's work "contains ideas not yet realized in our time, namely, that education of both young and adults is ineffective unless it grows out of the initiative of the people themselves, unless it speaks their language, and unless it influences not only isolated individuals but the life of the whole community" (Ulich 1954, 480).

In addition to being known as the founder of Kindergarten, Froebel has been hailed as "the prophet of the active nature of the learning process" (cited in Lawrence 1970, 244). Froebel made the self-activity of the learner the central theme of his pedagogy: "To stir up, to animate, to awaken, and to strengthen, the pleasure and power of the human being to labour uninterruptedly at his own education, has become and always remained the fundamental principle and aim of my educational work" (Froebel 1954, 525). With Froebel, we also see the emphasis on intrinsic motivation for autonomous learning activities. "Froebel's self-activity is necessarily coupled with joy on the part of the child. To him joy is the inward reaction of self-activity" (translator's note cited in: Ulich 1954, 557). The role of intrinsic motivation in active learning foreshadows the modern literature on the limitations of external motivators in education (e.g., Kohn 1993) and in work (e.g., McGregor and Deming, not to mention Ruskin). As the late philosopher of education David Hawkins put it:

> If we ask how the teacher-learner roles differ from those of master and slave, the answer is that the proper aim of teaching is precisely to affect those inner processes that, as Hegel (and the Stoic philosophers before him) made clear, cannot in principle be made subject to external control, for they are just, in essence, the processes germane to independence, to autonomy, to self-control. (Hawkins 2000, 44)

This theme helps account for the general ineffectiveness of direct methods in fostering mental transformation.

John Dewey and the Active Learning Pedagogy

John Dewey's (1859–1952) theory of education was based on the autonomy-compatible actions of the teacher and the activist role of the learner. As noted above in the context of the learning paradox in Augustinian Neoplatonism, Dewey notes that no idea "can possibly be conveyed as an idea from one person to another" and he evokes the horse-to-water metaphor. The reliance on extrinsic rewards or punishments, not to mention physical control, may yield conforming behavior but has little educative effect. Indeed, the threat to autonomy may lead to an adverse reactance effect. "His instincts of cunning and slyness may be aroused, so that things henceforth appeal to him on the side of evasion and trickery more than would otherwise be the case" (Dewey 1916, 26). An autonomy-compatible educational program needs to engage the person's more natural and intrinsic motivation.

> When we confuse a physical with an educative result, we always lose the chance of enlisting the person's own participating disposition in getting the result

> desired, and thereby of developing within him an intrinsic and persisting direction in the right way. (Dewey 1916, 27)

The students' active interest and involvement is a necessary component so one must consider the roots of engagement. Students do not construct knowledge in a void. Learning is contextual; it builds upon the context of previous knowledge, experience, and problems. Hence, Dewey's "pragmatic" emphasis was placed on learning in the context of the "social environment," albeit simplified and ordered in a school, so that the student would have a natural or intrinsic incentive to learn. Hence Paulo Freire's emphasis on dialogue as the prelude to, as well as the means of, learning (1970). By formulating a literacy campaign in terms of the peasants' daily concerns, the peasants are motivated to be involved and take ownership of the process. The cases, examples, and questions can be couched in terms that make sense from the student's viewpoint and are relevant to the student's interests. With this preparation, the student can take responsibility for actively reconstructing and appropriating knowledge with occasional prodding and questioning from the teacher as midwife. Knowledge obtained in this active way is truly the student's own; it is neither an imposition nor a gift. In general, one may try to "give" help to others or to impose "help," but in neither case are the others helping themselves. The latter requires indirect methods.

The most common error in an educational effort is for the one with superior knowledge (the teacher) to try to impose or imprint knowledge on the one with less knowledge of the relevant sort (assisted by manipulated rewards and punishments). These pedagogical errors are aided and abetted by the Lockean epistemology, which sees the mind as a passive waxed tablet upon which knowledge may be imprinted. Another common error is to think that the alternative role for the teacher is passivity (leaving the children to "free play"). Between these poles lie the autonomy-compatible mode of interaction that is Dewey's "direction by indirection" (Westbrook 1991, 107):

> When the parent or teacher has provided the conditions which stimulate thinking and has taken a sympathetic attitude toward the activities of the learner by entering into a common or conjoint experience, all has been done which a second party can do to instigate learning. The rest lies with the one directly concerned. . . . This does not mean that the teacher is to stand off and look on; the alternative to furnishing ready-made subject matter and listening to the accuracy with which it is reproduced is not quiescence, but participation, sharing, in an activity. In such shared activity, the teacher is a learner, and the learner is, without knowing it, a teacher—and upon the whole, the less consciousness there is, on either side, of either giving or receiving instruction, the better. (Dewey 1916, 160)

Martin Buber also tries to capture the subtlety of "direction by indirection" in his description of the relationship between educator and pupil:

> For if the educator of our day has to act consciously he must nevertheless do it "as though he did not." That raising of the finger, the questioning glance, are his genuine doing. Through him the selection of the effective world reaches the pupil. He fails the recipient when he presents this selection to him with a gesture of interference. It must be concentrated in him; and doing out of concentration has the appearance of rest. Interference divides the soul in his care into an obedient part and a rebellious part. But a hidden influence proceeding from his integrity has an integrating force. (Buber 1965, 90)

Such an indirect autonomy-respecting interaction is even more subtle when all parties concerned are adults with their own past education and formative life experiences.

Carl Rogers's Nondirective Therapy

The next example of an indirect approach comes from Carl Rogers's notion of client-centered therapy—which was also called "nondirective" theory echoing Dewey's notion of direction by indirection. The temptation for the therapist, as for the teacher and manager, is to "take charge" and to try to "produce" the right results. And as in the other cases, this overbearing approach cuts across the other person's internal resources for self-directed activities. On the other hand, a complete laissez-faire or hands-off approach would lead to no interaction rather than an autonomy-compatible interaction (a charge sometimes leveled against nondirective therapy). One key for the therapist, as for the educator, is to see the world through the client's eyes.

> This formulation would state that it is the counselor's function to assume, in so far as he is able, the internal frame of reference of the client, to perceive the world as the client sees it, to perceive the client himself as he is seen by himself, to lay aside all perceptions from the external frame of reference while doing so, and to communicate something of this empathic understanding to the client. (Rogers 1951, 29)

The client-centered therapist must guard against this "empathy" being used as a gimmick to control the patient "while pretending to let him guide himself" (Ibid., 30) just as the Theory Y manager needs to avoid seeing "participation" as a tool to get worker "buy-in" to management decisions. The basis in all cases is the respect for the autonomy of the client (student or worker):

> The sincere aim of getting "within" the attitudes of the client, of entering the client's internal frame of reference, is the most complete implementation which

has thus far been formulated, for the central hypothesis of respect for and reliance upon the capacity of the person. (Ibid., 36)

The therapist's role is to be a "catalyzer of change, rather than a director, controller, or external motivator. . . . In terms of causality . . . the goal of therapy is to be a strengthening of one's autonomy orientation, that is, one's capacity to be self-determining" (Deci and Ryan 1985, 291).

Rogers applies the client-centered approach to education where it becomes "Student-Centered Teaching" (chapter 9 of Rogers 1951), which acknowledges the debt to Dewey and develops the same themes and even some of the same metaphors ("You can lead a horse to water. . . "). Rogers also pointed out the connection to management theory:

> The grounds for the theory of administration which McGregor calls "Theory Y" have been exemplified in all of the preceding chapters of this book. The assumptions on which this theory is based, the kinds of evidence from the behavioral sciences which support it, the view of human nature which permeates it, constitute the backbone of what I have set forth. (Rogers 1969, 207)

Søren Kierkegaard and Ludwig Wittgenstein on Indirect Communication

Søren Kierkegaard (1813–1855) was the philosopher of the indirect approach par excellence. His approach to philosophical persuasion was steeped in indirect Socratic irony and his main message was that all direct objective approaches to spiritual insight must fall short; only subjective inwardness could appropriate the truth about questions of moral or spiritual value. For example, can he directly inform and persuade a conventional "Christian" that he is only under an illusion of being a Christian?

> No, an illusion can never be destroyed directly, and only by indirect means can it be radically removed. If it is an illusion that all are Christians—and if there is anything to be done about it, it must be done indirectly, not by one who vociferously proclaims himself an extraordinary Christian, but by one who, better instructed, is ready to declare that he is not a Christian at all (as S.K. did ironically in: 1992, 466) . . . A direct attack only strengthens a person in his illusion, and at the same time embitters him. . . . And this is what a direct attack achieves, and it implies moreover the presumption of requiring a man to make to another person, or in his presence, an admission which he can make most profitably to himself privately. This is what is achieved by the indirect method which, loving and serving the truth, arranges everything dialectically for the prospective captive, and then shyly withdraws (for love is always shy), so as not to witness the admission which he makes to himself alone before God—that he has lived hitherto in an illusion. (Kierkegaard in: Bretall 1946, 332)

Kierkegaard's main point was not just about the indirectness of persuading others but about the utter subjectivity of moral or spiritual insight even for oneself so that all direct objective or intellectual ("speculative") approaches were doomed to fail and could only produce a counterfeit approximation to insight. He poses the learning paradox about the extent to which truths, spiritual Truth in his case, can be learned from others. He reviews the old doctrine of recollection according to which "the Truth is not introduced into the individual from without but was within him all the time" (in Bretall 1946, 155). Hence, these matters need to be communicated indirectly or maieutically (as by a Socratic midwife). Kierkegaard also gives a spiritual interpretation of "Socratic ignorance" as the recognition that this inward subjective truth cannot be obtained objectively or speculatively.

We noted previously that actions have motives and beliefs have grounds. Kierkegaard is making the point that intrinsically motivated actions and inwardly subjective beliefs cannot be extrinsically or objectively obtained just as love cannot be bought. "But to be a lover, a hero, etc. is reserved specifically for subjectivity, because objectively one does not become that. . . . And . . . piety is rooted precisely in subjectivity; one does not become pious objectively" (1992, 132). It is not the "what" of one's beliefs that counts—as that can be learned by rote—but the "how" of the beliefs, that is, how the beliefs were subjectively appropriated. For instance, Kierkegaard satirizes an orthodox "Christian" gentleman who

> does everything in the name of Jesus and uses Christ's name on every occasion as a sure sign that he is a Christian and is called to defend Christendom in our day—and he has no intimation of the little ironic secret that a person, just by describing the "how" of his inwardness, can indirectly indicate that he is a Christian without mentioning Christ's name. . . . If anyone says, "Yes, but then one can in turn learn the 'how' of faith by rote and recite it," the answer to that must be: That cannot be done, because the person who states it directly contradicts himself . . . (O)ne human being cannot directly communicate this something else to another. . . . All ironic observing is a matter of continually paying attention to the "how," whereas the honorable gentleman with whom the ironist has the honor of dealing pays attention only to the "what." (1992, 613–14 and footnote)

In this sketch, no attempt is being made to capture the richness and scope of Kierkegaard's philosophical psychology or the particulars of his treatment of Christianity. For our purposes, he was the quintessential philosopher of the inner life; indeed, he was obsessed with the juxtapositions of the outer to the inner, the external to the internal, the objective to the subjective. In so doing, he saw clearly that the usual direct methods for dealing with the outer, external, and objective aspects of the world would not extend to the other side; indirect methods were needed to deal with the inner, the internal, and the subjective. Attempts to apply the direct methods to subjective transformation would only produce inauthentic counterfeits.[23]

Kierkegaard is widely considered as one of the founders of existentialism, but it is quite relevant to our theme to see the influence on Ludwig Wittgenstein (1889–1951). By analyzing Wittgenstein's intellectual and social background in early twentieth-century Vienna, Stephen Toulmin has persuasively argued for a more Kierkegaardian interpretation (with significant influence also from Schopenhauer and Tolstoy) than the conventional interpretations of the early Wittgenstein as a logical positivist or the later Wittgenstein as an ordinary language philosopher. This Kierkegaardian reading is important to understand the enigmatic ending of the *Tractatus* (1922): "Whereof one cannot speak, thereof one must be silent." Wittgenstein, like Kierkegaard, strictly separated the objective world of facts from the subjective world of moral and aesthetic values.

> In separating reason from fantasy, the mathematical representation of the physicist from the metaphor of the poet, straight-forward descriptive language from "indirect communication," Wittgenstein was convinced that he had solved "the problem of philosophy." (that is, in the *Tractatus*) . . .The implication of the model theory was that the "meaning of life" lay outside the sphere of what could be said; . . . So the model theory corroborates Kierkegaard's notion that the meaning of life is not a topic which can be discussed by means of the categories of reason.
>
> Subjective truth is communicable only indirectly, through fable, polemics, irony, and satire. This is the only way that one can come to "see the world aright." Ethics is taught not by arguments, but by providing examples of moral behavior; this is the task of art. It is fulfilled in Tolstoy's later *Tales*, which explain what religion is, by *showing* how the truly religious man lives his life. (Janik and Toulmin 1973, 198)

In a December 1929 conversation, Wittgenstein made the explicit connection to Kierkegaard:

> Nevertheless, we run up against the limits of language. This running-up-against Kierkegaard also saw, and indicated in a completely similar way—as running up against the Paradox. This running up against the limits of language is *Ethics*. I regard it as of great importance, that one should put an end to all the twaddle about ethics—whether it is a science, whether values exist, whether the Good can be defined, etc. In ethics people are forever trying to find a way of saying something which, in the nature of things, is not and can never be expressed. We know a priori: anything which one might give by way of a definition of the Good—it can never be anything but a misunderstanding. (Reported in: Waismann 1967, 68–69; quoted in: Janik and Toulmin 1973, 194–95)

In the turn from the early to the later Wittgenstein, his doubts about the efficacy of direct communication in ethical and aesthetic matters spread, albeit for different reasons, to descriptions of the world. Instead of mirroring or picturing facts, language acquired its meaning by its use in inherently social forms of life. When removed out of its embedding in such a language game, an expression might have many interpretations and might cause undue philosophical problems when it is assumed to have a meaning in a very different game. Wittgenstein would use indirect methods of stories and fables to dissolve philosophical problems resulting from lifting language from one form of life to another.

> What Tolstoy's *Tales* had done for the unsayable in ethics, these fables of Wittgenstein's did for the unsayable in the philosophy of language. So, in philosophy as in ethics, Wittgenstein believed, teaching could bring a man only to a point at which he recognized what you were getting at, for himself; and it was no good attempting to draw an explicit conclusion for him. (Janik and Toulmin 1973, 229)

This is expressed in the warhorse aphorism about the indirect way that "You can lead a horse to water but . . . ."

Wittgenstein's theory of meaning as use embedded in a form of life also gives a version of the Augustinian learning paradox that "no man ever does or can teach another anything."

> No-one can achieve my understanding for me, not for the trivial reason that it is mine, but because to internalize the requisite connections is to go beyond what is presented on any occasion of so-called teaching. Augustine does not have Wittgenstein's subtle arguments to bring out the multiplicity of ways in which I might seem (to myself and others) to understand and later turn out to have missed the point, which in turn demonstrates the multiplicity of connections in understanding itself. But we might read Wittgenstein as reviving the ancient understanding of the complexity of understanding. (Burnyeat 1987, 23)

Understanding comes from the listener's integration into the form of life where a linguistic expression is ordinarily used and where the "meaning is the use." This interpretation of Wittgenstein's use of indirect methods meshes well with our next topic—which takes us from Kierkegaard's unsayable "how" to Ryle's inarticulate "knowing-how."

Ryle, Polanyi, and Oakeshott on Uncodified Knowledge

Knowledge that can be directly communicated has already been codified, but much knowledge has the uncodified form of know-how, practical, or tacit knowledge. Gilbert Ryle (1900–1976), Michael Polanyi (1891–1976), and

Michael Oakeshott (1901–1990) have in different fields using various terminologies explored the special problems of uncodified knowledge, including alternatives to the naïve pedagogy of direct teaching as if all knowledge were the technical, explicit, codified, or knowing-that type of knowledge.

Polanyi (1962; 1966) juxtaposes personal, implicit, or tacit knowledge to codified knowledge, the latter being knowledge that can be said, written down, or transmitted over a wire. But "we know more than we can say," such as the knowledge implicit in using our native language, recognizing faces, or performing skilled physical operations such as riding a bicycle. Ryle (1945; 1949) earlier makes the distinction between knowing-that and knowing-how, while Oakeshott (1991) compares technical to practical knowledge.[24]

For Oakeshott, "Rationalism is the assertion that what I have called practical knowledge is not knowledge at all, the assertion that, properly speaking, there is no knowledge which is not technical knowledge" (1991, 15). Technical knowledge is codified and can be learned at least in a rote sense from a book, a correspondence course, or a transmission over a wire. But practical knowledge requires a more indirect process.

> On the other hand, practical knowledge can neither be taught nor learned, but only imparted and acquired. It exists only in practice, and the only way to acquire it is by apprenticeship to a master—not because the master can teach it (he cannot), but because it can be acquired only by continuous contact with one who is perpetually practising it. . . . Thus a pianist acquires artistry as well as technique, a chess-player style and insight into the game as well as knowledge of the moves, and a scientist acquires (among other things) the sort of judgement which tells him when his technique is leading him astray and the connoisseurship which enables him to distinguish the profitable from the unprofitable directions to explore. (Oakeshott 1991, 15)

As all knowledge has a practical as well as a technical component, the Rationalist tradition, according to Oakeshott, tends to systematically ignore the practical component. In what is even a caricature of engineering, Rationalist politics and economics is assimilated to a kind of social engineering based on technical knowledge.

> Thus, political life is resolved into a succession of crises, each to be surmounted by the application of "reason." Each generation, indeed, each administration, should see unrolled before it the blank sheet of infinite possibility. And if by change this *tabula rasa* has been defaced by the irrational scribblings of the tradition-ridden ancestors, then the first task of the Rationalist must be to scrub it clean; as Voltaire remarked, the only way to have good laws is to burn all existing laws and to start afresh. (1991, 9)

Indeed, Oakeshott remarks that it is characteristic of the Rationalist to think of getting rid of a law by burning it—as if the law were only the codified part written down.

Social engineering with carrots and sticks based on Rationalist precepts will try to directly implement change while ignoring the practical knowledge embedded in existing institutions and thus it will most likely fail.[25] To utilize that practical knowledge, change must evolve out of the existing configuration of customs and institutions. A more indirect nonengineering approach might foster that sort of change process. However, a die-hard social engineer might work to make the practical and inarticulate knowledge explicit in order to have social engineering with a human face. Thus, even if autonomy compatibility is not taken as a constraint, there is a practical-knowledge argument against enlightened social engineering based on skepticism about the "practicality" of turning the relevant practical knowledge into technique.

Michael Polanyi made the notion of tacit or personal knowledge into the centerpiece of his philosophical viewpoint. When one focuses on another face and recognizes it, the features of the face necessary for recognition were only attended to in a "*subsidiary awareness*" (1962, 55) and one would be hard put to articulate them. In one's *focal awareness* of the face, these features are brought together in a *gestalt*-like way so that the face is seen as a familiar one. One has a commitment to that tacit knowledge and relies on it for the recognition. If one tries to articulate the separate features of the face that make it recognizable, then one loses the *gestalt*. Polanyi generalized these aspects of tacit knowledge being utilized in a unifying way in all human actions including rigorous scientific activity.

The bringing together or integrating of the underlying tacit knowledge is a creative mental action, and thus it is reminiscent of the active (Kantian) role of the mind in Augustine's Platonism and in modern generative linguistics. Indeed, Polanyi describes the child's acquisition of language as the "early apprenticeship by which the child acquires the idiom of its native community" (1962, 322). Hence, on Polanyi's analysis, the problem with direct methods of teaching or transmitting knowledge is not simply that they neglect the tacit component but that they do not supply the active integration of the tacit knowledge into the focal act of knowing. Thus, what is naively seen as direct transmission is really the more indirect prompting of internal *gestalt* processes of learning and knowing.

Gilbert Ryle (1945; 1949) made an early distinction between knowing-that (propositional knowledge) and knowing-how, the latter being his treatment of practical and personal knowledge. How does Ryle's treatment of the different types of knowing illuminate the direct and indirect approaches to acquiring knowledge? Is the problem with the direct approach simply that it tends to leave out tacit knowledge which might be picked up by indirect means? Or does it relate back to the more passive role of the student under the direct method of teaching in contrast to an indirect approach which casts the learner in a more active role? For Ryle, the important thing was not the explicit/implicit or codified/tacit distinction but the difference between learning propositions (e.g., 7 x 8 = 56) essentially by rote and learning how to *do* something (e.g., to multiply as well as to ride a bike). And when the student learns by doing, then that inextricably active component in the student's role implies a more indirect approach, whereas the direct approach is based on a "semi-surgical picture of teaching as the forcible insertion into the pupil's memory of strings of officially approved propositions" (1967, 108).

In a by-now familiar manner, Ryle poses the learning paradox.

> How, in logic, can anyone be taught to do untaught things? . . . How can one person teach another person to think things out for himself, since if he gives him, say, the new arithmetical thoughts, then they are not the pupil's own thoughts; or if they are his own thoughts, then he did not get them from his teacher? Having led the horse to the water, how can we make him drink? (Ryle 1967, 105, 112)

Ryle's answer is along the lines of the motive inconsistency argument; there is no way to heteronomously impose autonomous action.

> How can the teacher be the initiator of the pupil's initiatives? the answer is obvious. He cannot. I cannot compel the horse to drink thirstily. I cannot coerce Tommy into doing spontaneous things. Either he is not coerced, or they are not spontaneous. . . . (1967, 112)
>
> How in logic can the teacher dragoon his pupil into thinking for himself, impose initiative upon him, drive him into self-motion, conscript him into volunteering, enforce originality upon him, or make him operate spontaneously? The answer is that he cannot—and the reason why we half felt that me must do so was that we were unwittingly enslaved by the crude, semi-hydraulic idea that in essence to teach is to pump propositions, like "Waterloo, 1815" into the pupils' ears, until they regurgitate them automatically. (1967, 118)

Ryle makes the case for the indirect approach crystal clear. The point is not the distinction between codified propositions and tacit practical knowledge; even to actually use and apply codified knowledge requires a knowing-how that needs to be acquired actively. Thus, the problem with the direct approach to teaching is the inconsistency of trying to "impose" active learning. The teacher can open the faucet but cannot supply the pressure for the water to flow (to use a Neoplatonic variation on the horse-to-water metaphor). At best, the teacher uses an indirect approach to bring the learner to the threshold; the self-activity of the learner must carry the process the rest of the way.

Gandhi and Satyagraha

In the case of Gandhi's method of social action called *Satyagraha* (truth-force), the relationship between the first party A (helper) and the second party B (doer) is openly antagonistic. The first party is an aggrieved person or group who feels that their rights have been violated by the second party who would typically be an established political or economic authority. With these caveats in mind, the helper-doer terminology will still be used—particularly in view of Erik Erikson's analogy between the method of *Satyagraha* and the therapeutic relationship (1969, 413, 439).

In the relationship of mind to mind, the main problem of direct methods of influence is motive inconsistency. Means are employed to bring about a change of mind in the doer when the motives are inconsistent with the desired change. Often the motive inconsistency will be of little concern if it is a one-time affair. If one is being attacked, then one would like the attacker (doer) to desist and one may not be fastidious about how the attacker's mind is changed. Ideally, one might want a potential attacker to refrain out of recognition and respect for one's rights, and one's defense might do little to bring about that recognition and motivation. This motivational inconsistency in one's defense would be of little practical consequence if the attack was a one-time matter. But if the situation is repeated as it would be in the case of group of people with a long-standing grievance against an economic or political power, then one might want to consider the motivational dynamics of one's method. Is there an alternative to the vicious cycle of tit for tat or eye for an eye (even the razor's edge of "exact" retaliation seems to lead inevitably to the downward spiral of unequal retaliation)?

The first criterion for an alternative strategy is that it be motivationally consistent with the desired actions on the part of the other party. That is the minimal basis for the passive "turning the other cheek," for not feeding the vicious cycle of attack and counterattack dynamics. The next step is to design an active response strategy that will not only be consistent with a desired motivation but will try to elicit a motive on the part of the doer that would lead to a mutually acceptable state of affairs. That goes beyond "turning the other cheek" to "Love your enemies and pray for those who persecute you" (Bible *Matthew* 5:45).

> Prior to reading Gandhi I had about concluded that the ethics of Jesus were only effective in individual relationships. The "turn the other cheek" philosophy and the "love your enemies" philosophy were only valid, I felt, when individuals were in conflict with individuals; when racial groups and nations were in conflict a more realistic approach seemed necessary. But after reading Gandhi, I saw how utterly mistaken I was.

> Gandhi was probably the first person in history to lift the love ethic of Jesus above mere interaction between individuals to a powerful and effective social force on a large scale. (King 2010, 84)

These strategies at the individual or social level go beyond the reach of direct carrot-and-stick methods. As Dewey remarked, "While we can shut a man up in a penitentiary we cannot make him penitent" (1916, 26). The "stick" at best deters and does not reform, and that may be the best that can be expected against a Tamerlane or a Hitler. But in most social situations there are other possibilities that might be obtained by more indirect methods.

By using indirect methods, mind can affect mind in ways that would be motivationally impossible with direct carrot-and-stick methods. Indirect strategies are designed not just to get the doer to change his behavior (e.g., for prudential reasons) but to change his "heart and mind" and perhaps to set off a more positive dynamics to the benefit of both parties. Changes at that deeper motivational level cannot be forced, and any attempt to crudely force such changes will only lead to resentment, resistance, and intransigence from the doer. Thus, indirect methods operate on the basis of respect for the integrity of the doer.

After exhausting conventional channels to resolve the conflict, the aggrieved party may decide to resort to *Satyagraha*. This party (the helper trying to help the doer change) believes it has been wronged on certain grounds by the doer; that is its "truth." The "truths" asserted by the helper must be heart-felt and not just tactics. To show that the claims are made for authentic reasons, the helper must be vulnerable to rational counter-arguments or new facts that might come to light and must under such circumstances change his mind. "A devotee of Truth may not do anything in deference to convention. He must always hold himself open to correction, and whenever he discovers himself to be wrong he must confess it at all costs and atone for it" (Gandhi 1957, 350). In this manner, arguments on the helper's side about these beliefs are kept on authentic grounds, not on the level of strategy and tactics, and the doer can then be authentically invited to reexamine his beliefs in the light of reason and evidence, not just self-interest.

The conflict is social and is carried out in public. In line with the old strategy to "fight a war to achieve a peace," the actions of aggrieved party must be compatible with the doer changing his mind while maintaining self-respect and self-esteem. While pressure will be brought on the doer to provide motivational backups, the pressure should not take the form of injuries that would derail the motivation for authentic change. That is the basis for the Gandhian doctrine of noninjury or *ashima*.

> Under the Babul Tree Gandhi announced the principle which somehow corresponds to our amended (Golden) Rule: "*That line of action is alone justice which does not harm either party to a dispute.*" By harm he meant—and his daily announcements leave no doubt of this—an inseparable combination of economic disadvantage, social indignity, loss of self-esteem, and latent vengeance. (Erikson 1964, 239)

In Joan Bondurant's authoritative treatment of *Satyagraha*, she noted: "If there is dogma in the Gandhian philosophy, it centers here: that the only test of truth is action based on the refusal to do harm" (1958, 25). Thus, Truth and *ashima* were two fundamental prongs in *Satyagraha.*

> *Ashima* and Truth are so intertwined that it is practically impossible to disentangle and separate them. They are like the two sides of a coin, or rather of a smooth unstamped metallic disk. . . . Nevertheless *ashima* is the means; Truth is the end. (Gandhi 1961, 42)

A third component is the self-suffering or *tapasya*, which works to elevate the motivation of the helper in the eyes of public opinion, if not in the eyes of the doer.

> Self-suffering, the third element of satyagraha, guarantees the sincerity of the satyagrahi's own opinions, the while it restrains him from propagating uncertain truths. The objective of satyagraha is to win the victory over the conflict situation—to discover further truths and to persuade the opponent, not to triumph over him. (Bondurant 1958, 33)

This last point—about winning the victory over the situation, not over the person—is particularly important as a means of maintaining respect for and the self-respect of the doer. When actions face constraints, it is very important whether or not the constraints are human-caused or "natural."

> In so far as poverty arises from the niggardliness of nature or the natural defects of human character, it is an evil, but it is not a grievance. . . . The fundamental grievance is not a mere deficiency of material resources. Hunger and cold cause misery, but men do not revolt against winter or agitate against the desert. (Tawney 1964, 102)
>
> "The nature of things does not madden us, only ill will does," said Rousseau. The criterion of oppression is the part that I believe to be played by other human beings, directly or indirectly, with or without the intention of doing so, in frustrating my wishes. (Berlin 1969, 123)

Thus, the doer will change his mind more easily if the conflict can be reframed as a depersonalized "situation" so that he is reacting to the situation rather than to specific pressure from the aggrieved party. In management theory, this is Mary Parker Follett's indirect method, the "law of the situation":

> Our job is not how to get people to obey orders, but how to devise methods by which we can best *discover* the order integral to a particular situation. When that is found, the employee can issue it to the employer, as well as employer to employee. (Follett 1992 (1926), 70)

Thus, unilateral command and pressure from another person is replaced by mutual recognition of the "law of the situation."

Direct carrot-and-stick methods on the part of the aggrieved party, the helper, are motivationally inconsistent with the motives that would bring about changes in the heart and mind of the doer. To keep the space open in the doer for those transformative motives to develop and come into the motivational foreground, the aggrieved party's actions should also be motivationally compatible. That means that those actions should be clearly based on shared principles, not tactical self-interest (a point dramatized by the self-suffering or *tapasya* of the aggrieved party), and that the arguments should appeal to shared reason and evidence. Then it is possible for the doer to yield to principles and reason with self-respect intact, not to be "defeated" by the other party.

However, in view of the human powers of self-righteous rationalization, particularly on the part of those who hold power, these appeals by themselves are not sufficient to bring about transformative changes in the doer. The point must be emphasized that just because external pressure should not be in the motivational foreground to force the change in the doer, that does not mean that external pressure should be absent. It is again a question of foreground and background. The basic idea of *ashima* is that the external pressures (e.g., economic boycotts) should be kept going in the background but should be designed so that they do not "take over" or crowd out the appeals to the better motives of the doer. Otherwise, the pressure might come into the foreground and ignite the downward spiral of retaliatory dynamics.

Moreover, if the circumstances of the doer should change so that they would have to yield to the extrinsic pressure alone, then, just as Gandhi put the drive for Indian independence on hold while England was involved in the World War II, the aggrieved party might reduce or temporarily suspend the pressure, to help ensure that the eventual changes on the part of the doer were made for the right reasons.

In summary, Gandhi's *Satyagraha*—abstracted from the particulars of the Indian case—is the development of the indirect method into a full-fledged methodology of change in the context of social oppression, and, as such, it is a social innovation of the first order.

CONCLUSION

My purpose in this chapter has been to try to discern the theoretical basis for the indirect approach by looking for the common themes in the use of the indirect approach in a wide variety of human endeavors over a long period of intellectual history. A common theme has emerged, once one allows for the many different vocabularies and diverse settings. Actions have motives just as beliefs have grounds. In the wide spectrum of human endeavor, there is only a fairly small "bandwidth" where the motives can be supplied by the carrots and sticks of the direct approach (including agency theory and market-driven activities as special cases of the direct approach to affect behavior). Outside of that spectrum of pecuniary and prudential behavior, the attempt to use direct methods in a controlling manner contradicts the motives for actions (and the grounds for beliefs). It is trying to "buy" love—trying to "impose" autonomy. The externally supplied carrots and sticks have a role only in the motivational background.

For those "higher" human activities, the motives must come from within, as rational beliefs need to be based on the exercise of our own critical judgment. People then have an active role to make the actions their own—or to make the beliefs their own. It is a variation on the old principle that people have a natural ownership over the fruits of their own activity. The helpers cannot externally supply the doers' own-motives or own-reasons. The helpers can at best use the indirect approach to bring the doers to the threshold; the doers have to do the rest—and that makes the results their own.

NOTES

1. See Ross (1973) and Stiglitz (1974) for early work. For surveys and applications, see Pratt and Zeckhauser (1991), Eatwell et al. (1989), or the text Campbell (1995). For earlier critical analysis of agency theory, see Perrow (1972), Hirsh et al. (1987), Pfeffer (1994), and the references contained in Eisenhardt (1989).

2. "It is hard . . . to learn to accommodate one's ends to those of others; to adjust, to give way here, and fit in there with respect to our aims. But difficult as this is, it is easy compared with the difficulty of acting *in such a way* for ends which are helpful to others as will call out and make effective their activities" (Dewey and Tufts, 1908, 303).

3. See Deci and Ryan (1985) for the notion of locus of causality. They differentiate it from the notion of locus of control (see Lefcourt 1976) as they interpret the latter as dealing with the outcomes rather than sources of action. Nevertheless, one may find that the notion of "locus of control" was often used to indicate the source of actions. We use the notions of having an internal locus of causality, self-determination, and autonomy as being synonymous for our purposes.

4. See Deci and Ryan (1985), Elster (1983), Lane (1991), Candy (1991), Kohn (1993), and Deming (1994).

5. See, for example, Ruskin (1985 [orig. 1862]). Mark Lutz (1999) gives an integrated treatment of Sismondi, Carlyle, and Ruskin.

6. See Titmuss (1970), Arrow (1972), Scitovsky (1976), Hirsch (1976), Sen (1982), Schelling (1984), Akerlof (1984), Hirschman (1992), Kreps (1997), and Prendergast (1999).

7. A classic example where economics has ignored crucial questions of motives for behaviors is the economic treatment of "cooperation" and "trust" based on repeated prisoner's dilemma games (Axelrod 1984 is the locus classicus). When a prisoner's dilemma game is repeated, the credible threat of being punished by the other party's defecting tomorrow may elicit cooperative behavior today. But this sort of cooperative behavior is quite different from cooperation and trust motivated by some fellow feeling for the other parties or some identification with the broader group which includes the other parties. Institutional design based on threat-induced "cooperation" would be rather different from design based on fellow feeling or identification where the penalties attached to noncooperation were not eliminated but played a secondary role as motivational backstops.

8. Thus, Milton (1957b [orig. 1659]) inveighs against "hirelings" in the church.

9. "Here is the radical fallacy of those who urge that people must use promises and threats in order to encourage opinions, thoughts, and feelings which they think good, and to prevent others which they think bad. Promises and threats can influence acts. Opinions and thoughts on morals, politics, and the rest, after they have once grown in a man's mind, can no more be influenced by promises and threats than can my knowledge that snow is white or that ice is cold" (Morley 1877, 199).

10. Kierkegaard used similar stories of putting a cap on a certain type of elf (1989, 12 or 468) or putting special armor on the god Mars to see how they looked (1992, 174), but in each case the act made them invisible. Elster points out similar notions in Gregory Bateson's double-bind theory (1972) and in the work of Watzlawick (1976) and Farber (1976). See also Parfit (1984) for a discussion of self-defeating theories.

11. McGregor (1948, reprinted in 1966, 152).

12. Peter Drucker (1954) developed essentially the same "Theory Y" ideas in his "Management by Objectives (MBO)" (also called "management by objectives and self-control") approach as opposed to "management by control" (as noted in McGregor 1966, 15–16 and in Drucker 1973). But the MBO theory was so popularized (indeed, vulgarized) by Drucker and others apparently in order to reach a mass market that it is commonly interpreted to mean "management by results" in a manner quite along the lines of Theory X and agency theory. Hence, we will rely more on McGregor's treatment of these ideas.

13. When the helper facilitates the doer finding a solution and refrains from "teaching" or otherwise imposing a solution, then the helper is perhaps engaging in "action by non-action" (*wu-wei*) of Taoist thought (see below).

14. In the same spirit, George Bernard Shaw quipped "if you teach a man anything he will never learn it" (1961, 11) and, as noted above, Ortega y Gasset suggested: "He who wants to teach a truth should place us in the position to discover it ourselves" (1961, 67).

15. One common metaphor is the two-sided problem of the grown teenager leaving the parents' "nest." The teenager needs self-confidence to release the parental hand and the parents need trust (and the willingness to forsake dependency and control) to let go of the grown teenager's hand.

16. "The successful psychotherapist is the one whose patients all believe they cured themselves—they internalized the therapy and it thereby became truly an integral part of them. Consultants suffer much the same dilemma of the psychotherapist—the problem of internalization. If they wish the client to use the right solution with full and lasting commitment then they must let him believe it is *his* solution" (Handy 1993, 145). This echoes the notion of the Taoist ruler who governs in such a way that when the task is accomplished, the people will say, "We have done it ourselves" (see Chapter 17 of Lao-Tzu's *Te-Tao Ching*).

17. This too was ancient Eastern wisdom. "When you know a thing, to recognize that you know it, and when you do not know a thing, to recognize that you do not know it. That is knowledge" (Confucius, *Analects*, Book II, 17). "To know you don't know is best. Not to know you don't know is a flaw" (Lao-Tzu, *Te-Tao Ching,* Chapter 71).

18. Clearly, Socrates used considerable knowledge to ask the appropriate questions, so one might quip that it takes a lot of knowledge to be as "ignorant" as Socrates. However, in the questions of human affairs, there is little reason then or now for this "ignorance" or intellectual humility to be just ironic. A common perversion is the pseudo-Socratic method employed by someone who has already decided upon the answer and is only trying to ask leading questions to bring the listeners to the same conclusion. As always, the difference is between the helper controlling ("helping") the doers or enabling the doers to better help themselves.

19. The theme that practicality was the road to engaging the interest and initiative of the students played a major role more recently in John Dewey's pragmatic philosophy of education. Interpreters of Dewey's pedagogy often think that his purpose was to urge "practical training" rather than to simply use practical problems as the source of student engagement so that the student's faculties of critical reason and social sympathy would be improved through active use.

20. This tendency to subvert indirectly in favor of direct methods is greatly aggravated by two more modern developments: teachers becoming employees of educational establishments who are held "responsible" for their students' progress (see McClintock 1982) and "evaluation" techniques geared to outward performance.

21. For instance, the Cambridge Platonist Ralph Cudworth writing in the late 1600s noted that "knowledge was not to be poured into the soul like liquor, but rather to be invited and gently drawn forth from it; nor the mind so much to be filled therewith from without, like a vessel, as to be kindled and awakened" (1996, 78). Cudworth also saw clearly the active nature of learning: "knowledge is an inward and active energy of the mind itself, and the displaying of its own innate vigour from within, whereby it doth conquer, master, and command its objects" (73).

22. This can't-push-on-a-string asymmetry was reflected in our previous discussion of extrinsic and intrinsic motivation. Extrinsic motivation can override and crowd out intrinsic motivation to control behavior, but removing the former will not automatically supply the latter. One cannot extrinsically bring about intrinsically

motivated action just as opening a faucet cannot itself supply water pressure. The oft-repeated ("warhorse") metaphor for this insight is: "While we may lead a horse to water we cannot make him drink" (Dewey 1916, 26).

23. For instance, there is the old insight that the "civil sword would make a nation of hypocrites but not a single Christian" (Gooch 1959, 74–75). There is now a whole literature on the problems of providing external incentives to try to achieve inward psychological results, for example Lepper and Greene (1978), Lane (1991), and Kohn (1993).

24. There is now something of a minor industry in making such distinctions. See Schön (1983) for a related treatment of professional versus instrumental knowledge, Marglin (1990) on *techne* versus *episteme*, and Scott (1998) on *metis* versus *episteme/techne*. The importance of the tacit/codified distinction is explored in Nonaka and Takeuchi (1995), and they note that Squire (1987) gives a dozen labels for similar distinctions.

25. See Scott (1998) for a less-conservative critique of "high Modernist" social engineering also based on an appreciation of the embedded practical knowledge that he calls *metis*.

Chapter 6

Knowledge and Autonomy-Compatible Development Assistance

INTRODUCTION

"Autonomous" comes from "self" (auto) "law" (nomos)—the property of having the "law" or principle of operation being derived internally as opposed to being imposed from an external source (heteronomous). How can external agents sponsor autonomy-enhancing development in individuals, organizations, regions within a country, or whole countries? At first glance, that seems like a contradiction in terms like "forcing spontaneity." While not impossible, external aid to autonomous development is nonetheless a subtle manner. Much development assistance is paternalistic in many obvious and not-so-obvious ways and increases long-run dependency. But the road to autonomy is also not autarky or isolation (e.g., communist Albania or North Korea). External relationships can bring the fruits of specialization and gains from trade without sacrificing autonomy (e.g., compare modern Japan to the closed society before the mid-nineteenth century).

Capital has played a central role in development assistance in the past, but today it is knowledge, the fourth factor of production, that is moving onto center stage (compare the knowledge-rich but resource-poor countries of the East Asian "miracle" with the resource-rich countries of the Middle East). Our analysis will therefore focus on the role of knowledge in shaping the methodology of autonomy-inducing development. On this general theme, we may start by recalling Kant's admonition at the beginning of his 1784 pamphlet *What is Enlightenment?*

> Enlightenment is man's release from his self-incurred tutelage. Tutelage is man's inability to make use of his understanding without direction from another. Self-incurred is this tutelage when its cause lies not in lack of reason

> but in lack of resolution and courage to use it without direction from another. *Sapere aude!* "Have the courage to use your own reason!"—that is the motto of enlightenment.

AUTONOMY-ENHANCING METHODS OF LEARNING

The Dimensions of Knowledge

How can we concretely understand the profuse forms and varieties of knowledge that drive development and that shape institutions? We must try to make do with rough measures of knowledge along many scales or dimensions such as explicit-implicit, specific-general, part-whole, local-global, analytic-synthetic, or external-internal dimensions. If we were to try to map out the domain of knowledge, then it is certain that the terrain would be quite uneven.

Methods of education and training for development as well as institutional capacity-building need to adjust to the local terrain. For instance, is the important knowledge in each area so explicit (like the rules of arithmetic or a computer language) that it can be transmitted vertically from those who know to those who don't? Or is the relevant knowledge more implicit (like knowing how to ride a bike) and best transferred through more subtle horizontal methods from those who have done it to those who have not yet done it? It is not a matter of an institutional form being "right or wrong" but of being well adapted or ill-adapted to the demands of knowledge acquisition and dissemination in a particular setting.

The Implicit versus Explicit Dimension of Knowledge

From the Enlightenment descends the image of modern science as giving knowledge that is explicit, objective, and intersubjectively transmittable. The architect prepares the blueprint of the house, and the blueprint contains the explicit information that is sufficient for the engineers and carpenters to build the house. The model of explicit objective knowledge (sometimes taken as a defining characteristic of "modernity") was often taken as contrasting with a model of mystical "knowledge" that was dominant in premodern times. But that may not be the most useful contrast. It seems to be much more fruitful to contrast explicit knowledge with knowledge that is implicit, tacit, and personal. The scientist and philosopher, Michael Polanyi, has particularly emphasized the importance of tacit or personal knowledge (1962).[1] Consider, for example, the blueprint that is supposed to contain the information to construct a house. In fact, there is relatively "little" information in the blueprint itself. Most of the knowledge about constructing the house is embedded in the practical skills and routines of the engineers and carpenters.[2] The blueprint transmits just the crucial cues to the holders of the necessary implicit knowledge to allow the latter to build the desired house.

Some training and education for development can be rather useless, if not dysfunctional, when it fails to pay attention to the explicit or implicit form of the important knowledge. Development experts in effect give "blueprints" to developing countries when in fact the missing knowledge may be the implicit "carpentry" skills to build the "house" from the "blueprint." The implicit practical knowledge might be best acquired "horizontally" by an apprenticeship or internship with those who have actually done it (which might not include the development experts).[3]

The Local versus General Dimension of Knowledge

Another important dimension of knowledge is the local-general dimension. Local knowledge is particular to the specific situation, while general knowledge would be more universal and would apply across a wide variety of situations. For instance, the carpentry knowledge to build a house might be partly location specific (the nature of the local building materials and site conditions) and partly general (applicable to building the house independent of location). Indeed, in some localities wooden buildings are considered appropriate only for farm animals, so the appropriate home-building knowledge might be more stone masonry than carpentry.

The local-general dimension of knowledge may provide another reason why expert knowledge from a developed country might be inappropriate. Some of the most important knowledge (whether explicit or implicit) in the design and implementation of institutions may be specific or local to the developing country and similar countries.[4]

THE LIMITED EFFECTIVENESS OF FOREIGN EXPERTS

The Relativity of "Best Practice"

Knowledge does not "travel" as well as money because of the importance of implicit, local, and practical knowledge as opposed to explicit, general, and theoretical knowledge. Foreign consultants' stock in trade is explicit and theoretical knowledge, whereas the problems might lie in the adaptation to the local situation. For instance, a foreign consultant in accounting might be able to transfer the logical structure of double-entry bookkeeping and the theoretical relationships between balance sheets, income statements, and cash flow statements. But these abstract accounting structures are always implemented in some localized way which takes into account specific data structures and regulatory frameworks. The foreign consultant's local knowledge would probably not extend to the client country's environment. The "devil might be in the details" of the local adaptation where the foreign consultant (no matter how highly paid and prestigious in his home country) is of little use.

These limitations even apply to technology transfer, which is often considered just a matter of transferring explicit technical knowledge.

> But in fact technology consists of complex "bundles" of information—both codified and tacit—as well as physical capital. Because tacit information is not readily transferable among firms and countries, technological blueprints do not contain inherent performance characteristics (such as set productivity levels). Instead, these blueprints have to be translated into specifications and procedures that are specific to particular applications—an uncertain creative process that can result in highly variable levels of performance. (Bell and Pavitt 1995, 74)

These limitations hold a fortiori for "expert knowledge" about social organizations and legal, economic, or political institutions. The dependency on local conditions renders the notion of "best practice" ambiguous. An institution that is a "best practice" under one set of local conditions might be rather dysfunctional in a different concrete setting. What is best practice in America might not be best practice all the world over.

A description of the perceived "best practice" is usually provided by a technical assistance expert.

> But, over time, development experience has shown that when external experts *alone* acquire, analyze, and process information and then present this information in reports, social change usually does not take place; whereas the kind of "social learning" that stakeholders generate and internalize during the participatory planning and/or implementation of a development activity *does* enable social change. (World Bank 1996, 5)

External consultants will tend to overestimate the relevance of the transferable technical information and to underestimate the need for the local adaptation and participation—which requires creativity, innovation, and autonomous action by the local counterparts.

The Self-Perpetuating Dynamics of Tutelage

Understanding some of the limitations of "expert knowledge" from developed countries (e.g., due to explicit-implicit or specific-general differences) is part of a developing country's "release from (its) self-incurred tutelage." Wilhelm von Humboldt reinforced Kant's dare-to-think argument:

> For nothing promotes this ripeness for freedom so much as freedom itself. This truth, perhaps, may not be acknowledged by those who have so often used this

> unripeness as an excuse for continuing repression. But it seems to me to follow unquestionably from the very nature of man. The incapacity for freedom can only arise from a want of moral and intellectual power; to heighten this power is the only way to supply this want; but to do this presupposes the exercise of the power, and this exercise presupposes the freedom which awakens spontaneous activity. (Humboldt 1969, 136)

Instead of maintaining the agents in perennial tutelage for fear that they might make mistakes, it seems best to promote autonomy through active "on the job" learning programs which include the "right" to make mistakes, to pay for them, and to thereby learn lasting lessons.

Yet there are institutional forces that operate to maintain a state of ongoing tutelage. The experts will not easily accept that their "blueprints" are not the most important "truths"—much less that the "blueprints" might end up having a dysfunctional role by confusing the situation, misdirecting very scarce organizational energies, and precluding other more fruitful lines of action. Any such recognition would tend to undercut and devalue the human capital of the experts or of the institutions sponsoring the experts. Surely (it will be said) the clients do not appreciate that the expert knowledge comes from "Harvard" (taken as a symbol of an elite university) or an elite development institution. It might be subtly suggested that the client's lack of appreciation of the "expert knowledge" is just another symptom of his backwardness and his need for further tutelage to continue the cycle.

The cycle of tutelage may also be sustained by institutional forms within the developing country. There may be individuals and institutions that specialize as the local "satellite relay stations" or "gate keepers" for the elite "expert knowledge." Their own legitimacy, prestige, and power is based in part on the belief in the "potency" of this esoteric knowledge which they can bring into the country. Devaluing the "knowledge" will undercut the power base of the local gatekeeper institutions. International development institutions naturally want feedback and evaluation from the client countries as to whether or not the proffered development knowledge is valuable and appropriate. The problem is that the feedback usually comes from the local satellite relay institutions which are more than willing to confirm the unique value and potency of the "expert knowledge" for which they are the gate keeper.[5] Thus, the knowledge system of feedback and evaluation between the development institution and the client country is closed and "locks in" to perpetuate the cycle of tutelage.[6]

One way to help break such closed feedback loops is to insist on a substantial local funding base (philanthropic, subsidized, or commercial) for any counterpart institutions. Fee-for-service business activities are particularly revealing because "in commercial activity economic return depends on correct assessment of local conditions" (Bauer 1981, 108). In any case, this might supply some reality check on the local applicability of the imported "expert knowledge" so that the "expertise" would not be propagated solely on the basis of blind faith. The pattern of tutelage can be particularly damaging to developing countries if it perpetuates the image that their problems can be solved by importing the right "magical" blueprint[7] (e.g., today's "capitalist blueprint" instead of yesterday's "socialist blueprint")—an image promoted by the expert proponents of each blueprint—instead of focusing on the development of the human resources that will enable autonomous development.

HORIZONTAL MODELS OF LEARNING

If the "vertical" transmission of "expert knowledge" from the developed to developing countries leaves much to be desired, then what are alternative models of learning? A model of learning might be called "horizontal" if it emphasizes learning from others from a similar background ("peers") who have had a head start or who have devised more successful methods. They have the relevant local knowledge, and local knowledge is best transferred through "apprenticeship" or other horizontal methods of learning. The potential (and pitfalls) of several models of horizontal learning, for example, study tours, cross-training, and twinning, will be considered.

Study Tours

Study tours can be a powerful instrument if done well. But often study tours end up being junkets to advanced metropolises for high-level officials with a thin educational gloss. The site of the tour might be chosen on the basis of its attractiveness to high officials rather than on the basis of its relevance to the developing country's real problems. The fundamental criterion for site choice should be whether or not the visited country offers a relevant and believable near future for the client country (so the countries are roughly "horizontal" peers). Trips of Russians to America, of Africans to Paris or London, and of Vietnamese to Tokyo do not seem to fall into this category. The gap between the visited and the client countries should not be too large. The gap should be small enough so that it could be plausibly traversed within the political horizon of the current generation in power. In short, study tours are too often seen as tools of vertical learning (the less-developed countries "learning" from the advanced countries), whereas they should be seen more as tools for horizontal learning (e.g., East-East or South-South) between slow-moving and fast-starting developing countries.

Top government officials, who smell a junket to Washington, Paris, or London, have carefully cultivated responses expressing shock and insult at the suggestion that they have anything to learn from lesser destinations.

"What could Russians possibly learn from their former satellite countries in Central Europe?" Study tours to the advanced metropolises will attract high-level officials (which adds to the importance of the activity) and such tours will get appreciative reviews from the participants in their evaluations. But the actual impact is rather minimal and hardly cost-effective. The participants hope they "see the future"—but right now it is a "science fiction" future. After returning home, they can think of thousands of reasons why "it wouldn't work here—at least not as things are now."

Horizontally oriented study tours show the participants how some of their problems had been solved by comparable countries. The tours show a plausible future. With such suitably horizontal tours, the reaction is, "If *they* can do that well, then we can certainly do it too."

Cross-Training Seminars

A variation on horizontally oriented study tours are cross-training seminars with the instructors being not experts from the advanced countries but experienced practitioners from countries that are plausibly "near-by" in terms of development. Such seminars are not always supported by experts from elite institutions. Why should a world-class development institution subsidize or promote seminars taught by "locals" who came from distorted environments, who were taught by the wrong textbooks, and who could not possibly have the depth and breadth of Western experts? What if they teach "the wrong thing"? Thus, paternalism is often couched in the language of "quality control" with "quality" defined by the Western experts.

In the early days of the transition out of socialism, lectures by Western experts were appreciated by the responsible authorities in the post-socialist countries. Certainly, they didn't want to embark on the transition without hearing what the experts had to say. But those times have now largely passed. The generalities proffered by the experts were easily mastered, and there was little concrete advice about how to implement the principles in such "distorted environments." That requires local knowledge. Such practical knowledge is best gleaned from comparable countries that have shown some measure of success. "Horizontal" seminars would gather together practitioners from the relative success stories to teach best practices to the relevant officials from the client country.

Twinning Projects

Horizontal cross-training in relevant best practices can be fostered on a long-term basis as a part of the design of development projects. The target of the project should be an organization, region, or country that is small enough for demonstration effects to be quickly transmitted and for cumulative bandwagon effects to be built up. Without allowing for some sort of cumulative causation or chain reaction, the beneficial effects of an otherwise well-designed project might soon dissipate. For example, instead of a restructuring project for all of Russia, there might be a project for a coherent and manageable region, oblast, or municipality (e.g., Nizhny Novgorod).

The target region could then be twinned with a similar region or country that has been relatively successful. The above-mentioned study tours and cross-training seminars are ways to start building the learning bridges between the two counterparts. Project design could also include business and restructuring consultants from the more successful country who would always be required to train and hand over the business to local counterparts as a part of the consulting contracts so as not to perpetuate a dependency relationship. Senior ex-government officials from the successful country could be retained to give advice and guidance to their counterparts now facing similar challenges.

The Market as the Prototype of Horizontal Learning

The topic of models of horizontal learning must include competition in the marketplace as perhaps the most ubiquitous form of horizontal learning. Friedrich Hayek has particularly emphasized the role of "competition as a discovery procedure"[8] (as opposed to textbook models of "perfect competition" which assume that the agents already have the relevant knowledge). Market relationships between self-standing entities (as opposed to ownership relationships between companies and subsidiaries) involves the useful exchange of information without sacrificing autonomy. To see the effect of market relationships on spurring development, the post-socialist starting positions of Yugoslavia (prior to the breakup and Balkan wars) and next-door neighbor Albania. Of all the socialist countries, Yugoslavia was most open, and Albania was the most closed to external market relationships, and accordingly today Slovenia (the part of Yugoslavia with most extensive exports and untouched by the wars) is per capita the richest and Albania is the poorest of the post-socialist countries.

LOCAL INSTITUTIONAL CAPACITY-BUILDING

Educational, Training, and Research Institutions

Regardless of whether knowledge was acquired vertically or horizontally, autonomous development requires local institutions that will retain, disseminate, and further develop the knowledge according to local conditions.

Otherwise the country would tend to remain in a continuing state of "import dependence" for this most crucial of inputs. There is a wide variety of local institutions, such as schools, colleges, universities, adult education institutions, professional associations, and industrial training institutes, that can be developed or strengthened in the client country to internalize the production and distribution of the appropriate and relevant knowledge.

Crowding Out and Hollowing Out

Here again relationships between international development institutions and client countries must be examined to see if they promote autonomy or sustain tutelage. The first question to consider is how and where do the international institutions invest their considerable training resources, in the institutions of the client countries or in already-developed centers of learning or training institutes in the West? When socialism collapsed in Eastern Europe and the Soviet Union, some argument could be made that emergency training programs needed to be mounted in existing facilities in the West. The needs were too urgent to await the longer process of reorienting the educational institutions in the post-socialist countries.

As these special programs and institutes were developed in the United States, England, Austria, and other Western countries, vested interests were of course created. Institutional inertia (or "momentum" depending on the viewpoint) sets in as the staff in these Western training centers and the international instructors naturally prefer the continuation of that arrangement (in spite of soft sunset clauses). Thus, the repository of the training capacity remains outside the client countries—which accordingly remain in a dependent state.

Here is a concrete example of the self-perpetuating feedback loop. The trainees from the post-socialist countries are, of course, delighted to have fully paid training programs for months at a time in Western metropolises. Program administrators can easily gather sheaves of ecstatic evaluations and letters of appreciation from this select cadre of participants attesting to how the programs have changed their lives (and how qualified they now are for the next segment of the multipart programs). A genuine evaluation of these programs would look not at the attestations of the select few who benefit, but at the opportunity costs of not investing similar resources in the training institutions of the client countries and at the many more people in those countries who thus did not have those training opportunities (and who are not asked to "evaluate" the programs). These dynamics are reinforced by the program administrators in the West who are not desirous of seeing their own budgets threatened by any "handover" of the programs to counterparts in the client countries. "How can we insure they would continue to teach the 'right things'?" "What about quality control?" Thus, the Western programs crowd out the development of indigenous training capacity, and the relationship of dependency and tutelage reproduces itself.

There is a second phenomenon that often occurs when the Western development institutions do put resources toward training programs in the client countries. Instead of figuring out how to give the program through the domestic training institutions, the Western trainers give the courses themselves using local institutions mainly for physical space, logistics, and coffee. This often takes the form of "training the trainers" which means that future trainers, perhaps from the local institution, attend the course so that they can reproduce it in the future. At first this sounds like a good idea, but it is typically implemented in a way that hollows out and weakens the local institution. In the second phase, the trained trainers are hired as individuals and paid by the Western institution to propagate or roll out the program. The capacity of the local institution is not built up and is in fact weakened as some of the most reform-oriented young professors are attracted away as private consultants ("private sector development") for the second-phase programs given by the Western institution that roll out across the client country. The professor or trainer would hardly forego such individual opportunities in favor of taking their newly acquired human capital back to their university or training institution to teach at their old salary.

Program administrators in the West also favor this form of "developing training capacity" which produces a "network of training partners" (i.e., the individual trainers on the payroll) in the client country. Instead of any handover, the whole program and budget remains in the hands of the task managers or their assistants—all of which promotes their own bureaucratic empire in the development institution. Here again such programs undermine the development of autonomous and institutionalized training capacity in the developing country.

Policy Institutes

What is the means by which the knowledge gained through vertical and horizontal modes of learning will finally be turned into practice? How is change finally implemented by the public and private sector organizations in the developing countries? On the model of the "blueprints" vertically transmitted from the developed to developing countries, it is a matter of bringing in "top experts" in senior policy seminars to reveal the best practices and the underlying principles to the assembled government leaders, officials, and parliamentarians. These seminars are best held in attractive resorts to improve the chances that top government officials will be able to find room in their tight schedules and to better insulate them from the day-to-day distractions of their high office. Yet after the experts fly back to the West, it is often the case that little actually changes.

The blueprint analogy helps to explain a basic weakness in the senior policy seminar approach. Assuming that the blueprint is appropriate and that the government has the will to change (two significant assumptions), the missing elements are the "engineering and carpentry skills" necessary to turn the blueprint into a reality. In the human sciences, the intermediate knowledge and skills to turn theory into practice is the subject matter of what are called the "policy sciences." Policy experts ("policy wonks" in the popular press) help to bridge the gap between academic research and concrete implementation. Since implementation depends in large part on the local concrete conditions, only policy advice of a rather abstract sort can be imported. A country needs to develop its own local public policy capacity to absorb the relevant theory and best practices from whatever the source, and to use their local knowledge to work out the myriad details for a successful implementation.

Public policy institutes are the organizations that have evolved to perform this function in developed countries as well as in developing countries. The development and implementation of successful policy initiatives require a lot of prior "spadework" to prepare the ground for transplantation. The Japanese have a word, "*nemawashi*," to describe such preparatory work.[9] When a tree is being transplanted, it is best to proceed slowly wrapping a major root and then waiting a while before wrapping the next root. It will take longer to transplant the tree, but this *nemawashi* will greatly increase the chances that the tree will survive. Policy institutes have the function in their respective countries of "public policy *nemawashi*." They work with policy-makers, technical staff in the ministries, academics, businesspeople, labor leaders, NGO staffers, and journalists to prepare the ground and help transplant worthwhile initiatives into their native soil.

The senior policy seminar approach as well as the more recent video or satellite TV versions of that approach have only limited success because the process of changing policies and implementing new ideas is usually rather messy and in need of "high maintenance" support. The officials or parliamentarians constantly need more information and advice—more "backup" and "hand-holding"—in order to carry out the process of new policy implementation. In the United States and the United Kingdom, there is a plethora of public policy institutes that constantly work with sympathetic officials and parliamentarians to carry new ideas through to practice. Development institutions can themselves learn from that "best practice" by promoting local public policy institutes in the developing countries rather than only the rather ineffective senior policy seminars. Since each institute cannot be expert in every policy area, horizontal networks of policy institutes in similar countries can be the vehicles for the natural mutual exchange of information that follows upon specialization. International development organizations can further leverage their resources by assisting organized networks of these policy institutes.

This policy institute approach is likely to be not only more effective (than the senior policy seminar approach) but also more conducive to developing the autonomy of the developing country. The institutes provide for indigenous production and accumulation of policy expertise, rather than complete "import dependence." Policy institutes always need to walk a thin line to maintain their own autonomy and professional integrity. If an institute based its legitimacy on being a local relay station for foreign blueprints, then it would lack incentive to work out the locally appropriate implementations which is probably wherein its own true niche would lie. Moreover, such a "parrot institute" would probably lack the social legitimacy and embeddedness in the country that would be necessary to function as an effective agent for change. There is the opposite problem of an institute simply being a part of the government (rather than a part of civil society). Then the institute will tend to be more a mouthpiece for government policy rather than a fulcrum for changing that policy.

A DEVELOPMENT INSTITUTION AS A KNOWLEDGE BANK?

With the growing importance of private capital for development projects, international development organizations are turning more to knowledge as the source of their comparative advantage. The World Bank, for instance, might function more as a "knowledge bank" than as a "money bank." But there are fundamentally different ways in which a "knowledge bank" might function, and these ways could have a powerful effect to enhance or hinder autonomous development.[10]

A "Knowledge Bank" Like a Church or Like a University?

Would a Knowledge Bank function like a church as the source of the "Truth" or like a university that would focus less on "truths" than on methods of reasoning and rational discovery to find and to corroborate theories? In the course of European history, the period dominated by an institution that possessed the "Truth" is today known as the "Dark Ages." During the Renaissance, Reformation, and Enlightenment, the West slowly emerged from its "self-incurred tutelage" to those who had the "Truth." Progress was made not by finding a new "Truth" as the object of devotion for the faithful, but by developing the scientific method which emphasized the will to doubt and be critical, the use of repeatable experiments to corroborate or disprove theories, and the general substitution of the inner light of reason for the external voice of authority.

All this sounds like old history, the repetition of well-worn clichés. Yet the modern commitment to the values of the Enlightenment or the values of an Open Society[11] is often only a veneer and has suffered major reverses within living memory. Communism, whose rise and fall has shaped much of the twentieth century, was a secular church that imposed its own Truth, and even tried to do so in the name of "Science." Even today, the defeat of communism is too often seen as the victory for the rival church whose Truths (as revealed, for example, in neoclassical economics) can now be disseminated ex cathedra by Western institutions to the developing countries. This is the frame of mind that yields what might be called the "church model" for the World Bank as a Knowledge Bank. The bank-as-church has little use for autonomy in the client countries because autonomy is then seen primarily as the license to err.

The defeat of communism should be seen not as the victory of an alternative dogma but as the victory for the methodology of critical reason (in addition to being a defeat for the communist theory for organizing an economy). That view yields what might be called the "university model" for the Knowledge Bank—where the emphasis is on developing the ability to think rather than on teaching "correct thoughts."

The Collision of Adverse Opinions

Intellectual liberty and tolerance are fundamental to the heritage of the Reformation and Enlightenment. Rather than a "Church" to protect "Truth" and suppress "Error," free discussion and debate fueled by the "collision of adverse opinions" (Mill 1977) is the best security against error. These principles of philosophical liberalism were first hammered out in the battle for religious freedom. Jefferson asked that his tombstone note that he was the author not only of the Declaration of Independence but also of the Virginia's 1779 "Bill for Establishing Religious Freedom," which argued in part that truth

> is the proper and sufficient antagonist to error, and has nothing to fear from the conflict unless by human interposition disarmed of her natural weapons, free argument and debate; errors ceasing to be dangerous when it is permitted freely to contradict them.

The toleration for dissent and debate is fundamental to the spirit of a university, not to the spirit of a church. Which would be the spirit of a "Knowledge Bank"?

A bank-as-university would be very different from a bank-as-church. A university as an organization does not set itself up as an arbiter of truth, but as an arena within which "adverse opinions" can be espoused and can collide in open debate. Yet it is quite easy to imagine a "Knowledge Bank" functioning as a repository and arbiter of truth by having the (implicit or explicit) "World Bank view" on the various economic and political questions of development. If each organization took a stand on the "truth" in each subject matter, then tolerance, discussion, and debate would tend to be only *between* such organizations, not *within* them. Reform would tend to come at the price of schism.

Within an organization that takes "official views" on questions, the genuine collision of adverse opinions and the rule of critical reason will tend to give way to the rule of authority and bureaucratic reason within the hierarchy of the organization. The authorities in the organization naturally decide "the views" of the organization that are expressed to the world and would tend to shut off any feedback loops that might expose any errors in the "official" views. Thus, if an organization decides that it is to officially espouse certain "views," then it has in effect decided to function more as a secular church than as a university. That bank-as-church frame of mind will in turn have many consequences for the possibilities of autonomous development in the client countries. The gardeners want only their own seeds to grow; all else are weeds.

The Bank-as-University Model

What is the alternative to a bank-as-church model? Surely much has been learned about development. What is wrong with espousing the best practices from successful development as well as promoting the underlying guiding principles? Should the World Bank or any other international development organization just be "agnostic" on the questions of development and treat all opinions as having equal weight?

To approach these questions, it is useful to consider the methodology of science. Science in any given area is hardly "agnostic" about the questions in that domain. All opinions are not given equal weight. Certain theories are the "received" or current theories in the field. The difference from a "Church" lies in the methodology used to sustain or overturn the hypotheses. In mathematics, it is proof, not authority, that is the basis for theorems. In the empirical sciences, hypotheses are developed on the basis of intellectual coherence and factual cues and are then openly subjected to experiments that can be intersubjectively verified and reproduced. The young or the uninitiated may "believe" scientific hypotheses on the basis of the "Authority of Science" but that is not the methodology of science based on critical reason. All who learn the language of science can read its "scriptures"; all who look at the record of experimentation can see its "revelations." There is no appeal to priests or prophets who have exclusive access to the "Truth."

This methodology of critical reason shows, at least in general terms, how a bank-as-university might operate. The important thing to teach is not the "Truth" but the methodology to find and corroborate or disprove "truths" (i.e., hypotheses and theories). In terms of the analogy with mathematics, the important thing to teach is not the theorem but its proof. The "proof" carries its own authority to the student, so the student does not have to accept the theorem based on the teacher's "authority." To teach the proofs and not just the theorems requires a certain humility on the part of the teacher who is thus foregoing the imposition of the result based on his authority. And it requires a certain respect for the intelligence of the student because the student is expected to understand the proof (or perhaps to find a flaw) rather than just accept the hypothesis based on authority. To teach the theorem without the proof would be to "short-circuit" and bypass the autonomous reason of the student, to substitute "authority" in its place, and thus to perpetuate the passivity of tutelage. "Truth, thus held, is but one superstition the more, accidentally clinging to the words which enunciate a truth" (Mill 1972, 103).

That methodology of critical reason can guide the World Bank if the staff and consultants are to be like "teachers" and the developing country officials are to be like "students" in that "university." If the World Bank wants to promote a certain doctrine, then it should be willing to share its method of corroborating the doctrine with the clients. Instead of asking the client country to accept the development doctrine based on authority (or based on conditionalities on loans), the World Bank would emphasize the means by which the country could experiment, test, and perhaps arrive at a similar corroboration of the doctrine—or arrive at a better theory for that institutional and cultural environment. The Knowledge Bank will need to discover that knowledge does not "travel" as well as money. The spirit needs to be "Experiment and test if it works for you," rather than "Trust my authority—particularly if you want to borrow my money."

For instance, if the World Bank wants to promote just one "best" method of privatizing the bulk of the enterprises in a post-socialist country, then it should be willing to share the source of that "knowledge" or to at least promote some experiments in the country to corroborate such a hypothesis before it is accepted as a "blueprint" for the country as a whole. Thus, the bank-as-university would promote "laboratory tests" in Nizhny Novgorod or Guangzhou or horizontal learning from similar experiments in other countries—rather than promoting the social engineering blueprints of the "authoritative experts" from elite Western universities.

The methodology of the bank-as-university would entail actually allowing its "experts" to disagree in public—and thus to publicly admit the lack of infallibility. Instead of acting like "parents" being careful not to disagree "in front of the children," the World Bank would drop the prerogative of imposing a "World Bank view" in favor of encouraging open debate with the public collision of adverse opinions—even in front of the clients.[12]

If little is known on a question, then real debate and honest experimentation are the best engines of discovery. If "partial truths" are known, then the same is necessary to ferret out a clearer picture and to better adapt theories to new and different contexts. But suppose we have the (near-impossible) case of a nontrivial thesis in the political economy of development that is so highly corroborated that it can be held with subjective near-certainty? Shouldn't the World Bank then "close" the public debate to conserve scarce internal resources and to avoid unnecessary confusion on the part of external clients? No, even in that quite hypothetical situation, debate and discussion serve to disturb the "deep slumber of a decided opinion" so that the opinion might be held more as a rational conviction rather than as an article of faith.

> So essential is this discipline to a real understanding of moral and human subjects, that if opponents of all important truths do not exist, it is indispensable to imagine them, and supply them with the strongest arguments which the most skillful devil's advocate can conjure up. (Mill 1977, 245)

In every case, open discussion and debate between the received opinions and the "legitimate opposition" (or "devil's advocate," if necessary) with frequent recourse to honest experimentation constitute the best methodology of all human organizations that are not blessed with infallibility.

Changes are no less required on the part of the developing country "students" if they are to grow out of their "self-incurred tutelage." Kant was careful to note that tutelage on the part of normal adults is always self-incurred. Indeed, that recognition is often the first step toward release from tutelage particularly on the part of those who draw comfort from blaming their backwardness on others. Taking responsibility for one's decisions can be a painful step for an individual or a government, but it is a necessary part of autonomous development. Parallel to the bank-as-university foregoing the role as the repository of truth, a developing country would forego the role of the "child" looking up to the "parent" to be told the truth, or the role of the refugee from a failed church looking for a new church to supply formulas with better potency. Instead, the country needs to establish the methodology by which it will test and corroborate the suggested theories of development, and then take appropriate action. As reform is not just a one-time occurrence, the government will need to study the consequences and then use that feedback to make further improvements.[13]

AUTONOMY-BASED STRATEGIES FOR INSTITUTIONAL CHANGE

Utopian Social Engineering

The opposite to change that is part of autonomous development is change that is imposed from the outside—heteronomously imposed change. What are the sources of externally imposed change? One source is well described in Karl Popper's treatment of utopian social engineering (e.g., see Chapter 9 in 1962). Not all utopian social engineering is externally imposed, but most externally imposed blueprints have their source in some project of utopian engineering. There are various dubious assumptions that underlie the utopian engineering orientation such as the assumption that there is "the knowledge" of a feasible first-best model or blueprint. Marxist-Leninism and neoclassical economics are both examples of this orientation.[14]

Misspecified "Optimal Model"

If there is a single first-best model or blueprint of any institution (like the Platonic "ideal"), then well-meaning reformers might take the imposition of "the best practice" as a natural means of development. The first problem is that the so-called first-best model might be misspecified. If the factors responsible for the relative success of the private property market economies was accurately specified in neoclassical theory (e.g., the Arrow-Debreu model), then it would be a relatively simple matter to reproduce or closely approximate that success under socialism. The failure of socialism in spite of considerable experimentation indicates that the success factors in a market economy are not well captured in neoclassical theory.[15] Thus, social engineering in the transitional or developing countries that is naively based on abstract neoclassical models may leave much to be desired.

Infeasible "Optimal Model"

Another problem is that the first-best model might be rather infeasible. Second-best feasible models might be highly dependent on local conditions and thus nonunique. Attempts to impose the first-best model might thus lead to third-best results or worse. A feasible second-best solution followed by its continuous improvement might be the first-best solution in the circumstances.

Unknown "Optimal Model"

There might be one best strategy to win from a given board position in a chess game, but it might be unknown due to the prohibitive costs of exploring all options. With such "bounded rationality," optimization based on local knowledge is the preferred strategy. In the more complicated and less well-defined "game" of institutional change, that strategy would be the piecemeal approach of "crossing the river by groping for the stepping stones."

Nonunique Models: Different Combinations of Interlocking Institutions

Finally, the assumption might be false because there is no unique first-best model, for example, the current global debate between Anglo-American-style capitalism and Japanese (or German-Japanese[16])-style capitalism (e.g., see Blinder 1995). One reason for the possibility of "multiple equilibria in the institutional marketplace" is the interlocking or internally coherent nature of institutional features. These features cannot just be mixed and matched to arrive at one optimal combination. Only certain combinations interlock and hold together in a mutually reinforcing whole, but there might be a multitude of incompatible combinations and no obvious way to rank them (except parochial predilections). Subsystems of one solution will interlock together but might malfunction if inserted into another solution.

The point is illustrated by a recent example in Europe (a still active battleground of different economic models). A rash of trucker wage disputes led to work stoppages and that had a particularly strong effect on a number of auto plants that had recently developed just-in-time (JIT) inventory systems. This showed the interconnectedness between the inventory system and the labor relations system. JIT worked best with a nonconfrontational cooperative system of labor relations, while confrontational labor relations required large inventories to buffer the effects of work stoppages. Table 6.1 illustrates how the subsystems fit together.

The interlockingness of institutional subsystems makes the job of the external adviser particularly delicate. The adviser might recommend a "best practice" subsystem that the adviser "knows" works well. But that is in the adviser's home country and other countries with similar institutions. The recommended subsystem might not fit well in the institutional setting of the client country, and it might be well beyond the powers of the clients to socially engineer a root-and-branch change in the whole system to fit the other model. Instead of helping, the well-meaning adviser who "knows the solution" might create a bit of a mess—a hodgepodge of system attributes that don't fit together. And those who are expert on one institutional solution will resist the devaluation of their human capital that is implicit in the recognition of multiple solutions. As in the old joke that a child with a hammer will find many things that "need hammering," so an expert in one solution will find a multitude of cases that "need" a few strokes of "the knowledge" whether appropriate or not.

Table 6.1 Inventory Policy and Labor Relations

	Confrontational Labor Relations	*Cooperative Labor Relations*
Large inventories	Anglo-American solution	Suboptimal due to unnecessary inventory carrying costs
Just-in-time inventories	Suboptimal due to vulnerability to labor stoppages	Japanese solution[a]

[a] See Aoki (1994) for a more systematic treatment of the interlockingness of system attributes in the Japanese case.
Source: Author.

PIECEMEAL VERSUS UTOPIAN INSTITUTIONAL CHANGE

"Big Bang" versus "Gradualism"

Piecemeal change is the Popperian opposite to utopian social engineering. In the debate about the transition from socialism, the contrasts were usually stated as "big bang" (or "shock therapy") versus gradualism with the implication that "big bang" was fast and gradualism was slow. But the fast-slow associations were often misleading. For example, in the much-debated Polish privatization program, the "big bang" solution supported by Western experts was the mass "privatization" program featuring national investment funds (NIFs). In contrast was the privatization by liquidation program designed by Poles without Western advice wherein the productive assets of firms were transferred on a lease-purchase arrangement to new companies (created usually by insiders) while the original legal unit was liquidated. The blueprint for the NIF plan, highly recommended by many Western academic advisers (not to mention financial sector advisers) and their eastern colleagues, took about five years of (rather predictable) parliamentary and bureaucratic torture to be implemented. Even then it only accomplished a formal "privatization" to the citizens of shares in what are in effect parastatal funds run by Western portfolio managers under lucrative management contracts. The "big bang" ended as a rather long-drawn-out whimper. Meanwhile, the privatization by liquidation program privatized to flesh-and-blood owners well over a thousand small and medium-sized firms (SMEs) and thus jump-started the SME sector in Poland. Thus, the "big bang" ended up being anything but fast, while the "gradual" privatization by liquidation program was hardly slow. Similar remarks apply to the quite rapid changes in China resulting from the non-big bang family responsibility farming system and the system of township-village manufacturing enterprises in the Chinese nonstate sector. With popular participation, "*change can come quickly*—far more quickly than the tired and disillusioned ask us to believe" (Lilienthal 1964, 10, quoted in Mason and Asher 1973, 332).

If big bang versus gradualism is not the best way to parse the conceptual issue (due to the inaccurate fast-slow connotations), then what is a better contrast? There is probably no simple way to characterize these complex issues so we will settle for "cluster concepts" on each side of the issue (see Murrell 1992 for a table applied to mass versus piecemeal privatization).

When is "Big Bang" Change Appropriate?

Instead of trying to argue that one approach or the other is best or correct, we will try to delineate the situations where each approach is appropriate. One broad class of cases where the big bang approach is appropriate can be characterized using a part-whole framework. The "whole" is divided into many "parts." Due to neighborhood or contagion effects, if only some of the parts of the whole are changed or "reformed," then the remaining "unreformed" parts will tend to undo the changes. Thus, all the parts or all parts beyond some "critical mass" have to be changed in order for the changes or reforms to stabilize (i.e., for the whole to change).

One simple example would be a "majority process" represented by an odd number of variables $x_1, \ldots, x_n$, where each variable has one of two values such as "unreformed" or "reformed." There are a number of time periods. During each time period, a variable may change its value, but at the end of the period and start of the next period, each variable is reset to the majority value. Thus, starting in an "unreformed" state for all the variables, if less than a majority of the variables were changed, then the "reforms" would be reversed at the end of the period due to the "distorted" initial conditions of the "unreformed" variables. Only a "big bang" or "shock" of changing a majority of the variables to a "reformed" state would break down or break through the barriers opposing system change and stabilize the "reforms" at the end of the period.

One model would be an epidemic caused by a contagious disease. Piecemeal application of an antidote would allow reinfection by the untreated parts or would allow the treated "germs" to rally their forces and overcome the medicine. Only a wholesale application of the medicine or antidote would achieve the necessary "breakthrough" to stop the epidemic. A military metaphor is sometimes used. Small incursions can be repulsed but a Normandy-style or blitzkrieg-style invasion can break through the defenses and succeed. Another metaphor was the change from driving on the left to driving on the right side of the road. One cannot have the cars switch sides this week and the trucks next week. One of the models of shock therapy favored by economists was for stopping hyperinflation. Unless applied across the board, anti-inflation measures would be soon undone by the contagion effects of the remaining inflationary trends and expectations.

The anti-inflation therapy, the more general epidemic-stopping therapies, and the related military metaphors were generalized into all manner of "shock therapy" or "blitzkrieg" prescriptions for institutional change in the transitional economies. Without a root-and-branch or canvas-cleaning change, the legacy of communism was seen as outweighing, reinfecting, and defeating piecemeal reforms. Thus, the transitional economies became fertile grounds for Western-inspired utopian social engineering (e.g., "market Leninism").

When is "Piecemeal" Change Appropriate?

Utopian engineering is often based on rather heroic assumptions about what is known while the alternative piecemeal approach emphasizes limited (explicit) knowledge and bounded rationality. The limitations on knowledge apply to the strategy of change away from the status quo and to the perhaps hidden or taken-for-granted properties of the status quo.

When there is knowledge only about the local surroundings of one's starting point in a journey, then it is foolhardy to rush off with all one's forces or resources into the darkness. One's local knowledge becomes increasingly useless the further one is away from the starting point. Smaller, tentative, and reversible forays or experiments will allow one to gather knowledge about possible paths by trial and error, and to plot a better course to move forward. To continue the metaphor, the starting point might also have some underappreciated virtues (such as a food or water supply or a defensible position) that would be lost by impetuous advances into a different terrain.

When working to establish certain relationships in a complex interdependent system, it is best "to define 'isolable subsystems,' that is, subsystems among which there is a minimum amount of interdependence, and then to adjust the resulting partial designs to each other" (Hirschman 1967, 24). Indeed, that is why it is called the "piecemeal" approach.

Applied to social change, the piecemeal approach emphasizes experiments and trial-and-error to obtain knowledge about the best way to proceed—all the while trying to have the appropriate continuity to preserve the social capital or other embedded institutional virtues[17] which once lost to ill-considered schemes cannot be readily recovered.

APPLICATIONS TO AUTONOMOUS INSTITUTIONAL CHANGE

Minding the Gap Between De Jure and De Facto Institutions

It is quite useful to differentiate between the de jure institution (described in the laws and regulations) and the de facto institution (the actual practices, routines, and habits that are the activity of the institution). There is often a considerable gap between the de jure and de facto institutions in transitional and developing countries, and it is wise to follow the advice of the conductor on the London subway to "Mind the gap." One might think of an elastic band as stretching across that gap. Small legislative or regulatory reforms will change the de jure institution and then the elastic band might pull along the de facto institution. Incremental reforms will not suddenly devalue the skills and knowledge of the people involved in the organization so they might respond to the other incentives to shift the de facto institution into compliance.

"Utopian" reformers and advisers tend to extrapolate and conclude that great changes can be similarly induced by "writing new laws" (perhaps modeled on the best practices in the developed countries). "Why compromise with the distorted environment and write substandard legislation?" "Don't our clients deserve the best?" For such large "shock" changes, the elastic band might snap as the participants dig in their heels and refuse to "ratify" the de jure changes by corresponding shifts in the de facto organization.[18] Instead of the "utopian" reforms, some bizarre noncompliant de facto institution evolves which might be worse than the status quo ante. The machinery of law is devalued by the utopian "law-based" reformers, and extralegal mechanisms evolve to take its place. A surreal and grotesque landscape develops as a hodgepodge of dysfunctional institutional attributes, and the course of reform is itself threatened (e.g., Russia today).

Paving the Paths

Utopian social engineering is typically imposed by "experts" from above in a manner that "short-circuits" the judgment of the participants. There is an alternative that is not only more piecemeal and incremental, but which is based on respect for the autonomy of the participants in the organizations. The alternative can be illustrated with the "paving the paths" example (see Williams 1981 for a description of the example). A number of office buildings were built in the middle of a large field. Where should the sidewalks be? A central planner would design the sidewalks to "address human needs," specify where the sidewalks should be built, and prescribe penalties for "walking on the grass." Instead, the area was filled with grass for several months. By that time, paths had been worn in the grass by the self-directed activities of the users of the buildings. The paths were then paved to create a system of sidewalks that addressed actual human needs by using knowledge generated by the spontaneous activities of the users (rather than the a priori conceptions of the planners).

The morale of the story is that reformers would be wise to pay more attention to the spontaneous activities of the participants or users. Those activities will reveal knowledge that is difficult to obtain otherwise. Of course, not all "spontaneous" activity should be legitimized or "paved" by changes in the de jure institutions. The "paving the paths" might take the form of designing the new de jure institutions to be nearby the spontaneous de facto institutions but with certain modifications to respect the rights of others or to guard against certain abuses—as has long been promoted by Hernando de Soto (1989) to formalize the informal property rights in Latin America.

Paving the Path of Spontaneous Privatization

The utopian versus piecemeal attitudes of Western advisers to the post-socialist transition is strikingly revealed by the reactions to spontaneous or "wild" privatization. The all-too-typical reaction was to condemn spontaneous privatization, to urge governments to quickly stop the "premature" entrepreneurship in all its forms, and to renationalize any such privatized companies. Then grand schemes were devised that were "fair" in the abstract sense of dividing everything equally among the citizens (e.g., giving babies and pensioners equal claims on the fruits of past labor).

A piecemeal approach takes a different attitude toward spontaneous privatization. As the power of the communist governments weakened in the decades leading up to 1989, many decentralized reforms were implemented that devolved power to the enterprises and local municipalities. The self-management system in Yugoslavia was the leader in this decentralization movement but it was followed by goulash communism in Hungary with its enterprise councils, by the Solidarity Movement in Poland and the Polish self-management councils, and by the Gorbachev reforms (e.g., the State Enterprise Reform Law of 1987) which significantly increased enterprise autonomy and self-accountability. These reforms represented something of a halfway station between the state and the market. When the socialist governments were finally overthrown, the spontaneous tendency was to continue the decentralization in the same direction all the way to the market with forms of insider-controlled enterprises. Those were the clear paths of spontaneous privatization. "Paving the paths" would mean devising a legal mechanism for management-employee buyouts (MEBOs) that put the process into a legal framework usually with some changes such as installment payments over several years for the endowment originally received from the state (see Murrell 1992 for a similar argument).

The lease buyout privatization program in the Soviet Union (see Rutgaizer 1989; Lloyd 1993; EBRD 1993; or Logue et al. 1995) and the Polish privatization by liquidation program (also known as "Polish leasing") are examples of following the flow of entrepreneurial activities by "paving the paths" to the market. Many countries chose the alternative path of mass privatization. In some countries, the residual power of the decentralization movements compromised the recentralizing and redistributive intents of the mass privatization programs. That resulted in voucher-based partial MEBOs (e.g., in Russia and Slovenia) that were confused mixtures of institutional attributes (and probably inferior to well-focused MEBO programs).

The piecemeal reform strategy in China also provides examples of "paving the paths." Long before Deng blessed the agricultural family responsibility system as a de jure institution, it had evolved as a de facto institution. By allowing many de facto experiments, the government learns where the paths are trodden in the grass, and then it can pave them and extend the results to other locales. The township-village enterprises grew out of similar experiments and are only now being "paved" with various legal forms (e.g., "employee stock cooperatives"). There is no small irony in the fact that the Chinese seem to be following the generic advice of Burke and Popper in their transition to the market, while so many other countries that hew closely to external advice are still devising their own Great Leaps Forward.

> The Chinese were wise enough to realize that they did not, in fact, know what they were doing. No one had ever successfully done what they were attempting, and so no one was an expert. Thus they set out in an experimental way, trying out different kinds of small changes and seeing what worked best. That "practice was to be the sole criterion for determining truth" was stressed again and again in the early reform documents. This was, naturally, intended mainly to rid the Party of the excesses of doctrinaire Maoism. It appears to have saved them from neo-classical orthodoxy, as well. (Benziger 1996, 6)

The Social Embeddedness of Change Agents

External advisers and reformers with "utopian" predilections tend to overestimate the power of the government to change institutions by passing a law—even a law "with teeth." Institutions can display remarkable forms of overt or, more to the point, covert resistance to sabotage change. It usually takes much more than passing a law and then trying to enforce it to bring the institutional players along and to effect lasting change.

These points might be particularly evident at the enterprise level. Some foreign consultants or external advisers might have the formal power to "implement" their recommended "best practices" to, say, restructure a distressed enterprise. The "best practice" might be locally inappropriate, and the external agent would ordinarily not have enough leadership authority to bring the enterprise personnel along.

> Corporate restructuring requires much effort and time, often years of intensive, single-minded concentration of resources. It cannot be imposed successfully from the outside (by shareholders, governments, or the public). It can only be instigated from within by managers able to carry the organization with them. (Wilson 1994, p. 167)

It is most difficult to implement and sustain basic change by "giving orders." Foot-dragging and slow sabotage will take their toll. Forced compliance will at most yield external conformity and will not bring about sustainable changes in basic structures.

The entrepreneur is often characterized by the ability to innovate and raise financial capital, but there is another component or requirement for the success of a project or enterprise which the entrepreneur cannot easily purchase with financial capital.

> This other component involves the ability to engineer agreement among all interested parties, such as the inventor of the process, the partners, the capitalists, the suppliers of parts and services, the distributors, etc.; the ability—so important in the undeveloped countries today—to enlist cooperation of official agencies in such matters as customs duties, permits, exchange control regulations, etc.; the ability to bring and hold together an able staff, to delegate authority, to inspire loyalty, to handle successfully relations with labor and the public, and a host of other managerial talents. (Hirschman 1958, 17)

Today, these forms of cooperation might be termed "social capital" following Putnam (1993). The point is that such social capital cannot generally be imposed by diktats or purchased with ducats; it is the means as well as the outcome in the virtuous circle of autonomous development.

These lessons from the enterprise would hold true, a fortiori, for institutional change in a society as a whole. To get more than sullen external compliance to legally enforced reforms, the reform leaders must have a certain "embeddedness" in the society or social organizations that they aspire to change. That, in turn, requires that the people in those organizations participate in an autonomy-respecting way in the change process. Such autonomy-respecting participation was essentially automatic in the previous example of "paving the paths" where the reform leaders "followed" the successful spontaneous activity of the changing organizations.

When reformers aspire to lead the change process, then certain forms of participation will actually increase the effectiveness and power of the leaders—rather than form a drag on the process. Various deliberation councils, consultative groups, and associations are intermediating forms that can give the leaders an embeddedness necessary to sponsor change and can give people the participation necessary to enable internal compliance or "buy-in" to the change process.[19] Without autonomy-respecting participation by the people that need to change, a long process of foot-dragging, recalcitrant compliance, and petty sabotage may slowly grind down and neutralize the reforms.

The Limitations of Diktat

Surely the maximum power of heteronomous "diktat" would be held by an occupying military power. While that power can destroy much, it is quite limited in its capacity to create and sustain new institutions. It is useful in this regard to compare the changes effected in Japan and West Germany by the occupying Allied Forces to the changes that Western advisers and institutions hope to effect in Russia. In Russia, the Western authorities do not have the power of an occupying force, and Russia did not suffer a military defeat.

In Japan, the Occupation destroyed the old family-controlled *zaibatsu* and turned the *zaibatsu* firms into publicly traded companies with most or all of the shares in the stock market (like large companies in America). But within a short time, the companies had bought each other's shares to form groups called *keiretsu*. That took most of the shares off the stock market so that the companies would not be vulnerable to foreign takeovers, and it reformed industrial groupings of companies on a new basis. The attempt of the Occupation to dictate the Anglo-American form of stock market-based corporate governance was not successful. Time will tell whether or not Western institutions have more success in Russia where they lack the power of an occupying army.

It is also interesting to consider foreign ownership in this context. It would have been a relatively simple matter to auction off West German or Japanese assets to the "highest bidders" (which would be mostly from the conquering power) in much the way that East German assets were auctioned off mostly to West German companies and individuals. Yet that did not happen to West Germany or Japan. Without significant foreign ownership, those countries were nevertheless quite successful in rebuilding and modernizing their economies to become economic superpowers today. Far from conforming to the Anglo-American model of the occupying powers, these countries have autonomously evolved an alternative German-Japanese model for a market economy.

Given this recent history, it is perhaps remarkable that Western institutions are rather uniform in recommending foreign ownership as the most important path for Russia and the other post-socialist countries to obtain expertise and capital for modernization and redevelopment.[20] In view of the German/Japanese precedent and in view of the fact that these countries are not defeated and occupied, it is unlikely for Russia (or any of the other transitional economies aspiring to autonomous redevelopment) to allow major foreign ownership. Movement in the German/Japanese direction of interlocking industrial groups or bank-led groups is much more likely. Anglo-American-inspired models designed to maximize the potential for external takeovers of ownership will not find fertile ground in Russia (as they found little in Germany and Japan). Insistence on such models will only hinder more autonomy-enhancing models of development for Russia and the other post-socialist countries.

CONCLUDING REMARKS

If knowledge is power, then tutelage is a form of intellectual colonialism. This chapter has focused on modes of learning and institutional change that will enhance autonomy, self-confidence, and self-reliance in developing countries. Furthermore, these methods will allow international development institutions to play a knowledge leadership role without setting up the dynamics that could perpetuate the tutelage of the client countries. By these methods, countries can pursue the inward transfer of knowledge without creating a debilitating dependency on the external sources of knowledge—so that they could also learn that knowledge is freedom.

NOTES

1. See Oakeshott (1991) for a similar distinction between technical and practical knowledge.
2. For related economic theorizing, see Nelson and Winter (1982).
3. Often experts from developed countries will take the required implicit knowledge quite for granted and think that transmitting the "blueprint" is enough. To use a baseball metaphor, people who are "born" on third-base may not be the best "experts" on how to hit a triple. More relevant expertise might be held by people who are only on second or first base but who actually hit a double or a single, that is, by people who got on base by their own efforts. They are likely to be better coaches for others to follow. We will later consider the additional problem that the local game might not even be "baseball."
4. The "best" baseball coaches in the world may not be so useful if the local game is soccer.
5. There is an analogy with the role of the local governments in East Europe during the communist era as the local "mirrors" to feed back to Moscow the great value and importance of the socialist blueprint and other benefits of the relationship with the leading example of socialism.
6. Hirschman notes a similar self-reinforcing dynamics when skills are imported because local skills are lacking and then "the local people whose inability to perform certain tasks is taken for granted and as unchangeable may come to be systematically excluded . . . from the skilled positions and the occupations by the newcomers who will acquire an interest in being retained as 'indispensable' in the elite positions they have come to occupy" (1967, 132).
7. See Hirschman's discussion of "*la rage de vouloir conclure*" (1965, 315) (the mania for wanting to conclude) wherein the developing country policy-makers are anxious to believe that the latest imported blueprint will solve their problems.
8. See chapter 12 of that name in Hayek (1978).
9. "It is a time-honored Japanese gardening technique to prepare a tree for transplanting by slowly and carefully binding the roots over a period of time, bit by bit, to prepare the tree for the shock of the change it is about to experience. This process, called *nemawashi*, takes time and patience, but it rewards you, if it is done properly, with a healthy transplanted tree" (Morita 1986, 158).
10. Paulo Freire has extensively criticized the "banking" concept of education where "knowledge" is transferred like money from the institution that has it to those who need it (see Freire 1970, chapter 2).
11. Popper's two volumes *The Open Society and its Enemies* (1962) are the "classic" modern restatement of the values of critical reason.

12. In one of my first assignments in the educational wing of the World Bank, I conducted a seminar for the Privatization Ministry in Kazakhstan as a debate between alternative views. When the Country Manager back in Washington heard about it, I was banned from the country.

13. There are deliberate analogies with the firm-level methodologies of continuous improvement such as the Plan-Do-Study-Act or Shewhart-Deming cycle (see Deming 1982, 88).

14. See Murrell (1992) for an excellent discussion of the economic transition from the viewpoint of the conservative Burke-Popper-Oakeshott tradition.

15. See Stiglitz (1994) for a development of this argument paying particular attention to the informational assumptions of the neoclassical model.

16. See Albert (1993) for a German-flavored "Rhine model."

17. See Edmund Burke's 1790 *Reflections on the Revolution in France* for the classic statement of the conservative case for judicious social change that will preserve the virtues of the past and see Ralf Dahrendorf's modern restatement of the ideas for the post-socialist transition *Reflections on the Revolution in Europe* (1990).

18. If the carrot is too far out in front of the donkey, then the donkey might turn elsewhere for food.

19. See Campos and Root (1996) for a discussion of these themes. Those intermediating groups and associations are the social versions of the enterprise-level worker committees, quality circles, management-labor consultative groups, and the like which are normally associated with Japanese-style business enterprises.

20. The major post-socialist countries need "redevelopment" since these countries were more misdeveloped than underdeveloped.

Chapter 7

Investment Climate for Whom?

Rethinking Globalization

INTRODUCTION

The improvement of "the" investment climate has become a major strategic focus of Western advice to developing countries. I will take the World Bank's recommendations to be representative of this advice. However, we might "complicate" the discussion by recognizing that there are trade-offs between different groups with different capabilities, interests, and assets. Making the investment climate better for one group may well be at the cost of making it worse for another group. Western advisers, for example, from the World Bank or IMF, tend to ignore these trade-offs and to implicitly identify with one group (usually external or foreign investors) and then to count an improvement in the investment climate for that group as being an "improvement" per se.

What are the other groups whose "investment climate" tends to get ignored? Private enterprise, particularly in difficult environments, is based on commitment to building the enterprise both on the part of the managers and workers. Over the course of time, they have to make a range of commitments or "investments" in people for firm-specific activities where they will not be able to reap the benefits of their sowing if they do not have some stability and longevity in the enterprise. If you don't know as to who will be around tomorrow or next week, then you are not going to make the type of effort commitments or firm-specific investments of human capital that are really necessary for success; you will focus your efforts to grab what you can while you can.

INVESTMENT CLIMATE FOR WORKERS

One person's "stability" is another person's "rigidity." Let us take the workers and managers separately. The World Bank tends to see the legislated or organizational sources of employment stability for workers (e.g., limitations on at-will contracts, not to mention trade unions) as "labor market rigidities" to be reduced or eliminated. Indeed, the Bank has not even been able to conceptualize the role of labor-in-the-enterprise or "human resource management" in its sectorial roadmap, only the "labor market" (which automatically directs the intelligence to the matter of "perfecting the labor market"). Thus, little or no attention in actual Bank practice (in the trenches, not in the rhetoric) is given either the learnings of the academic literature of the "What do unions do?" tradition (Freeman and Medoff 1984) or the human relations strategies of building worker commitment to the firm through commitments by the firm to the workers so that the workers put forth their best efforts, that is, make their largely firm-specific human capital investments in the firm (e.g., Blair 1995).

For instance, Japanese economists have developed a whole theory about how the "barriers to exit" (i.e., neoclassical "rigidities") work to generate organizational commitment.

> The way in which underpayment of wages in the early years of service and the acquisition of firm-specific skills create barriers to exit is obvious. These exit barriers perform several important functions for the firm as an organizational entity. The first is the incentive function whereby the interests of the firm and the interests of the individual are linked. Unable easily to exit, people can only protect their interests by working to ensure that the firm prospers. . . . The interlinking of interests means that when crisis looms, efforts are redoubled. The option of leaving the sinking ship is not freely available, either to the crew or the captain. (Kagono and Kobayashi 1994, 94)

This thinking, however, has not made much inroad into neoclassical economic thinking in the Bank. In constantly prodding client countries to improve "labor market flexibility," the Bank is in fact working *against* the investment climate for human capital investment within the firms. Hence, one way in which the discussion of investment climate might be complicated is to recognize that certain policies promoting labor market flexibility in the interests of short-term efficiency tend to cut against the human capital investment climate within firms and to promote grab-what-you-can short-termism.

INVESTMENT CLIMATE FOR MANAGERS

Analogous considerations hold for hired managers, except now it is the owners who are the source of uncertainty. The Bank has an almost exclusive focus on the "investment climate" for external financial investors so, from that perspective, it is key to have ownership always "up for grabs" so that those assets are always "transparently" available to the investors with the highest effective demand. Any restrictions of the ownership being up for grabs is a barrier, impediment, imperfection, rigidity, and all-around negative thing. Thus, the top and middle managers also tend to live "hand to mouth" rather than make long-term firm-specific human capital investments since one never knows who the boss will be tomorrow.

It is like a farmer with an at-will rental contract on the land where the land was always "on the market" so the farmer would have little incentive to make nonrecoupable investments. Bank staff are quite capable of understanding this point when reading de Soto's, *The Mystery of Capital* (2000). Without stable property rights, asset users will avoid nonrecoupable investments. But this point tends to be forgotten when the Bank's own Capital Market Department is trying to jump-start stock markets all over the world or when voucher privatization was recommended to the transition economies. Managers have problems making long-term commitments to firms in Siberia when they don't know what deals will be made tomorrow by stockbrokers in Moscow.

Here again, it is the Bank's own programs that are discouraging the sort of investment that requires stable mutual commitments where the value of investment is not recoupable other than by staying in the relationship. The conventional wisdom sees such commitments as rigidities and barriers that need to be eliminated to "perfect" the market for corporate ownership and control. The Bank's thinking and much standard economic advice does not recognize the conundrum in the *trade-off* between the logic of exit and the logic of loyalty and voice (see Hirschman 1970).

INVESTMENT CLIMATE FOR OWNERS

The same logic plays out for the owner. We can distill this wisdom from the academic scribblings of the defunct economist, John Maynard Keynes. Lord Keynes was much concerned with the adverse effects of the stock exchange on real investment. Investment in productive enterprise is largely irrevocable, and the management of enterprise requires a long-term commitment and the application of "intelligence to defeat the forces of time and ignorance of the future" (Keynes 1936, 157). In short, it is based on the logic of loyalty, commitment, and voice. But when investment is securitized as a marketable asset on the stock exchange, then it "is as though a farmer, having tapped his barometer after breakfast, could decide to remove his capital from the farming business between 10 and 11 in the morning and reconsider whether he should return to it later in the week" (Keynes 1936, 151). The stock exchange panders to the "fetish of liquidity" and thus continually undermines the bonds of long-term commitment that are so important to problem-solving and productive enterprise.

It is fine for Bank managers to "promote the investment climate," but do they really face up to this dilemma—the trade-off between commitment and liquidity? Improving the investment climate for financial investors on the stock market may undermine the sort of long-term investment in productive enterprise by nonspeculative owner-managers—particularly in complex and volatile environments.

Which of these investment climates is most important for economic development? The answer seems clear, and yet the Bank emphasized jump-starting stock market development with such policies as voucher privatization in the transition economies. The Czech Republic threw their companies onto the stock market with voucher privatization to maximize the opportunities for "investors" and the Bank and other aid agencies such as the United States Agency for International Development (USAID) promoted that policy all over the transition economies (see the later chapters on voucher privatization and the privatization debates).

Instead of belatedly learning something about these matters, the Bank even sponsored a voucher privatization program in the war-destroyed economy of Bosnia in the late 1990s. Voucher investment funds that profited handsomely from the programs in other parts of East Europe then acted as vulture funds swooping into Bosnia to buy vouchers at about 6 cents on the dollar to then get control of Bosnian assets. After they have "tunneled" out the value and stripped the assets, there will be an even poorer investment climate in that country. Here again, the Bank operates to worsen the domestic investment climate, not to improve it—unless one speaks of the investment climate for vulture funds as "foreign investors."

INVESTMENT CLIMATE FOR DOMESTIC DIRECT INVESTMENT

There are several ways in which Bank/Fund policies have worked against domestic direct investment.

High Interest Rate Policies

One way was emphasized by Joseph Stiglitz in the way the IMF policies, particularly in crisis situations, tend to push up interest rates to attract foreign capital with the predictable effect of choking off domestic investment and increasing bankruptcies.

Overvalued Exchange Rate Policies

Another policy is the pressure for "over-valued" exchange rates. The net effect is that domestic demand is expended on foreign imports. In theory, this could create healthy competition for domestic industry, but where the gap is too large, it tends to bankrupt domestic industry first. The best thing to happen for Russian industry at the end of the 1990s (aside from high oil prices) was the collapse of the Bank's and Fund's "protect the ruble corridor" policies in the fall of 1998 so that foreign-imported products were priced out of the market. The increased domestic demand for Russian-manufactured products led to a revival of Russian industry. Thus, growth came from the collapse of the Bank's policy framework in favor of the non-Bank framework of de facto protectionism and import substitution.

Blackhole Government Bond Markets

Another way in which Bank policies tend to spoil the conditions for domestic direct investment is the promotion of government bond markets. For instance, early in the post-socialist reforms, great symbolic or totemic significance was attached to creating active securities markets in stocks and bonds. When the government's budget was not covered by tax collections (it was often cheaper to "buy" an exemption that to pay taxes), then the primary noninflationary source of domestic finance was the market for government bonds. The high rates offered on government bonds operated as a financial black hole sucking in funds from banks, firms, individuals, and even foreign speculators. That, in turn, skyrocketed the interest rates available for loans to SMEs so that loan market was throttled in the crib.

When the Russian market for their high-yield government bonds (GKOs) was booming, it was celebrated as a success for the reforms that included bringing "investment capital" into the country. The common criticism in retrospect is that the market developed into an overheated Ponzi scheme and eventually collapsed. But there is a more basic criticism. Even without the overheating and collapse, the GKO-type markets massively diverted funds away from productive investment, and a similar story played out in other transitional economies with government bond markets not quite as spectacular as the GKO scheme. Those analysts who celebrated the "improvement in investors' confidence" that brought in footloose portfolio investors to the GKO market had their eye on the wrong indicators. By diverting funds away from direct productive investment (e.g., the SME loan business), the high-return government bond markets detract from, rather than improve, the real direct investment climate. Have the parts of the World Bank Group that were cheerleading the growth of the "vibrant Russian securities markets" learned any lessons or changed any policies after this debacle?

Open Capital Account Policies

Another Bank/Fund policy that detracts from domestic direct investment is the promotion of open capital accounts. These opportunities generate capital flight out of Russia and many other post-socialist countries. Great harm is done to domestic investment when government officials do not enforce the country's laws against illegal transfers of capital out to secure and discreet havens in the West. One of the biggest assists that the West can give to investment in these countries is to enact and/or enforce the laws to stop the illegal hemorrhaging of domestic capital from these countries. That, of course, is a second-best policy in the sense that we would all prefer to make the investment climate so attractive that the capital would remain in Russia of its own accord. But after the 1990s decade of de facto open capital accounts and the yearly exodus in excess of $20 billion, one might consider a second-best policy.

Financial Games versus Production?

Another area where international financial institution (IFI) policies have been detrimental to real investment is in the promotion of the financial sector schemes such as the voucher investment funds. These funds were nonstarters to supply capital or restructuring to troubled companies; they would end up siphoning or tunneling value out of the companies. Government officials all across the map quickly saw "the possibilities," so these Bank policies had "true government ownership." Voucher privatization and its progeny, mandatory second-pillar pension "reforms," were not "imposed" on Kazakhstan; the government officials *truly* wanted these "reforms."[1] When the complying government officials finally leave office in these voucherized countries, they tend not to become chemical or electrical engineers in manufacturing companies; they tend to go through the revolving door into the "financial sector" as board members, deal-makers, and the like. The same "motivation" reaches young people. Why go through all the years of study to become an engineer when very little study and a few connections can get one into the Klondike of "financial engineering" where the real fortunes are being made?[2]

INVESTMENT CLIMATE FOR FOREIGN DIRECT INVESTMENT

I have taken some pains to emphasize that improving the "investment climate" for one group may make it worse off for some other groups. In spite of some nods in the direction of domestic investors, Bankthink (i.e., groupthink within the Bank) tends to interpret "investment climate" in terms of the foreign investors who are supposed to bring capital, technology, and management/marketing know-how. But does Bankthink at least understand foreign direct investors?

Buying Shares on the Market versus Private Transactions

One common but persistent fallacy is the idea that foreign investors will want to come into the country through the stock market. This belief is one of the (non-cargo-cult) reasons for all the push in the World Bank Group for stock market development. But once a company is broadly owned on a stock market, why would a well-heeled foreign direct investor want to start buying shares off the market? Share owners would start holding out for higher prices from the deep-pocketed buyer or might even hold onto shares looking forward to large capital gains in the future. In either case, the foreign investor would find broad stock market ownership as an impediment, not a help, to obtaining 100 percent ownership. The investor would much prefer a clean private transaction for the whole company than the self-frustrating attempt to buy bits and pieces on the open market.

Indeed, some companies in the post-socialist world have deliberately worked with IFI support to do a public offering as a way to fight off being purchased by a foreign company. Once the stocks were scattered to the four winds on the stock market, the foreign company would be discouraged from trying to put all the pieces together again.[3] Here again, my point is not to argue that this was good or bad but to complicate the discourse by highlighting the trade-off. When the IFIs are promoting the flotation of the better companies, they are at the same time thwarting foreign direct investment in the companies of the most interest to the multinationals.

Share Deals or Asset Deals?

Indeed, most foreign investors would think twice before doing a share deal at all. If the investor really wants 100 percent ownership, then an asset deal (e.g., part of a greenfield or brownfield investment) might be far cleaner with no complications of hidden liabilities or employment expectations in enterprises that will need some restructuring. For instance, when IKEA bought a furniture company in Romania as a going concern, they made it clear that one of the plants was problematic and that if it was not profitable in one year, they would have to shut it down. The Federal Government was in full agreement and the deal went through. After a year, the plant was not profitable, so IKEA announced the closing (while continuing to operate other plants). The next day the local police arrived to notify the IKEA managers that they had violated local laws and would have to leave. The Federal Government said it was a local matter. IKEA ended up negotiating a new agreement and learned a hard lesson about buying a company as a going concern.

Dating Before Marriage?

Another persistent fallacy is the idea that foreign companies will come in and buy a company without having some prior trust-building getting-to-know-you relationship. This might take the form of a trade relationship, subcontracting production agreements, technology licensing agreements, or sales/service representation. And if that is one of the main paths to investment, then the investment climate work should include *the climate for trade relationships as well as production, technology, and sales/service agreements*.

There seems to be considerable implicit resistance in the IFIs to recognizing that companies can acquire export markets, technology, and know-how all without selling equity—as did the Japanese or Koreans. Whatever the reason, this leads to the underemphasis in the IFIs on these intermediate forms of involvement which are beneficial in their own right and which may or may not lead to foreign equity investment. A comprehensive program to promote the benefits of "foreign investment" would include the promotion of these forms of foreign involvement. Dating before marriage—involvement before investment.

Transfer Pricing versus Dividends: Misdirected Corporate Governance Policies

Another area of misdirected "investment-climate"-related policies is in the sphere of protecting minority shareholders. There seems to be the remarkable assumption that majority or controlling shareholders who are trade related to a company "should" take value out of the company only through dividends to be equally shared with the free-riding and passive "minority shareholders." However, it is quite normal and to be expected for controlling trade-related shareholders to take their value out in a variety of other ways such as transfer pricing and licensing agreements. It is hopeless to try to extend the scope of "corporate governance problems" to somehow control and exclude these hard-to-monitor-or-verify business practices.

The problem lies in the minority shareholders who exhibited less than brilliant judgment in investing in a company with a trade-related controlling shareholder without any other safeguards such as mandatory buy-back clauses that would be normal for a minority position in a closely held company in the West. That would be a foolish investment, and the World Bank Group should not broaden the "corporate governance" agenda to include "protecting" foolish investors.

LOGIC OF EXIT VERSUS THE LOGIC OF VOICE, LOYALTY, AND COMMITMENT

My remarks on the theme of investment climate promotion have focused on complicating the discourse by arguing that there are often trade-offs between different types of investment. A better investment climate for one group may create a worse one for another group. There is also a theoretical structure common to most of the comments. Neoclassical economics focuses on markets, and (arms-length) markets are driven by the logic of exit. The areas where I argued that the focus on investment climate was one-sided were those areas where the Bank tends to adopt a "Wall Street" view of business. Then "investment" is taken as investment in securities. The logic of markets in general and securities markets in particular is the logic of exit, liquidity, mobility, and flexibility.

There is another logic of voice, loyalty, and commitment (see previous chapter) that comes more into play *within organizations* that is usually neglected by economists in general and in Bank policy-making in particular. The investment climate trade-offs come from the cases where investment goes hand in hand with commitment and is *undercut* by the logic of exit, liquidity, mobility, and flexibility.

In the face of decline, there are always two different strategies for renewal: replacement or transformation.

- After a few years when the family car starts to emit strange clunking sounds, one has the choice of replacing it or trying to fix it (transformation).
- Many years ago, there was a cigarette ad about the loyal (or perhaps addicted) consumers who would "rather fight than switch"—the other option being "rather switch than fight."
- Albert Hirschman, in his 1970 classic, *Exit, Voice, and Loyalty: Responses to Decline in Firms, Organizations, and States*, developed these two strategies as the logic of exit (replacement, the quintessential logic of the market) and the logic of loyalty, commitment, and voice (transformation, the quintessential logic of stable organizations).

When facing decline, a commitment-based strategy "fights" for renewal by fostering the transformation of the given people and structures. An exit-based strategy sees renewal as coming primarily and initially from the outside through "switching," the replacement of the existing people (or at least the top people) and structures by new ones. Transform the old into the new—or throw out the old (to create a *tabula rasa*) and then import the new; that is the question.

The pure logic of exit applies only to the ideal model of a perfectly competitive market imagined in economics textbooks. And there is no human organization with "No Exit." All real-world situations of decline will call for appropriate combinations of transforming the homegrown old into the new (transformation strategy) and replacing the homegrown old with the imported new (replacement strategy).

CONCLUSION

Much of the conventional Western thinking about improving the investment climate is informed by a market-oriented exit-based vision of the markets and organizations system. This vision leaves out half the story and thus yields rather one-sided policy recommendations that seem to favor investors from advanced countries to invest in developing countries. The market-oriented exit-based vision leads to policies that do not support and may even worsen the investment climate for the members of organizations or even countries to invest in building organizational and productive capacity.

We have also seen that in the face of decline, there are essentially two strategies for renewal: transform the old into the new (transformation strategy based on logic of commitment and voice), or throw out the old (to create a *tabula rasa*) and then import the new; that is the question (replacement strategy based on logic of exit).

If the local decision-makers are to stay in control of the country's own development, then enough of the homegrown old must be transformed into the new so that they do not "lose their footing" and become so estranged from the change process that his only response is to cling to the old.[4] From that sound footing on the homegrown but transformed old, they can then take charge of throwing out part of the old and to appropriate and adapt the imported new to make it their own. The alternative is a process externally driven by replacement of the old with the imported new where people are "blown off their feet" and are being swept along without any real ownership of the new realities that were established outside of their control.

This analysis supplies a perspective on the current debate about globalization. Often that debate is posed in simplistic terms of whether or not a country should be "open" to globalization. This seems to be the wrong question. Of course, a country needs to be open to whatever is compatible with and will augment its independent development. Gandhi used a good metaphor for the openness that is compatible with one's autonomy. "I do not want my house to be walled in on all sides and my windows to be stuffed. I want the cultures of all lands to be blown about my house as freely as possible. But I refuse to be blown off my feet" (quoted in Datta 1961, 120). By building on enough transformation of their old into the new, the local change-agents could remain "on their feet" and have the self-confidence to seek out, assimilate, adapt, and own the external knowledge, experience, and relationships available to them in a globalized world.

NOTES

1. After the Bank sponsored and funded "pension reform" in Kazakhstan, more than a billion dollars have been taken by law out of workers' paychecks and fed into the "pension funds" controlled by the main financial/tribal groups in the country.
2. A private sector development team took a tour in the late 1990s around Russia visiting companies to help prepare the new strategy for Russia. One of their striking observations was the number of bright young people who had recently come into manufacturing after originally being in "financial engineering" but then had to leave after the financial collapse in August 1998. Here again, it was the collapse of the Bank/Fund protect-the-ruble-corridor policies and the related financial schemes that help redirect the "best and brightest" human capital into the real sector.
3. One example of this strategy to thwart foreign direct investment was the flotation of the Croatian pharmaceutical company Pliva on both the London and Zagreb stock exchanges—when a large Western drug company was in hot pursuit.
4. For a case study based on this theme, see Ellerman and Kreacic (2002).

Chapter 8

Revisiting the Privatization Debates

HISTORICAL INTRODUCTION

More than a quarter century has passed since the privatization debates raged in the international financial institutions (IFIs) and in academia concerning Russia and the other transition economies. There has been plenty of time for reflection and evaluation of these debates. Have the Western advisory institutions learned any significant lessons from the Russian debacle, or have they essentially adopted the Sachs-Summers-Shleifer[1] strategy of quietly closing an embarrassing chapter in their history and moving their attention (and hopefully the public spotlight) on to the breathless pursuit of more immediate and pressing concerns? This note addresses two questions: the overall institutional change strategy and the arguments against and the alternatives to voucher privatization.[2]

There was a rough consensus view of privatization among post-socialist reformers and their Western advisers. I would paraphrase the stylized story as something like this:

> Privatize quickly and irreversibly to prevent a comeback of the *nomenklatura*. The quickest and most politically popular technique is mass voucher privatization.[3] However without intermediaries, this would spread the ownership too wide and would thus create the problem of "corporate governance." Therefore, voucher privatization needs to be augmented by voucher investment funds to provide the necessary corporate governance for the restructuring of the privatized enterprises.

The first throughgoing voucher privatization in the post-socialist transition period of the early 1990s was carried out in the Czech Republic.

> By 1996 Prime Minister Klaus could state that the transition was more or less complete and henceforth the Czech Republic should be viewed as an ordinary European country undergoing ordinary political and economic problems. He characterized the voucher privatization program as "rapid and efficient." Most observers and most World Bank staff working on the real sector in transition agreed. (Nellis 2007, 98)
>
> The World Bank was far from alone in this; most other donors, including the EBRD, the EU, USAID, and several other bilaterals, endorsed, advanced, and supported this approach. (Ibid., 129)

A footnote then adds concerning the World Bank staff:

> Not all, for example, David Ellerman (1998) had long expressed doubts as to the utility of the approach, and later wrote a strong critique of the approach. (Ibid., 129)

John Nellis was one of the key participants in the debates about privatization in the World Bank during the 1990s. After he retired and after more than a decade of evidence accumulated, he reluctantly concluded:

> The faith in the voucher approach was misplaced, or at least heavily over-emphasized. Stiglitz and others are correct to admonish the external advisory community; it—we—should have been searching earlier for ways to introduce concentrated owners; we should have paid more attention (earlier than we did) to prudential regulations in capital and financial markets and other institutional development matters. (Nellis 2007, 123)

The Stiglitz critique was forcefully given in his "Whither Reform?" paper delivered at the 1999 All Bank Conference on Development Economics (ABCDE) in Washington. As Stiglitz's speechwriter at the time, I coauthored the paper but, in accordance with standard practice, was not listed as the coauthor. The official Bank's published version was somewhat edited, but the full version was later reprinted in Stiglitz (2001). The conclusions have held up quite well over the years.

INSTITUTIONAL CHANGE STRATEGIES

History offers few "crucial experiments" but the contrast between the Russian and Chinese transitions is probably the best one could ask for to contrast an institutional shock therapy or blitzkrieg approach with an incremental, step-by-step, or staged approach to institutional change. As the Yeltsin reformers such as Anatoly Chubais did use rather "Bolshevik" methods to try to storm the ramparts during the few windows of opportunity, Stiglitz (2001) and Reddaway and Glinski (2001) have called this "market Bolshevism." A wise commentator has described these Bolshevik tactics well.

> We have a fearful example in Russia today of the evils of insane and unnecessary haste. The sacrifices and losses of transition will be vastly greater if the pace is forced. . . . For it is of the nature of economic processes to be rooted in time. A rapid transition will involve so much pure destruction of wealth that the new state of affairs will be, at first, far worse than the old, and the grand experiment will be discredited. (Keynes 1933, 245)

These words are as true today as when they were written. And they were written by John Maynard Keynes about the original Bolshevik transition, not today's market Bolshevik transition in the opposite direction.

What was the alternative strategy? In this case, the incremental non-Bolshevik/Jacobin alternative has long found its sophisticated expression in the work of Albert Hirschman about incremental reform-mongering change driven more by endogenous pressures, bottlenecks, and linkages rather than by exogenous "carrots and sticks" embedded in IFI loan conditions.[4] The reform experience in China—which has never had an IMF program—represents something like this incremental approach in practice, crossing the river groping for the stepping stones rather than jumping over the chasm in one last "great leap forward." As Deng Xiaoping put it in 1986: "We are engaged in an experiment. For us, it (reform) is something new, and we have to grope around to find our way. . . . Our method is to sum up experience from time to time and correct mistakes whenever they are discovered, so that small errors will not grow into big ones" (see Harding 1987, 87). When experiments had positive results, the idea was to then catalyze the process. As Chinese reformer Hu Qili put it at the same time: "We allow the little streams to flow. We simply watch in which direction the water flows. When the water flows in the right direction we build channels through which these streams can lead to the river of socialism."[5]

One of the important misformulations of the transition question was "Fast versus slow?" "Incremental" might be misleading if it is construed as "gradual" or "slow." The Chinese reforms were neither gradual nor slow, and the Russians will not soon climb out of the chasm they failed to jump over in one leap. The point is to find and build step-by-step upon the reform efforts of the past (which requires taking into account past conditions) rather than trying to wipe the slate clean and legislate ideal institutions in one fell swoop. Murrell (1992) explored the connections between incrementalist strategies and conservative political philosophies. In Lau, Qian, and Roland (2000), the Chinese "two-track" system of reforms is analyzed where a second track, step, or stage is inaugurated and can then grow to eventually render the earlier stage obsolete. Black et al. (2000) use the word "staged" in much the same sense. In Joseph Stiglitz's *Whither Reform?* (2001), the two "ideal types" are compared as a battle of metaphors, as shown in table 8.1.[6]

Another part of the incremental approach, also evident in China, is the willingness to allow experiments in different parts of the country and then foster horizontal learning and the propagation of the successful experiments. This is an important part of the alternative to the Bolshevik/Jacobin approach of legislating the brave new world from the capital city to be applied uniformly across the country. The transition from socialism to a market economy had not happened before in history so the situation *clearly* called out for

Table 8.1 "Battle of Metaphors"

	Shock Therapy	*Incrementalism*
Continuity versus break	Discontinuous break or shock—razing the old social structure in order to build the new.	Continuous change—trying to preserve social capital that cannot be easily reconstructed.
Role of initial conditions	The first-best socially engineered solution that is not "distorted" by the initial conditions.	Piecemeal changes (continuous improvements) taking into account initial conditions.
Role of knowledge	Emphasizes explicit or technical knowledge of end-state blueprint.	Emphasizes local practical knowledge that only yields local predictability and does not apply to large or global changes.
Knowledge attitude	Knowing what you are doing.	Knowing that you don't know what you are doing.
Chasm metaphor	Jump across the chasm in one leap.	Build a bridge across the chasm.
Repairing the ship metaphor	Rebuilding the ship in dry dock. The dry dock provides the Archimedean point outside the water so the ship can be engineered to blueprint without being disturbed by the conditions at sea.	Repairing the ship at sea. There is no "dry dock" or Archimedean fulcrum for changing social institutions from outside of society. Change always starts with the given historical institutions.
Transplanting the tree metaphor	All at once transplantation in a decisive manner to seize the benefits and get over the shock as quickly as possible.	Preparing and wrapping the major roots one at a time (*nemawashi*) to prevent shock to the whole system and improve chances of successful transplantation.

Source: Author.

experimentation and pragmatism.[7] Instead the World Bank succumbed out of its own arrogance and "la rage de vouloir conclure" (the rage to conclude)[8] to the social-engineering Bolshevik/Jacobin mentality (complete with cold warrior moral fervor to wipe the slate clean of past evils), with help from elite academic advisers, and supported Moscow legislation to apply the dreamed-up solutions across all of Russia.

Today, any passively voiced "mistakes-were-made" admissions are invariably accompanied by TINA pleadings—"There Is/was No Alternative." But not only was it feasible for experiments to take place, they *were* taking place and were stopped in the market Bolshevik frenzy to legislate the brave new world during the window of opportunity. I will focus on the alternatives or "counterfactuals" available concerning privatization.

THE PRIVATIZATION DEBATES

After some initial limp resistance, the World Bank quickly succumbed to the public relations image[9] of the Czech voucher privatization as being "successful" and then promoted that model in other countries. In the rather standard model of voucher privatization, vouchers were distributed to all citizens, but it was expected that individuals would only invest the vouchers in mutual-fund-like voucher funds in return for shares in the funds. The funds would, in turn, use the vouchers to buy shares in the companies being privatized at state-run voucher auctions. But the voucher funds were run by fund management companies that could be completely owned by a few individuals or even by state-owned banks (e.g., in the Czech case). The voucher funds were supposed to be "controlling owners" who would supply "corporate governance" to the privatized companies. The companies were called "privatized" since their shares were predominantly held by the voucher funds which in turn were "owned" by millions of private citizens. But the funds were in fact controlled by the fund management firms which had negligible ownership interests[10] so the net effect was the "tunneling" of assets out various "back doors" to the benefit of the fund managers and their colleagues. Such was the scheme promoted by the IFI and academic experts in institutional design for "private property market economies."

In a World Bank working paper later published in *Challenge* (Ellerman 2001), which, incidentally, circulated for several years around the Bank in *samizdat* form before Stiglitz arrived and allowed it to be brought out as a working paper as Ellerman (1998), I argued that the economic case for voucher privatization was remarkably superficial and that the basic rationale was political. Stiglitz (2001) and Stiglitz-Ellerman (2001) develop an additional argument as to why the voucher privatization programs such as the

Russian scheme actually contributed to the debacle. This argument can be developed in different vocabularies.

The Argument in Terms of Agency Chains

One approach is via the notion of agency chains.[11] Long agency chains are very difficult to police and maintain. Information economics emphasizes the "asymmetric information"[12] and monitoring failures in principal-agent relationships.[13] The longer the agency chain, the more is the asymmetry and the greater are the chances for opportunistic behavior. It took most of the twentieth century to develop the array of watchdog institutions (e.g., accounting/auditing firms and the SEC) to police long agency chains in the West. A glance at runaway executive compensation in America, the ENRON-like scandals, and the collapse in 2008 shows the continuing problems in making the system work. The market Bolsheviks tried to legislate and install institutions such as stock markets, watchdog agencies, and publicly traded companies as if all that could be done practically overnight.[14] Voucher privatization which threw most medium and large-sized companies into the stock market was an extreme "pathological" example of trying to legislate well-functioning long agency chains.[15]

Economists who are not blinded by ideology should know that market economies start with short, not long, agency chains—indeed, they start with the identity of principal and agent in owner-operated firms and farms. The decentralization that is part of building a market economy in transitional countries needs to similarly start with agency chains as short as possible, not as long as possible. In the Czech-style "model" of voucher privatization with investment funds generally preferred by the Western advisers, the principal-agent "layers" in the long agency chain were the following:

1. the millions of citizen-shareholders of voucher investment funds who were to control;
2. the boards of the funds which were supposed to control;
3. the fund management companies which were supposed to control;
4. the boards of their hundreds of portfolio companies which were supposed to control;
5. the managers of the portfolio companies who were supposed to control;
6. the middle managers and workers who were supposed to actually produce something that people were willing to buy.

Historians may find it hard to believe that the "experts" in the IFIs and in elite academia actually thought that such agency chains could be legislated and "installed," and would then work reasonably well in economies after seventy years of communism.[16] And today, the comic book version of the Russian debacle that is promulgated for public consumption is not the farcical nature of trying to legislate five-linked agency chains overnight. Instead, the story is that "It didn't work as planned" because of the rapacious managers and state officials who did not respect property rights. Thus, the fault lies not in the architects of the defenseless chicken coops but in the rapacious nature of the foxes.

The Argument in Terms of De Facto Property Rights

This analysis can also be approached using the notion of de facto property rights. Neoclassical economics tends to follow Ronald Coase and to emphasize the importance of establishing clear formal property rights (and then perhaps the market will do the rest). And the cartoon picture of the transition used by the IFIs and allied experts is one that hammers away on the importance of respecting "private property rights." Never mind if the "clear-cut private property rights" are the ownership of junk shares in voucher investment funds on the tail end of many-layered agency chains. And never mind that in the US economy (i.e., the experts' implicit mental model) there has been a "separation of ownership and control" (Berle and Means 1932) for most of the twentieth century so that the top managers who command the heights in this paradigm "private property market economy" do so on the basis of their organizational role (much like Communist Party officials) and de facto control of the board—*not* on the basis of their private property rights. Neoclassical cartoons tend to ignore such troublesome aspects of reality.[17]

Progress has been made on this question in Hernando de Soto's books (1989; 2000). Although this was little noticed by the cheerleaders who wrote blurbs for his book jackets, including Ronald Coase, de Soto did not just argue for formal property rights but for the formalization of de facto property rights. That's a horse of another color. After all, all the land occupied and farmed by peasants or occupied and used by slum dwellers already had formal owners; it was not part of some "commons." The idea is that by using and improving these assets (formally but absentee owned by others), people have established certain de facto property rights which give them the capability to sow and reap. Any "reform" that would take away those de facto property rights (and the capabilities they represent) to assert absentee formal property rights would in fact be disempowering and antidevelopment. To promote market-driven development, the reforms should find out ways to formalize some socially acceptable approximation to those de facto rights so that the people then encounter the market and the private property system as something that empowers them—rather than the opposite.

Now transpose this argument over to the transition economies. In the decentralizing socialist reforms over the years and decades before 1990, the workers, managers, and local communities had developed a range of de facto property rights (or "use rights") over their enterprises. Central planning never worked well and, as it got worse, forms of decentralization took hold in varying degrees across much of the socialist world. These reforms included the Yugoslav self-management system, the enterprise self-management councils of Hungarian "goulash" or reform communism, the Polish Solidarity-dominated self-management committees, and the Gorbachev *perestroika* reforms to increase enterprise self-accountability. One way or another, in often bizarre ways, people learned to do things in a twilight half-centralized and half-decentralized system. They developed de facto property rights that represented their capabilities to actually get a few things done and to squeak by.

When the spell was finally broken in 1989–1990, the alternative to institutional shock therapy and market Bolshevism—the counterfactual—would have been to formalize the nearest approximation to the de facto property rights that would accepted as socially fair and thus continue the decentralizing thrust going "straight to the market" (e.g., through the lease buyouts discussed later). If that alternative approach had been taken, then people would have encountered the market as something that would recognize and formalize the capabilities they had already developed and would allow them to do even better.

Instead the market Bolsheviks designed the so-called market reforms with the exact opposite purpose to deny the de facto property rights accumulated during the "communist past," to righteously wipe the slate clean by renationalizing all companies of any size, and to start afresh with formal property rights deliberately unrelated to the previous "vestiges of communism."[18] Sometimes these "ideal reforms" were compromised in getting legislation passed but, by and large, the "reforms" were successful in denying the de facto property rights acquired during the earlier decentralizing reforms. For instance, outside of a small elite, most Russians encountered the market not as something that strengthened their capabilities and empowered them to do more but as something that took away what they were capable of doing and left them in a position where the rational choice was to grab what they could in the face of a very uncertain and uncontrollable future.

These points are perhaps easier to understand when applied to dwellings. Here pragmatism tended to prevail over market Bolshevik ideology. People acquired various de facto property rights over their flats in the socialist countries (analogous to "squatters' rights" in de Soto's work). Since the distribution of housing also partially reflected the power relationships under communism, one might pursue the same logic to suggest that the slate should be wiped clean of the communist past and all apartments should be put on the market and auctioned off to the highest bidder. Just think of the efficiency gains by jump-starting the housing market! Instead most of the post-socialist countries figured out ways to arrive at formal rights that were the closest socially fair approximation to the de facto rights.

Moreover, this analysis and critique is not just "hindsight." The following was written in 1992 and published (outside the World Bank) in 1993:

> After the collapse of the socialist idea in the late 1980s and early 1990s, the question of institutional change strategies came to the forefront. Broadly speaking, two opposed strategies emerged. The Big Bang approach advocated just drawing a big **X** over the old half-reformed institutions and then legislating new "ideal" institutional forms (figure 8.1).
>
> The old *de facto* property rights embodied in the half-reformed institutions would not be recognized in any significant way, and the new *de jure* property rights would be legislated by the new "revolutionary" democratic government.
>
> What is wrong with moving in one great leap to some desired ideal form? Nothing—if institutional change could actually take place in that manner. But it usually does not. People will resist and "drag their feet" in countless ways when their *de facto* property rights are canceled or trivialized. The imagined great leap breaks down in chaos. Instead of disappearing overnight in favor of the new ideal institutions, the de-legitimated old institutions break down in favor of a shadowy anarchy of *ad hoc* opportunistic forms. The Big Bang becomes a Big Bust.
>
> The alternative is a strategy of incremental institutional change. Instead of an imagined great leap forward over the chasm between socialism and capitalism, incentives would be devised to move people incrementally but irreversibly from the existing quasi-reformed institutions towards the "ideal" institutions. Instead of just negating the de facto property rights of managers and workers, they can arrive at a nearby set of legitimized de jure property rights by moving in the right direction (figure 8.2).

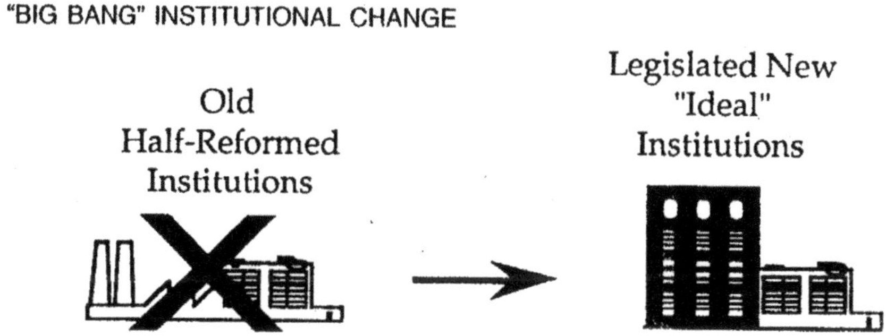

Figure 8.1 Big Bang Institutional Change.

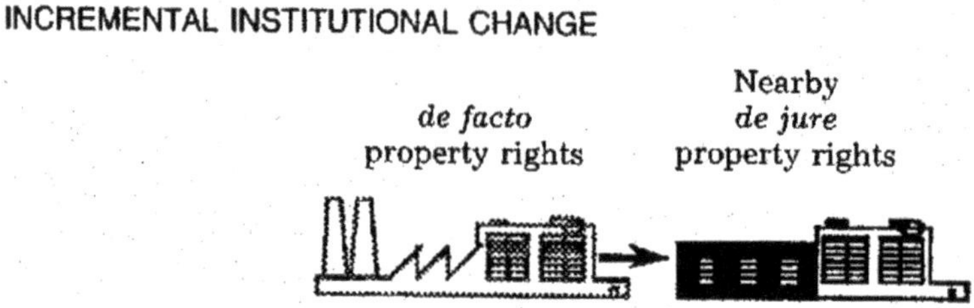

Figure 8.2 Incremental Institutional Change.

> These two strategies are posed as opposites. No country would adopt a totally pure strategy, and one country might use both strategies in different parts of its reform program. For instance, the privatization-by-liquidation program in Poland is based on an incremental strategy while the Polish mass privatization plan originates from a Big Bang approach. The Czech voucher plan is a Big Bang strategy, while small business privatization in the Czech Republic (and in most other countries) is based on an incremental approach. Aside from the lease buy-outs and other MEBOs, the Russian mass privatization program is a Big Bang program, while the Chinese reforms in agriculture and industry are the clearest example of a thoroughgoing incremental approach. (Ellerman 1993, 27–28)

The Lease Buyout Counterfactual

What are the forms of privatization that try to move to a set of formal property rights that are a socially acceptable approximation to the de facto property rights that resulted from the earlier reforms during the socialist era? In Stiglitz's *Whither Reform?* (2001), the general strategy was called "stakeholder privatization." Look at the parties which actually have to cooperate in order for an enterprise to succeed regardless of the "ownership structure." This includes the workers, managers, and local authorities. It does not include voucher fund managers sitting in Moscow. Then "shrink-wrap"[19] the ownership structure around those stakeholders to arrive at a minimal agency-chain structure where the owners have to cooperate on a day-to-day basis. In the above passage written in 1992, the Polish privatization-by-liquidation (also called "Polish leasing") program, the Soviet lease buyouts, and the Chinese reforms in agriculture and industry (i.e., household responsibility system and township-village enterprises, or TVEs) were all picked out as examples of this strategy to strive for formal rights close to de facto rights and to minimize the distortions of information and effort involved in long agency chains and absentee ownership.[20]

What was a counterfactual or alternative to the market Bolshevik program in Russia? If the logic (minimizing agency chains and building on de facto property rights) is sound, then the Soviet lease buyouts and related experiments seem to be the closest thing to a counterfactual to grow out of the reform experience in the former Soviet Union (FSU).[21]

> It's ironic that the Russian Communists of a decade ago, knowing that central planning was a dead end but not fully trusting markets either, likely built through enterprise leasing a better means for enterprises to manage privatization than the privatize-now approach that Western advisors later promoted and Russian reformers enthusiastically followed. The Russians who blame Western advice for destroying their economy are not entirely wrong. (Black et al. 2000)

As noted above, this option was argued for at the time and on the basis of roughly these arguments. The late Martin Weitzman also at the time gave a pragmatic argument for the worker ownership version of stakeholder privatization.

> Under worker ownership, the workers themselves, or their agents, will have to control pay and negotiate plant shutdowns. The most acute "us vs. them" stalemates may be avoided. Ownership is more concentrated relatively close to management decisions and can put more immediate pressure on performance. Regulatory capture may be avoided. Hard budget constraints may be more acceptable. There is less opportunity for financial manipulation. (Weitzman 1993, 267)

Note Weitzman's version of the minimal agency chain and "shrink-wrapped ownership" argument in his statement: "Ownership is more concentrated relatively close to management decisions and can put more immediate pressure on performance." Unfortunately, the IFIs chose to promote privatization in the way that Soviet-expert Weitzman recommended "How Not to Privatize."

Moreover, the IFI specializing in the region, the European Bank for Reconstruction and Development (EBRD), was not only aware of the leasing option but sponsored a set of pilot projects to show how lease buyouts could be done using modern corporate forms (Lloyd 1993). The structure of these deals and a host of other examples were presented in an EBRD technical note (1993), so all these ideas were known in the early 1990s to those in the IFIs who wanted to know and who were not blinded by anti-worker animus.[22]

The counterfactual is often caricatured as arguing "that institutional and regulatory reform should have preceded privatization." However, the point is that stakeholder privatization minimizes the need for the institutions to police long agency chains so that the *appropriate* forms of privatization can go forward as those institutions are being developed and can, indeed, drive that institutional development through the endogenous Hirschmanian linkages (in contrast to the IFI conditionalities).

For instance, it might be argued against the Russian lease buyouts that "Russia did not have a sufficiently well-developed national or regional institutional environment, as in Poland, to prevent large-scale managerial expropriation of assets under such a scheme." But the stakeholder theory did not depend on a "well-developed national or regional institutional environment" (such as securities and exchange commissions and auditing agencies) to protect the self-interest of those who have to cooperate together on a daily basis to earn their economic livelihood. The stakeholders are all "mutual hostages" to the success of the enterprise so that they can exercise their de facto property rights directly, not by trying to get "national or regional" institutions to enforce any formal rights.

Unfortunately, the "experts" did not seem to have understood the argument then—or now.[23] When the "experts" have a quasi-religious faith in *ersatz* national or regional watchdog institutions enforcing long agency chains and fail to see how people will try to enforce their de facto property rights in their concrete day-to-day self-interest, then the "experts" seem to have "failed in their understandings of the core elements of a market economy" (Stiglitz 2001).

There is also the argument that the stakeholder privatization option would have been too slow. In the Bank, we often heard a specious dichotomy of mass privatization (meaning vouchers) versus "case-by-case privatization" where the latter meant painstaking negotiation of each deal. Yet the lease buyout schemes were a form of "mass" privatization in the sense that each deal simply had to satisfy certain cookie-cutter requirements in order to go through. Polish leasing was not slow, and the 10,000 or so Soviet lease buyouts before 1992 when the door was shut indicate that they were also not slow.

Indeed, one of the "problems" with the lease buyouts is that they were too fast and too popular at the firm level, not that they were too slow. The stream might swell to a river. If the lease buyouts had not been stopped, then the market Bolsheviks feared that there would not be any good firms left to go into the voucher auctions. Thus, the stream was dammed, and the waters diverted into the Kremlin-preferred channel of voucher privatization.

"Employee Ownership" in the Voucher Program

But, it is asked, if stakeholder privatization such as worker ownership was such a good idea, what about the substantial employee ownership that resulted from the Russian voucher program (Blasi et al. 1997)? Didn't "employee ownership" get its chance and fail? The advice of advisers favoring employee ownership (the author included) was unanimous that any genuine attempt to use a worker ownership as a part of the voucher program would require a mechanism for collective decision-making such as the US or the UK employee stock ownership plan (ESOP) (as was roughly built into the lease buyout firms).

Repeated attempts to allow an "ESOP option" in the Russian Mass Privatization Program (MPP) as "Option 4" were specifically prevented by the GKI (Russian Privatization Agency) and Western advisers in the IFIs who wanted the worker ownership to be strictly temporary and not subject to collective decision-making. All at least agreed that by allowing individual sell-outs, there would be a prisoners' dilemma situation with the eventual noncooperative solution of most workers selling out individually (particularly when helped by managers withholding wages and offering to buy shares instead). The GKI even outlawed shareholder agreements, which might have functioned as "home-made ESOP trusts" to prevent individual share sales without a collective decision, since the GKI wanted to avoid workers having any enforceable collective decision-making about selling shares.

Moreover, the Dream Team, the Kremlin's arch-defenders of shareholder rights, pushed through a Yeltsin executive order that restricted the employee-owners to at most one-third of the board of directors—even if the workers had majority or super-majority (e.g., 80 percent) share ownership.[24] Thus, the stakeholders who could have helped to prevent managerial looting in the voucherized firms were deliberately prevented from legally coalescing as a stable decision-making group with a common interest in bettering the enterprise.

Those who deliberately designed the MPP to prevent the collective empowerment of the stakeholders in the enterprises were not simply displaying anti-worker animus (although that should not be discounted). They entertained the hope that this would lead to the concentration of ownership ("real owners") and the top-down power to restructure enterprises and reallocate assets. The MPP often worked as planned to concentrate ownership—in this case, usually in the hands of the top enterprise managers. But the top managers had little reason to follow out the rest of the hoped-for "logic" since they had little confidence that any increased value of the enterprise as a profitable going concern could be capitalized upon their impending retirement. This created the situation where many managers felt the most rational response was just to grab what they could while they could. Since the stakeholders were formally disempowered, they were somewhat less assertive to stop the attempted plunder (although there have been hundreds of plant occupations in Russia by workers trying desperately to stop managerial looting). New schemes of plunder could be arranged with the other major holders of formal rights (called "tunneling" in the Czech context).

Since the MPP was deliberately designed and implemented to undo insider social capital and to legally disempower the insider coalition of stakeholders (even if workers were majority owners) with the collective interest in preserving and improving the enterprise as a going concern (all dismissed as "impediments to restructuring"), it is a bit disingenuous to picture the asset stripping by the top managers and their outside colleagues as an failure of "employee ownership." After deliberately tying up the watchdog at hand (in favor of some *ersatz* and distant "watchdog institutions"), the Russian "reformers," the IFIs, and the Western advisers shoulder much of the responsibility for the foxes having the run of the chicken coop.

"CARGO CULT" ECONOMIC REFORMS: WHERE IS THE ROAD TO CARGO?

There is a certain self-reinforcing vicious circle that leads the World Bank and other agencies to try to "install" inappropriate institutions in developing and transitional post-socialist countries. Let us begin with the supply side of this unhappy transaction.

People from advanced developed countries are, in effect, "born on third base and think they hit a triple."[25] Such "natural-born development experts" may be graciously disposed to teach developing countries how to "hit a triple." The developing country should redraft its laws to describe the institutions seen from the vantage point of "third base" (e.g., "like in America") and then after passing these new laws, everyone should wake up next morning as if they too were born on third base.

Societies, however, tend to operate on the basis of their de facto institutions, norms, and social habits, not their formal laws—and particularly not the formal laws "pulled out of the air" with little relation to past experience. When such a gap between formal and de facto institutions is introduced, then the bulk of the population can rarely "jump over the chasm" to suddenly start living according to the new formal laws—so the rule of law is weakened. Semilegal ("gray") and illegal ("black") activities become more prominent as the connection between legal and actual behavior is strained to and beyond the breaking point. The advice from the natural-born development experts thus becomes more part of the problem than part of the solution. More relevant institutional information could be provided by people who were only on first or second base since they might actually know how to hit a single or a double.

Now consider the demand side—the demand for impossible "overnight" jumps to institutions copied from technologically advanced developed countries. The people and the politicians of the developing and the transition economies are constantly bombarded by the mass media with images of life in the "First World." They want to get there "tomorrow" (if not "yesterday").

Consultants and academics from elite universities with no real development experience badger the government officials to have the political courage and will to undertake a shock therapy-style change in institutions, to jump over the chasm in one leap (i.e., jump directly to third base)—*as if* such institutional change were actually possible. Those locals who caution against radical leaps are dismissed as only trying to protect their privileges and "rents" from the past regime. "How dare you think you know better than professors from Harvard!"[26] The idea is to "escape the past," not to study the past to better develop incremental change strategies. If the scientific experts from the First World give this advice, how can the benighted officials from the Third World or the post-socialist countries resist? All people have to do when they wake up the next morning is to start behaving according to the new laws drafted by the experts!

For instance, in a southeast European post-socialist country that had been particularly isolated in the past, government officials wanted to jump to modern corporations "like in Europe." This was an example of an "iceberg" institutional reform; the "above the water-line" laws could be quickly changed but the problem was the "below the water-line" long-term changes in behavior. They located a European foundation that was willing to fund an "adaptation" of the corporate laws of a west European country. The new draft laws were quickly passed by the Parliament so that the government officials and legislators could brag that they now had "European corporate statutes." All they needed now was a few lawyers, a few judges, a few accountants, a few regulators, a few businesspeople, and a few decades of institution-building experience so that the new statutes could actually be used. Any attempt to get the country to adopt laws similar to those in neighboring countries that had incrementally evolved toward a market economy for several decades was angrily rejected. "Why do you try to get us to use these second-best or third-best laws when we can adopt the *best* European statutes?" Surely the natural-born development experts from the First World want to provide the *best* laws for their clients?

Thus, the government officials demand that they do not want some second-best model; they want the "very best" for their people—like in the advanced countries. The third-basers in the international aid bureaucracies then can reap the seeds they have sown by "listening to the clients" and "responding to the clients' desires" by trying to set up "public joint stock companies" in Albania, a "stock market" in Mongolia, "defined contribution pension plans" in Kazakhstan, and "modern self-enforcing corporate laws" in Russia. Thus, the circle is completed; supply responds to demand in a self-reinforcing vicious circle to waste untold aid resources on the attempted instant gratification of a nonevolutionary "Great Leap Forward" to First World institutions.[27]

Perhaps the common focus of Western advice was to set up a "stock market." One primary purpose of a public capital market is to provide a bridge so that personal savings can flow into the investments of businesses.

> To a large extent equity markets are an interesting and fun sideshow, but they are not at the heart of the action. Relatively little capital is raised in equity markets, even in the United States and the United Kingdom. One cannot expect equity markets to play an important role in raising funds in the newly emerging democracies. (Stiglitz 1994, p. 228)

Furthermore, the voucher privatization process does not "jump-start the capital market" since the whole process of distributing vouchers to citizens and firms distributing shares in return for vouchers does not move one ducat of capital from savings into investment. An ersatz "stock market" in a transitional economy for the secondary trading of voucher-based shares does not perform that most basic function of a capital market—in spite of the strong symbolism of the "stock market" in the popular mind.[28] If public stock markets in the West play such a small role in net finance and if the stock markets in the transition economies don't even have that role, then it is difficult to explain the enormous attention and resources devoted to stock markets in the transition economies by Western advisers and domestic reformers.

> I think developing and ex-Communist countries should go slow in copying the financial institutions of the United States or the United Kingdom, or of Japan for that matter. When I read that Wall Streeters are visiting Beijing to help the People's Republic establish a stock market, I shudder. It is far from clear that the proliferation of financial instruments, market arbitrage opportunities, and paper transactions in advanced countries has created social product to justify the high-quality human capital resources it devours. (Tobin 1990, p. 233)

The finite Western technical and financial assistance would probably be better used in building up a sound banking system and an effective commercial court system—than in promoting disinvestment-oriented "investment funds" and largely symbolic "stock markets."

The failed attempts at utopian social engineering might be usefully viewed from an anthropological perspective. Many of the First World institutions such as "The Stock Market" have a certain totemic or "religious" significance. The Wall Street mentality found in the post-socialist world is reminiscent of the cargo cults that sprung up in the South Pacific after World War II.[29] During the war, many of the glories of civilization were brought to the people in the southern Pacific by "great birds from Heaven" that landed at the new airbases and refueling stations in the region. After the war, the great birds flew back to Heaven. The people started "cargo cults" to build mock runways and wooden airplanes in an attempt to coax the great birds full of cargo to return from Heaven.

Peter Berger has pointed out the cargo cult mentality in development that promises a great magical leap to modernity. "Indeed, one recurrent assertion of revolutionary propaganda is that its program can deliver the 'cargo' more surely or more swiftly than the gradualistic development models" (Berger 1976, 21).

Postcommunist countries, with hardly a banking system worthy of the name, nonetheless opened up Hollywood storefront "stock exchanges," which were kick-started by the listing of shares in almost all companies in a voucher privatization program. Government officials in East Europe, the FSU, and even Mongolia proudly showed the mock stock exchanges, complete with computers screens and "Big Boards," to Western delegations of Bank, Fund, and USAID officials (with enthusiastic coverage from the Western business press) in the hope that finally the glories of a private enterprise economy will descend upon them from Heaven. An earlier generation of misguided development efforts left Africa dotted with silent "white elephant" factories, and the present generation of revolutionary reforms in the post-socialist world left the region dotted with dysfunctional "cargo cult" institutions—the foremost among them being the largely totemic stock markets.

SOME POLITICAL CONSIDERATIONS

In summary, the Soviets (and the EBRD) experimented with the lease buyouts as a more homegrown option but the Yeltsin-era Russian reformers, with the full support of the IFIs and other Western advisers, stopped those experiments and deliberately stopped attempts to include some reasonable version of stakeholder privatization in their new Master Plan for Russia. Instead, they wiped the slate clean of people's accumulated de facto property rights and capabilities (in favor of vouchers worth a few bottles of vodka) so that most Russians "met the market" as an alien and disempowering force—which has repercussions to this day. The so-called reformers legislated a new system of corporate governance using long multilinked agency chains and *ersatz* watchdog institutions that don't even function that well in advanced economies after many decades of development.

Intellectual historians, from the perspective of history, will see how little the neoclassical Washington consensus understood the critique of Bolshevism-Jacobinism by the conservative or "Austrian" tradition of Hayek, Popper, and Burke. So many of our best and brightest economists seem to have just thought the Bolsheviks had the wrong textbooks. With the right textbooks in their briefcases, the "market Bolsheviks" thought they could fly into the socialist countries and use a peaceful version of Leninist methods to make the opposite transition.

But the task was not resetting inflationary expectations with a dose of "shock therapy." The task was deep-lying transformation of many complex interconnected institutions. These institutions had evolved through decades of communism, so the deeply rooted interconnections were not apparent, particularly not to the market Bolsheviks parachuting in from the West. The origin of what became known as the "shock therapy" approach to the transition was not only a bad analogy with inflation-stopping therapies. I fear the origin also lay the moral fervor of cold warriors who sought to "wipe the slate clean" of the institutions of communism and to socially engineer in their place (using the right textbooks this time) the new, clean, and pure "textbook institutions" of a private property market economy.

Interestingly, in this context, "Western" seems to mean "American" (or "Anglo-American"). German or Japanese economists seem to have felt uncomfortable as intellectual evangelists (or "imperialists") preaching to the post-socialist countries even though they may actually have more relevant experience to offer than their Anglo-American counterparts (e.g., Blinder 1995). Only the mixture of American triumphalism and the academic arrogance of neoclassical economics could produce such a lethal dose of gall. If the economics of Pinochet's Chile was attributed to the "Chicago Boys," then the economics of Yeltsin's Russia might be attributed to the "Harvard *Wunderkinder*."

We have seen, time and again, that the "arguments" for voucher privatization were blatantly poor—indeed quite unworthy of the most worthy elite advisers from the West and their reformer counterparts from the East. What was going on? The holes in the Swiss-cheese arguments are akin to Sherlock Holmes's "dog that didn't bark"—the absence tells the story. The advisers and reformers were following another logic that was less defensible in public.

The effort to pull power and ownership back to the state to be "properly" redistributed revealed the underlying *political* battle. It was not the battle between Light and Darkness presented to Western onlookers; it was the conflict between two very different strategies out of communism. The battle was between the following:

(1) the new "clean" post-socialist revolutionaries—those who emerged from internal or external exile, relatively untainted by the old system, armed with free-market rhetoric, and well connected to Western aid sources—to take over after the democratic revolutions of 1989–1990; and
(2) the old "embedded" decentralizing reformers—those who worked against the old system from within and who generally had social

democratic views but were dismissed as "nomenklatura" by the new "clean" revolutionaries.

In a nutshell, "voucher privatization" was essentially the cover story for the power plays of the new "clean" post-socialist revolutionaries against the old "embedded" decentralizing reformers.

In the years and, in some cases, decades before 1989–1990, many of the socialist countries had decentralizing reforms with varying degrees of success: self-management in Yugoslavia, goulash communism with the enterprise councils in Hungary, Solidarity with the self-management councils in Poland, and *perestroika* with the decentralized management, cooperatives, and lease buyouts in Gorbachev's Soviet Union. When the dam finally broke in 1989–1990 and the new "clean" post-socialist revolutionaries were elected, what was the best path to the market? The most direct and continuous route would have been to push the halfway decentralizing reforms in the same direction all the way forward to the market. That would have meant transforming the quasi-ownership of the workers embodied in the various self-management councils into management and employee buyouts (MEBOs) as in the ESOPs of the United States and the United Kingdom, or as in the Mondragon cooperatives of the Basque region in Spain. Then the people in the post-socialist countries would have met the market and the private property system as empowering instead of disempowering them in favor of the oligarchs, tycoons, and returning émigré cronies of the new governments.

But the clean post-socialist revolutionaries and their Western advisers each had their own reasons for opposing this direct route to the market where employee ownership would have been a major theme. The clean post-socialists had won electoral victory over the older generation of embedded reformers, but the older reformers were still represented in the management of the enterprises and on the worker councils. The new generation having obtained political power needed to secure and enrich it by also obtaining economic power. They needed a grand scheme to stop the drive toward decentralization and the market so that economic power could be pulled back to the state now controlled by the clean post-socialist revolutionaries and then redistributed to their allies or cronies.

For instance, the public story in Slovenia was that the existing managers (after decades of successful marketization) were still bad managers and that is why they should be replaced. But Jeff Sachs was then advising the Slovene government and let it slip in an American interview that the underlying reason was political; "Even if they are all Lee Iacoccas, does it make sense to simply give the country's industry to them?"[30] (quoted in Warsh 1991, G3). After some debate and experimentation, voucher privatization with voucher investment funds emerged as precisely that grand scheme—and Western *wunderkind* economists emerged as the ideal shills with world-class credentials to testify that it was the True Path to the market.

Just what was the role of the Western advisers and to what extent were they responsible for the debacle? Western economists seem to have had little or no important role in the Czech voucher privatization (although not for lack of trying). In other countries, the prominent Western advisers served as a credible shill for the policies of the clean post-socialist revolutionaries. There had been a collapse of intellectual self-confidence in the many postcommunist countries which was often coupled with a "self-hatred" of their past. Redemption had to come from the outside. In particular, the new governments needed some prestigious Western spokesmen to "sell" such a bizarre idea as voucher privatization to their own populations. Thus, the union of the self-important Western economists and the intellectually dependent post-socialist governments was a marketing marriage made in heaven. The clean post-socialists needed to market their scheme to finesse the earlier decentralized reforms (so the changes could be "done right" the second time), and the Western advisers were marketing themselves as the intellectual saviors of the benighted East by putting the scientific prestige of neoclassical economics behind one of the most cockamamie social engineering schemes of the twentieth century.

Aggressive self-promotion is not a sin—at least not for Americans. The problem lies elsewhere. When the spell broke in 1989–1990, the populations in the socialist countries turned in earnest to the West for guidance and assistance. Western scholars with knowledge of the Soviet Union understood the enormity of the task and did not leap forward to offer nostrums (e.g., Harvard's Martin Weitzman or Marshall Goldman). Economic *wunderkinder* had no such "hindrance" of noncartoon knowledge about socialist economies so they felt little compunction in offering themselves as experts in the transition from socialism to capitalism. Being an expert in neoclassical economic theory seems to qualify one as an "expert" in something that has never before happened.

Having been constrained from enjoying the Western "good life" for so long, the people of the socialist countries really wanted to escape their history and make a sudden great leap forward to a Western consumer economy and lifestyle. Giving up the socialist economic security and pace of work was a "different question" and hence the jokes about wanting to be a "consumer in the West and worker in the East." The embedded reformers had a fair sense that this would take many years of determined but incremental transformation. As the clean post-socialist revolutionaries had little or no practical experience or track record, the Western advisers had a key role to establish credibility and to offer hope. Any local embedded reformers who cautioned incrementalism were undercut by the shock therapy advice of the Western professors on how to jump over the chasm from socialism to capitalism in one great leap. How could "socialist ignoramuses" be wiser than Western professors from top universities and with world-class credentials in the science of economics? Thus, in the transitional countries, the charge against the Western advisers was that their thirst for self-promotion led them to undermine more pragmatic local advice, to undercut the intellectual self-reliance of the countries, and to plant false hopes of jumping over the chasm in one great leap.

CLOSING REMARKS

Those who wish to learn from the Russian debacle should not wait for any deep understanding to come from the institutional experts and academic advisers who engineered it. Tawney noted well that historical understanding requires the perspective of distance.

> The student can observe the results which these cataclysms produce, but he can hardly without presumption attempt to appraise them, for it is at the fire which they kindled that his own small taper has been lit. (1954, 227)

The institutional and academic advisers whose torches seem to burn with the same fire as the Russian conflagration cannot be expected to shed much new light on those events; their inclination is to blame others and to move on to other places and concerns.

Perhaps the last word on what was largely Harvard's role in the debacle should be given to one of Harvard's leading economists who was not involved.

> According to the 2002 World Development Report (World Bank 2002), from 1990 to 2000, China's real GDP grew at an amazing 10.3 percent per year. Meanwhile, Russia's output fell at a rate of 4.8 percent per year. Such a shocking contrast cries out for an explanation. (Mankiw 2003, 256–57)

Gregory Mankiw of the Harvard Economics Department and then (2003) head of the Council of Economic Advisors made this parallel comparison in the course of reviewing a book by John McMillan (2002).

> Russia leaned on lawyers, economists, and bankers from the West for advice on how to privatize state firms, develop capital markets, and reform the legal system. . . . China by contrast called little on foreign consultants. (McMillan 2002, 207–08; quoted in Mankiw 2003, 257)

McMillan, a Stanford economist, roundly condemned the near-unanimous consensus on the shock therapy strategy.

> If McMillan is right that shock therapy was the problem, then the economics profession must accept some of the blame. Our profession lent some of its best and brightest to the transition effort, such as my former colleague Jeffrey Sachs.[31] Most of these advisors pushed Russia to embrace a rapid transition to capitalism. If this was a mistake, as McMillan suggests, its enormity makes it one of the greatest blunders in world history. (Mankiw 2003, 257)

NOTES

1. The "Harvard *wunderkinder*," Jeffrey Sachs, Larry Summers, and Andrei Shleifer, together with the Kremlin "Dream Team" (Summers' memorable label) led by Anatoly Chubais played a role in Yeltsin's Russia roughly analogous to the "Chicago Boys" in Pinochet's Chile. Peter Murrell has referred to their general strategy as "The Transition According to Cambridge, Mass." (1995) but (as an M.I.T. alumnus) I must point out that the *wunderkinder* were all at Harvard.

2. My main focus is on privatization prior to the Russian reformers' "loans-for-shares" scheme—the latter of which played a major role in creating today's oligarchs and which was not publicly opposed by the IFIs. Many commentators seem to avoid learning difficult lessons from the earlier voucher privatization by focusing on the loan-for-shares scheme as the "Mother of all Debacles," instead of simply as "Dream Team: The Sequel."

3. While voucher privatization gives away for free the bulk of the assets on the asset side of the public balance sheet, one needs to consider the liabilities side of the balance sheet which includes the following:

- funding the daunting pension liabilities and health care needs of the aging population,
- meeting the interest and principal payments of the public and foreign debt,
- funding the social safety net and other economic dislocation costs,
- modernizing the education system to face the new challenges of a competitive market economy,
- paying to clean up after the environmental neglect of the past, and
- rebuilding the infrastructure needed for a modern economy (see Ellerman, Vahcic, and Petrin 1991).

4. See the "two basic approaches" in Hirschman (1973, 247–48) where he contrasts an ideological, fundamental, and root-and-branch approach to reform with an incremental, step-by-step, piecemeal, and adaptive approach.

5. Quoted in: Harding (1987, 318). Thus, Chinese socialists do instruct market Bolsheviks on the non-Bolshevik methods of institutional transformation. A related "pave the paths" metaphor is used by Christopher Williams (1981, 112). In a complex of new buildings, let grass grow between them, see where footpaths develop, and then

pave the paths. While voicing Hayek's ideas about the market as a spontaneous order, many market Bolsheviks (such as Václav Klaus) labored to totally stop spontaneous privatization instead of trying to find the closest socially acceptable channel so that those market forces might swell from a stream to a river (see Ellerman 1993).

6. See Benziger (1996) on the Chinese "not knowing what they were doing," Elster et al. (1998) for the use of Otto Neurath's "rebuilding the ship at sea" metaphor in this context, and Morita (1986) on *nemawashi.*

7. Deng Xiaoping's pragmatism, "It is not important if the cat is black or white, but that it catches the mice," was echoed by Ralf Dahrendorf's 1990 call "to work by trial and error within institutions" (41; quoted in: Sachs 1993, 4). Dahrendorf's book was a deliberate updating of Edmund Burke's anti-Jacobin tract *Reflections on the Revolution in France* (1937 [orig. 1790]). Sachs argued against Dahrendorf's pragmatism, noting: "If instead the philosophy were one of open experimentation, I doubt that the transformation would be possible at all, at least without costly and dangerous wrong turns" (Sachs 1993, 5). To avoid "costly and dangerous wrong turns," the then-Harvard *wunderkinder* promoted the scheme of mass privatization through voucher investment funds.

8. See (Hirschman 1973, 238–40).

9. Actually it was more than PR, at least in the usual sense. Some Bank economists churned out reams of accommodating econometric studies "scientifically" showing how "successful" the Czech privatization and restructuring was. Later, when Stiglitz had the econometrics redone outside the Bank, the results were negative or insignificant (see Weiss and Nikitin 1998). For a thoughtful rethinking of the Bank's experience by the then head of the Bank's thematic group on privatization, see Nellis (1999; 2007).

10. The voucher funds were typically restricted by law to owning at most 20 percent or 30 percent of a portfolio company, and the annual payoff of the fund management companies was typically fixed at 2 percent of the value of the portfolio under management. Hence, the "ownership interest" of the controlling fund management firms was on the order of 2 percent x 30 percent = 0.6 percent or six-tenths of 1 percent. This was not some "secret" design flaw discovered later; this was in the legislation of the voucher programs. Surely the experts, *wunderkinder* or not, could "do the math." Yet the globe-trotting "institutional design experts" seemed surprised to later find in their voucher programs all across the transition economies that the fund management companies devised more efficient ways to "tunnel" funds (getting 100 percent rather than 0.6 percent) out various "back doors" of the firms. See Coffee (1996) for these and other typical details of voucher investment funds.

11. An "agency chain" is a multilinked chain of principal-agent relationships. For instance, in the large publicly traded US companies, the theory is that the shareholders are the ultimate principals who "supervise and control" the board of directors as their agents (in theory through board elections but, in fact, dissidents tend to use exit—selling shares—rather than voice). The board, in turn, is supposed to select and supervise the top managers (rather than the other way around) in another link in the agency chain. Then the top managers supervise the middle managers and so forth eventually down to the workers on the office or shop floor.

12. For instance, managers have much more relevant information about what they are doing and about the company than their "principals," the board members, and the shareholders.

13. In 2001, Stiglitz received the Nobel Prize in Economics for his work in information economics.

14. The superficiality of interpreting "passing laws" as institutional change (unfortunately, a common practice in the IFIs) was noted long ago by Richard Tawney after visiting China in 1930. "To lift the load of the past, China required, not merely new technical devices and new political forms, but new conceptions of law, administration and political obligations, and new standards of conduct in governments, administrators, and the society which produced them. The former could be, and were, borrowed. The latter had to be grown" (Tawney 1966 (orig. 1932), 166).

15. See "Corporate Law from Scratch" (Black, Kraakman, and Hay 1996) for a remarkable example of trying to etch first-best laws as if on a blank slate in Russia. Even more remarkable is that after much bitter experience with corporate governance in Russia, Black and Kraakman later reversed themselves (Black et al. 2000) and argued for a more pragmatic "staged" approach to legal and institutional development (see below on lease buyouts). The third author of "Corporate Law from Scratch," Jonathan Hay, was a legal specialist from the Harvard Law School who worked with Shleifer in Russia on USAID contracts through Harvard. Shleifer and Hay were later indicted by the US Department of Justice for corrupt practices in that work and were convicted and fined on some counts and settled out of court on other counts. See McClintock (2006) and Warsh (2018).

16. The attempts to use vouchers to kick-start "stock markets" in transition economies from the Czech Republic to Mongolia are best viewed as "cargo cult" reforms driven by the totemic or "religious" significance of "Wall Street" rather than by any real economic function (see Ellerman 1998; 2001). In this case, USAID presented a strong challenge to the World Bank/IMF to be "more Catholic than the Pope"—to be the true "Vatican" of the stock market cargo cult. Political appointees to ambassadorships in US embassies in post-socialist countries had little patience with any incremental institution-building strategies; they wanted to see a "stock market" as soon as possible—even if it was little more than a Hollywood storefront or cargo cult copy.

17. James Scott's book *Seeing Like a State* (1998) argues persuasively that states use simplified pictures of reality to administer their affairs but that these simplified pictures lead to disaster when they are the basis for large-scale social engineering schemes to change reality. Global development bureaucracies have even less contact with local realities than national governments and thus they tend to be even more driven by bureaucratic common-denominator stereotypes or cartoon models of reality.

18. It is of some historical interest that (to my knowledge) no conservative or Austrian economist, political thinker, or social scientist publicly raised their voice to oppose the market Bolsheviks. This intellectual "prudence" (a nice euphemism for cowardice) was probably due to their fear of being seen as soft on communism since the market Bolsheviks had framed the task as the great leap over the chasm between communism and capitalism. Otherwise, conservative and Austrian thinkers can be very vocal in using their "principles" to criticize any institutional change considered

"socialistic." Critiques of the Bolshevik methods in the early 1990s came from Dahrendorf (1990), Kornai (1990), Murrell (1992), Weitzman (1993), and the author (1993), none of whom would be considered as conservative or Austrian thinkers.

19. "Shrink-wrapped ownership" is a metaphor denoting a structure where owners are those "stakeholders" who—independently of any formal ownership—have an "up close" functional relationship to the operations of a firm that would include the staff and major suppliers (including finance) or customers and perhaps local authorities but not, say, absentee buyers of second-hand shares. The idea is to match ownership to function with the firm rather than treat "ownership" as a tradable commodity that can be bought by otherwise unrelated parties. By "firm" I mean the de facto firm that meets every working day, not the formal legal entity that meets once a year. The strikingly successful Chinese TVEs (Weitzman and Xu 1994) function with a "shrink-wrapped" ownership/control structure even without Western-style formal ownership—much to the bewilderment of the Western experts.

20. In the transition literature (e.g., Dabrowski et al. 2001), one sometimes finds the view that the industrial TVEs somehow sprung up de novo in the nonindustrial countryside of China during the 1980s and 1990s. In fact, they started as the conversion and expansion of the commune (= township) and brigade (= village) enterprises left over from the earlier attempts to decentralize industry to the rural areas (see Byrd and Lin 1990).

21. In a lease buyout, the enterprise staff—who developed de facto property rights in the decentralizing reforms—were allowed to proceed "straight to the market" by purchasing the company with seller-supplied credit on an installment or lease-purchase basis. As in US-style leveraged buyouts, the installment payments are made by the company (not the individuals) to the seller. The lease buyouts worked best as medium-sized (or smaller) firms. But the Soviet dinosaurs typically needed to be busted up into a related set of medium-sized firms, so lease-buyout "spin-offs" or "break-aways" could also be used to restructure and privatize large firms.

22. One finds rather crude expressions of anti-worker animus in private conversation. During my years in the World Bank in the mid-1990s, I supported the proposed privatization policy whereby the people in the post-socialist countries should meet the market and private property system by getting some ownership in their place of living and their place of work—instead of it going to the oligarchs and other government cronies. On a flight from Tallinn Estonia to Moscow, a high-ranking official in the World Bank's privatization program leaned across the aisle (after a few drinks in the Tallinn exit lounge) to tell me why the Bank would never support worker ownership privatization. She said that once workers got control of a factory, they would start cutting out the electrical wiring and unbolting the machinery to get some quick money in the market for scrap metal. As factory after factory would subsequently shut down, the blame for the damage to the economy would fall on whoever advocated worker ownership privatization, and that was not going to be the World Bank. When I asked what it would sound like if she attributed similar idiocy to blacks or women, the conversation ended.

23. The failure of elite academic and bureaucratic economists to "understand" this mutual hostage argument surely derived in part from their fundamental anti-worker

animus. This was clearly shown in the behind-the-scenes arch-paternalist view that "worker ownership" would just lead to workers destroying their own livelihood by stripping the assets of their own firms. They argued for strong concentrated owners who would be "interested in maintaining the long-run health of the assets" and who would act as "asset advocates." And then the elite advisers supported voucher investment funds—funds which, together with ENRON-style managers, showed their great devotion to assets by promptly tunneling them out of the firms. However, some Polish critics of the "Stiglitz perspective" (Dabrowski et al. 2001) allowed that "workers' self-management played an important part in limiting the fall in output and the amount of criminal asset stripping in the state sector in Poland," and thus they are "Not Poles Apart" on the short agency chain and mutual hostage arguments (Stiglitz and Ellerman 2001).

24. Yeltsin Executive Order N. 2284, "About the National Program of Privatization of State and Municipal Enterprises in the Russian Federation" was issued on December 24, 1993 (thanks to John Simmons and Olga Klepikova for the reference—particularly §9.10.4). One can surmise the hue and cry that would have been raised by the IFIs and other assorted "defenders of stockholder rights" had such a decree been directed at foreign investors instead of worker-owners.

25. The baseball metaphor was used by the Texan populist and political commentator Jim Hightower to describe President George H. W. Bush.

26. See Wedel (1998) for more on the role of the Harvard *wunderkinder* in Eastern Europe and in Yeltsin's Russia. Jeffrey Sachs was the first young Harvard economics professor to gain notoriety in this regard, but he was soon eclipsed by his colleagues Lawrence Summers (who during the early 1990s become chief economist of the World Bank and later secretary of the Treasury in the US government) and, his protégé, Andrei Shleifer (born in Russia but emigrated to America as a teenager).

27. Tawney put it well. "What makes modern industry is ultimately not the machine, but the brains which use it, and the institutional framework which enables it to be used. It is a social product, which owes as much to the jurist as to the inventor. To regard it as an ingenious contrivance, like a mechanical toy, or the gilded clocks in the museum at Peiping made by London jewellers for the amusement of Chinese emperors, which a country can import to suit its fancy, irrespective of the character of the environment in which the new technique is to function, is naïve to the point of absurdity. It is like supposing that, in order to acclimatise Chinese script in the West, it would be sufficient to introduce Chinese brushes and ink" (Tawney 1966 (orig. 1932), 130).

28. This may help explain why the standard Western advice ignored nonequity corporate securities in voucher privatization. Why distribute equity as opposed to debt instruments in quasi-bankrupt companies to the citizens when equity has the lowest claim on corporate asset value? Aside from the role of the stock market in popular consciousness in the East and West, the main reason was probably to keep equity control out of the hands of insiders (seen as *nomenklatura*) and, if possible, to distribute it to financial intermediaries seen to be in "reform-oriented" hands.

29. See the chapter on "Cargo Cult Science" in Feynman (1985). See the foreword by J. K. McCarthy in Lawrence (1979) for the cargo cult formulation of the question

of development assistance: "Where is the road that leads to cargo?" Jan Knippers Black also uses the cargo cult metaphor for some recent development thinking (2000, 137 or 280).

30. Lee Iacocca was then seen as the great turnaround manager who saved Chrysler.

31. The other two Harvard *wunderkinder*, Larry Summers and Andrei Shleifer, made more direct contributions to the Russian debacle than Jeffrey Sachs (now with a reinvented persona at Columbia University) but Shleifer is still a colleague of Mankiw's at Harvard and Summers was then president of Harvard University.

Chapter 9

The Logical Fallacy in the Kaldor-Hick Principle and Cost-Benefit Analysis

INTRODUCTION: TWO CONCEPTIONS OF ECONOMICS

There are, broadly speaking, two different visions of economics: one divides the subject matter into production and distribution (essentially the classical view) and the other emphasizes exchange. John R. Hicks (1975) has usefully juxtaposed the two visions of economics. One vision goes from the classical economists through Marshall and Pigou, and it emphasized the production and distribution of the social product (Pigou's "national dividend"). The other vision of economics was ushered in by the marginalist revolution of the Lausanne and Austrian schools, and it focused on exchange (catallactics).

Catallactics studied the decentralized or polycentric system of market exchange, but the production and distribution approach could be viewed as an overall maximization of wealth or welfare that did not imply but was compatible with centralized control.

> Robbins offered the widely accepted definition of "the economic problem," as the allocation of scarce means among alternative ends. With this definition, the way was set for the disciplinary domination of the maximizing paradigm at the expense of the almost total neglect of "catallaxy," which offers the only mind-set from which the implications of the science of economics for sociopolitical order can emerge. (Buchanan 2005, 66)[1]

As formulated in the Marshall-Pigou tradition, the economics of welfare was based on a fundamental distinction between the size versus distribution of the "social pie," for example, Pigou's "production" versus "distribution" of the "national dividend" (Pigou 1960). This social pie was *not* to be identified with overall welfare (e.g., Pigou's "economic welfare") since the quantity of overall welfare could be affected by both the size *and* the distribution of the pie (e.g., Pigou's "national dividend"). The pie that economists would be "professionally" concerned with maximizing is an intermediate aggregate usually expressed in the measuring rod of money and variously known as the national dividend (or product), net social benefits (e.g., in cost-benefit analysis [CBA]), and social wealth (e.g., in the law and economics literature). An increase in "efficiency" was identified with an increase in the size of that social wealth pie, whereas the distribution of the pie was a question of "equity" outside of the scientific bailiwick of economics.

At first, the marginalist revolution and the catallactic notion of Pareto optimality displaced the older welfare economics that analyzed the production and distribution of social wealth. Since the notion of a Pareto-superior change (a change where no one becomes worse off and some better off) was considered rather "theoretical" and impractical, there was a counterreformation led by Hicks and Kaldor to rehabilitate in more modern terms the older vision based on the production and distribution of social wealth. The austere criterion of a Pareto-superior change in social state was to be replaced by the Kaldor-Hicks (KH) Principle (Hicks 1939; Kaldor 1939). For any proposed change in social state, the gains of the gainers and the losses of the losers were to be measured in terms of the numeraire and added up. If the total was positive, then the change would represent an increase in social wealth where, in principle, the gainers could compensate the losers with transfers in the numeraire so that there were no post-compensation losers. The change in social state plus the hypothetical redistribution would constitute a Pareto improvement.

> This argument lends justification to the procedure, adopted by Professor Pigou in *The Economics of Welfare*, of dividing "welfare economics" into two parts: the first relating to production, and the second to distribution. (Kaldor 1939, 551)

Having thus parsed the total change into the wealth-increasing part and the redistributive part, the KH Principle would recommend the wealth-increasing part on efficiency grounds since efficiency is the professional concern of economics, while leaving to one side the equity question involved in the redistributive part.

At first, there were some fine-grained technical objections raised against the KH Principle based on some very special cases—where making a change recommended by the principle would change the situation in such a way that the reverse change would then be recommended (Scitovsky 1941; Samuelson 1961; Chipman and Moore 1978). But since these objections (like the majority voting paradox in political science) had little relevance to ordinary applications, they have not affected the practical use of the KH Principle. With the technical objections being largely irrelevant, the remaining objections have been largely on "humanistic" grounds (see Nussbaum 2001; Richardson 2001)—which have also had little effect on practical applications.

THE KH PRINCIPLE AND COST-BENEFIT ANALYSIS

The Pareto Principle holds that a proposed change is an increase in allocative efficiency or a *Pareto-superior* change if it makes some people better off and no one worse off. Since there are no "losers" in a change recommended by the Pareto Principle, it has not been very controversial for that reason. The case usually made against the Pareto Principle is simply that it is impractical. Social choices rarely come in the form of "some winners and no losers" so economics needs some more practical principle in its applications.

The KH Principle is intended to fill this need. Given a proposed change, such as a change in policy, a new law, or an economic project, one could in theory get those who gain (the winners) to specify the monetary value of the gain to them, and one could in theory get those who lose (the losers) to specify the monetary value of their losses. The methods used to estimate these monetized benefits and costs is part of the science and art of CBA.

> CBA utilizes an alternative decision rule with somewhat less conceptual appeal, but much greater feasibility, than the actual Pareto efficiency rule. It is based on what is known as the *Kaldor-Hicks criterion*: a policy should be adopted if and only if those who will gain could fully compensate those who will lose and still be better off. (Boardman et al. 2011, 32)

If those total benefits exceeded those total costs, then one could in theory have the winners compensate the losers with some net benefit left over. Hence, the proposed change plus the compensation payments from the winners to the losers would constitute a Pareto-superior change. Therefore, the proposed change where the monetized benefits exceed the monetized costs—but without the compensation payments—is sometimes called a *potential* Pareto-superior change.

The KH Principle is based on the characterization of the potential Pareto-superior change as an *increase in social wealth* or economic welfare (in terms of the numeraire usually taken as money) while the compensation payments are only a *redistribution of social wealth* between people which does not change the total of social wealth. The increase in social wealth is termed a question of "efficiency" while the redistribution is termed a question of "equity." The KH

Principle then calls upon the social division of labor between the economics profession, which is taken as focused on efficiency, and the other fields which might want to render a judgment about the equity effects of (not) making the compensation payments (e.g., moral philosophy or politics). The KH Principle then specifies that qua economists, the practitioners of CBA can recommend the potential Pareto-superior change while leaving the question of the redistributive effects to ethicists, politicians, and others.

> The purpose of considering hypothetical redistributions is to try and separate the *efficiency* and *equity* aspects of the policy change under consideration. It is argued that whether or not the redistribution is actually carried out is an important but *separate* decision. The mere fact that is it possible to create potential Pareto improving redistribution possibilities is enough to rank one state above another on efficiency grounds. (Boadway and Bruce 1984, 97)

Economic theory has no grounds to assign relative weights to the efficiency and equity considerations. The point is simply that as an applied science, CBA can recommend the potential Pareto-superior change on efficiency grounds while leaving equity considerations to others.

> But to the extent that distributive justice can be shown to be the proper business of some other branch of government or policy instrument . . . it is possible to set distributive considerations to one side and use the Kaldor-Hicks approach with a good conscience. This assumes . . . that efficiency in the Kaldor-Hicks sense—making the pie larger without worrying about how the relative size of the slices changes—is a social value. (Posner 2001, 318–19)

The CBA is actually a rather big deal now. It has been supposedly vetted by many economists and public policy experts (Boadway 1974; Squire and van der Tak 1975; Stokey and Zeckhauser 1978; Pearce 1983; Drèze and Stern 1987; Layard and Glaister 1994; Adler and Posner 2001; Mishan and Quah 2007), and even Cass Sunstein has written a book about it (2018). There is a professional society with the slightly more upbeat name, the Society for Benefit-Cost Analysis, and there are many standardized textbooks on the topic (Irvin 1978; Campbell and Brown 2003; Brent 2006; Zerbe and Bellas 2007; Boardman et al. 2011). The economic analysis of law or "law-and-economics" has swept through the law schools of America like syphilis in Hawaii—creating much resentment but finding no cure—and is now influencing the American judiciary (Posner 1972, 1983, 1990; Bork 1993; see analysis by Glick 2018).

But in spite of all this, the KH Principle is based on a fairly simple logical fallacy that vitiates the disciplines based on it such as the wealth maximization school of law and economics as well as CBA. The KH analysis commits a basic logical error which vitiates the parsing of the whole Pareto-superior change into the "efficiency + equity" parts (i.e., the potential Pareto-superior change plus the compensations payments). The point is not the simple observation that everything depends on everything else in economic affairs so that there is no clean parsing into efficiency and equity parts. It is an error in the whole parsing itself. The error is so basic that in simple cases one can even reverse the description of the same total change so that the so-called equity part becomes the "efficiency" part and the so-called efficiency part becomes the "equity" part. Thus, with a mere redescription of the exact same changes, the KH Principle would make the reverse recommendation. In other words, the KH Principle breaks down in incoherence and arbitrariness since its recommendations change when the exact same situation is merely redescribed with a different unit of account. When the analysis is reformulated so that the error is avoided, then it reduces to the Pareto efficiency analysis that the whole KH program was designed to avoid.

DEFINITIONAL STATEMENTS AND THE SAME YARDSTICK FALLACY

The logical fallacy behind the KH Principle occurs in many other contexts so we will first give some more obvious examples of the fallacy. To understand how the so-called efficiency-equity parsing changes under a redescription, we must outline what might be called *definitional statements* that appear to be nontrivial empirical statements but turn out to be only empirically vacuous or tautologous statements about the definition of the measurement or coordinate system.

Empirical statements often involve the use of some coordinate or measurement system. Nontrivial statements like "the intersection of the supply and demand curves has the coordinates (23, 40)" will use the coordinate system but will tell us something about the world being described (if true). But there are other statements which are superficially similar, like "the X-axis crosses the Y-axis at the coordinates (0,0)," which are just trivial definitional statements about the coordinate system itself and have no empirical content beyond that.

Perhaps the most famous definitional statement would be: "The standard meter bar in Paris is one meter long." Attention was directed to such statements by Wittgenstein with suitable obscurity or, perhaps, profundity:

> There is *one* thing of which one can say neither that it is one metre long, nor that it is not one metre long, and that is the standard metre in Paris—But this is, of course, not to ascribe any extraordinary property to it, but only to mark its

> peculiar role in the language-game of measuring with a metre-rule. (Wittgenstein 1958, Section 50)

The point of a statement like "the standard meter bar in Paris is one meter long" is only to "fix the reference" (Kripke 1980, 55) as to the measurement system being used, and is thus quite unlike the statement: "This stick is one meter long," which uses the metric system to make a nondefinitional empirical statement. "As Wittgenstein says, the standard is a means of representation in the language game of measuring with the metric system, not something that is represented in the system" (Pollock 2004, 155).

Saul Kripke notes that another statement of the same type is: "Water boils at 100°C at sea level" (1980, 56). The statement is true by the definition of the Centigrade measurement scale and has no empirical content unlike "The temperature outside is 30°C."

Fallacious arguments can be easily constructed which use definitional statements as if they had empirical content. Here are some examples.

A "Proof" That Yardsticks Cannot Change

Perhaps a yardstick has expanded or contracted and is thus not accurate. In order to determine if it still measures a true yard, we mark off its distance on, say, a table. Then we measure the distance using the (same) yardstick as the standard and conclude that the yardstick is truly a yard long. But the conclusion that the distance on the table was a yard long (aside from negligible measurement error) was a definitional statement since we were using the yardstick as the true measure of a yard. The statement gives no new information since the distance was measured by the same yardstick used to mark off the distance. Hence, the argument that the yardstick had not changed was fallacious. This sort of argument might be called the *same yardstick fallacy*.

A "Proof" That Inflation Is Impossible

In the year, say, 1900, a dollar would buy a dollar's worth of goods. Would a dollar buy more or less in the year 2000? We find that a dollar still buys a dollar's worth of goods, so we conclude that a dollar has the same value at these two times. The same argument works for any two times so we must conclude that inflation is impossible. But the statements that a dollar buys a dollar's worth of goods is a definitional statement with no empirical content. A dollar was used as the measure of what a dollar would buy instead of, say, some standard set of commodities. Hence, the argument that "a dollar has the same buying-power at any two times" is fallacious.

A "Proof" That the Earth Does Not Move

Let *S(t)* be the coordinates of the Sun and *E(t)* the coordinates of the Earth at time *t* where we are using the geocentric coordinate system. We observe that the coordinates of the Sun change over time, while the coordinates of the Earth always stay the same (at the origin of the geocentric coordinate system). Hence, we conclude that the position of the Earth does not change so the church is vindicated, and Galileo refuted. But the statement that the Earth does not move in geocentric coordinates is a definitional statement about the origin in geocentric coordinates and thus has no empirical content. Hence, this empirical conclusion that "the Earth does not move" does not follow.

A "Proof" That an Apple Has the Same Value to All Consumers

If Mary had an apple, then it would be worth one apple to Mary—using apples as the *numeraire* (i.e., the units in which value and prices are stated). If John had the apple, then it would also be worth one apple to John. An apple's an apple for all that. Since the same argument could be repeated for any potential consumer, we must conclude that an apple has the same value to any consumer so any exchange involving an apple would be pointless. But the statement that an apple is worth one apple to any consumer using apples as the numeraire is only a definitional statement with no empirical content. One needs a different yardstick of value, that is, a different numeraire, to meaningfully determine if the apple had different values for Mary and John.

A "Proof" That Compensation Payments Do Not Change Social Wealth

While the above argument using the apple may seem obvious, our point is that exactly the same sort of definitional statement is involved in the "proof" that the hypothetical compensation payments in the numeraire (which would turn a potential Pareto-superior change into an actual one) do not change social wealth measured in the same numeraire (and thus are a question of equity rather than efficiency). *Any unit of the numeraire will have the same value to anyone in terms of the same numeraire—by definition.* Any argument based on the statement "transfers in the numeraire (compensation payments) do not change social wealth when measured in terms of the same numeraire" is only a definitional statement and only gives an illusion of being a substantive statement—an illusion might be called *numeraire illusion* (Ellerman 2009).

The KH methodology was based on numeraire illusion—using the definitional statement that the potential compensation payments in the numeraire were only redistributive (i.e., did not change social wealth measured in terms of the same numeraire) to set aside that part of the total Pareto-superior change and to recommend the other part on efficiency grounds.

When a noninvolved numeraire is used, then one cannot definitionally set aside any part of the Pareto improvement as being merely redistributive so all that can be recommended on efficiency grounds is the total Pareto improvement. Then we are back to the Pareto criterion, and the attempt to establish a different notion of "KH efficiency" is seen to be based on a logical error. Hence, the parts of applied welfare economics based on the KH Principle—such as CBA—are rendered baseless.

A SIMPLE EXAMPLE IN THE LAW AND ECONOMICS LITERATURE

CBA is often applied to proposed changes or projects that are quite complex. It offers the hope of the "scientific" reduction of the problem down to a simple quantified criterion: Is the net monetized benefit positive or not? But the same analysis, and the KH Principle behind it, could also be applied to very simple situations, for example, for pedagogical purposes. Then the above criticism shows how the conclusions can be drastically changed, if not reversed, simply by redescribing the exact same situation using a different unit of account or numeraire. The same logic or illogic applies to the more complex cases but is more disguised by the complexity of the situation.

The John and Mary example outlined above comes from David Friedman's law and economics text: *Law's Order: What Economics Has to Do with Law and Why It Matters* (2000). Mary has an apple which she values at fifty cents while John values an apple at one dollar. There might be a voluntary exchange where Mary sold the apple to John for, say, seventy-five cents. There are two parts to that whole Pareto-superior change: the transfer of the apple from Mary to John (the "proposed project or change") and the transfer of seventy-five cents from John to Mary (the "compensation payments"), as shown in figure 9.1.

Let us apply social wealth maximization reasoning to the transfer of the apple using money as the numeraire. Since the apple was worth fifty cents to Mary and a dollar to John, social wealth would be increased by fifty cents by the apple transfer from Mary to John. That is an increase in efficiency. The other part, the transfer of seventy-five cents from John to Mary, is a question of distribution or equity. Social wealth (measured in dollars and cents) would

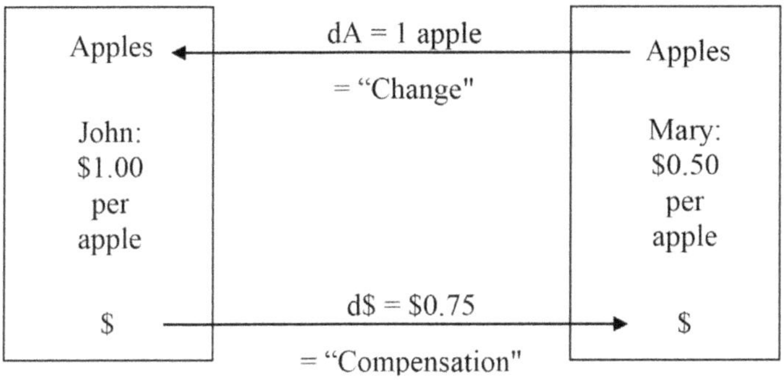

"Change" dA gives \$0.50 = \$1 – \$0.50 = Δ\$ increase in social dollar pie.

"Compensation" d\$ gives \$0 = \$0.75 – \$0.75 change in the dollar pie.

Figure 9.1 The Transfers Described with \$ = Numeraire.

be unchanged by the mere transfer of seventy-five cents from one person to another.

> It would still be an improvement, and by the same amount, if John stole the apple—price zero—or if Mary lost it and John found it. Mary is fifty cents worse off; John is a dollar better off, net gain fifty cents. All of these represent the same efficient allocation of the apple: to John, who values it more than Mary. They differ in the associated distribution of income: how much money John and Mary each end up with.
>
> Since we are measuring value in dollars it is easy to confuse "gaining value" with "getting money." But consider our example. The total amount of money never changes; we are simply shifting it from one person to another. The total quantity of goods never changes either, since we are cutting off our analysis after John gets the apple but before he eats it. Yet total value increases by fifty cents. It increases because the same apple is worth more to John than to Mary. Shifting money around does not change total value. One dollar is worth the same number of dollars to everyone: one. (Friedman 2000, 20)

Note that Friedman's last statement, "One dollar is worth the same number of dollars to everyone: one," is a perfect example of a vacuous definitional statement.

Now describe exactly the same situation but from an inverted perspective with a numeraire reversal from dollars to apples. Changing the numeraire does *not* mean the trivial conversion of the net benefits in one numeraire to another one at some fixed public price ratio; it means summing again the benefits and costs using each person's (marginal) evaluations.

Mary was at a point of trading one-half a dollar for an apple so her price of a dollar in terms of apples was two apples per dollar. John was at a point of

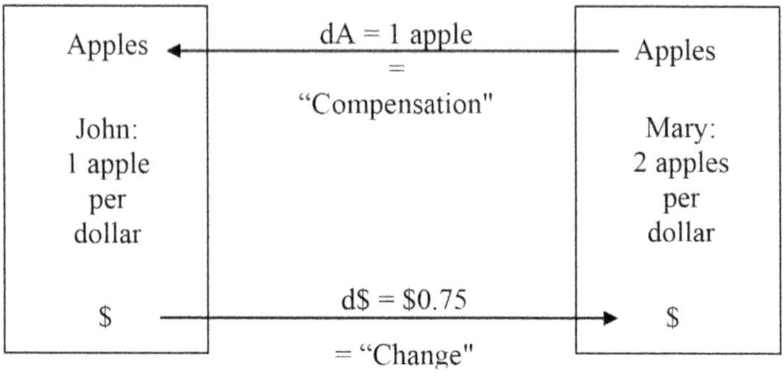

"Change" d$ gives 0.75 = 1.5 – 0.75 = Δapples increase in social apple pie.

"Compensation" dA gives 0 = 1 – 1 = no change in apple pie.

Figure 9.2 Same Transfers with Apples as Numeraire.

trading apples and dollars one for one so his price of a dollar in terms of apples was one apple per dollar. Now apply the reasoning of social wealth maximization (measured in apples) to the proposed change of transferring seventy-five cents from John to Mary. The seventy-five cents are only worth three-fourths of an apple to John while the seventy-five cents are worth one and one-half apples (2 x 0.75 = 1.50) to Mary. Hence, the social pie (which is now an apple pie) is increased by three-fourths of an apple by the transfer of seventy-five cents from John to Mary. Hence, *that* money transfer is now the *efficient* change (the increase in social wealth). Whether or not an apple is actually transferred from Mary to John is now the question of equity or redistribution, which leaves the social (apple) pie unchanged. Paraphrasing Friedman's definitional statement of numeraire illusion; one apple is worth the same number of apples to everyone: one. An apple's an apple for all that (figure 9.2).

There has been no change in Mary's or John's preferences or evaluations; exactly the same underlying situation is described first using dollars as numeraire and then using apples as numeraire. Yet the results of the social wealth maximization reasoning (and the underlying KH logic) changed completely between the two descriptions. The "efficiency" part and the "equity" part of the total change reversed themselves under the numeraire reversal (table 9.1).

Table 9.1 Reversal of Efficiency and Equity Parts under Numeraire Reversal

	Normal Description (Money = Numeraire)	*Inverse Description (Apples = Numeraire)*
Increase in size of "social pie"	Transfer of apple from Mary to John	Transfer of seventy-five cents from John to Mary
Redistribution of "social pie"	Transfer of seventy-five cents from John to Mary	Transfer of apple from Mary to John

Source: Author.

ANALYSIS OF THE METHODOLOGICAL ERROR

Of course, the KH Principle is usually applied in CBA to much more complex changes than a simple exchange. But the logic is exactly the same. For instance, Friedman's definitional statement "One dollar is worth the same number of dollars to everyone: one" in the context of a simple transaction is mirrored in the much more complex case of the economic evaluation of projects in CBA where one finds the same definitional statement that "pure transfers of funds among households, firms and governments should themselves have no effect on project benefits and costs" (Boadway 2000, 35). Or again: "It should be emphasized that pure transfers of purchasing power from one household or firm to another per se should be typically attributed no value" (Boadway 2000, 30).

The arguments that a "dollar is worth the same number of dollars to everyone: one" and that numeraire transfers "have no effect on project benefits and costs" are measured in terms of the same numeraire—pinpoint the problem of "numeraire illusion"—taking a definitional statement as being a statement about the economic realities.[2] Transfers in whatever is taken as the numeraire will always leave the size of the pie unchanged (since the pie is measured in the same unit of account) and thus to be merely distributive. Changes in a yardstick will never be revealed by *that* yardstick; one needs to use a different yardstick.[3]

Although applications of CBA are more complex, they do not change the underlying logic or illogic of the methodological error. Change the numeraire to another involved good, and the recommendations of the KH Principle will change—although not as dramatically as the reversal seen in the case of a simple exchange.

Change the numeraire to an *uninvolved* good to avoid the definitional statements, and the whole project cum compensations will then become the "efficiency part" and will be recommended (assuming the total change in "social wealth" is positive) and there will be no definitional statement or "equity part" since the numeraire is then not involved in the proposed changes or compensation. But then we are back to the Pareto-superior criterion which recommended the changes *together with* the compensation.[4]

For instance, if the mutually beneficial exchange had been Mary's apple in exchange for John's three-fourths of a pound of nuts (instead of three-fourths of a dollar), then in terms of some third commodity such as dollars we could say symmetrically that John values the apple more than Mary and that Mary values the three-fourths of a pound of nuts more than John. Each of the transfers (apples and nuts) increases social wealth, and there is no definitional statement since the numeraire (money in this case) is not involved in the swap. But by computing in the metric of one of the goods involved in the potential exchange, we are misled into the definitional statement that one part of the exchange is a mere redistribution—an illusion that is exposed by changing the numeraire.

When the KH criterion differs from the Pareto criterion due to the use of an involved numeraire and the resulting definitional statements (mistaken as empirically significant numeraire-invariant statements), then the KH argument breaks down in giving different and perhaps even reversed recommendations under a mere redescription using a different numeraire. When the error is avoided by using a noninvolved numeraire, then the KH Principle just reduces to the Pareto criterion. Since the point of CBA was to be able to recommend the proposed changes on efficiency grounds without the compensation payments that would make the total change Pareto-superior, we see that the cost-benefit methodology is fatally flawed.

CONCLUSIONS

Aside from pointing out practical difficulties, perhaps the most common criticism of CBA is that it sets questions of redistribution or equity to one side (and thus implicitly assigns them little or no weight). But that the so-called criticism already accepts as significant the definitional statement that the potential transfers in the numeraire (compensation payments) are merely redistributive and do not affect "social wealth." The analysis given here shows that the whole parsing into an "efficiency" part and an "equity" is only an artifact of the choice of numeraire or unit of account used in the description of the total changes. Hence, the problem in CBA lies deeper than a supposedly excessive concern for "efficiency" and disregard for "equity." It is not a question of a "hard-hearted" efficiency orientation versus a "soft-hearted" equity orientation. The KH Principle fails on technical and logical grounds. Change the numeraire and the efficiency-equity parsing itself changes so that whole framework of analysis breaks down in incoherence.

The CBA is the best practical offering of neoclassical (as opposed to catallactic) economic theory to fulfill the old dream of reducing public policy questions to a technocratic exercise aloof from the often-messy process of democratic decision-making. Moreover, it is the basis for the rather standard "Chicago" approach to the economic analysis of law (Posner 1972) based on social wealth maximization. The exposure of CBA as being based on a fatal logical-methodological error calls that whole technocratic and economistic dream into doubt. The collapse of the KH Principle gives a return to the notion of a Pareto-superior change or to Wicksellian unanimity of consent in the language of James Buchanan's Public Choice School (Ellerman 2014). But such unanimity of consent implicitly assumes that a person's consent is only required for a certain "sphere of consent," essentially the individual's person and property. That in turn raises the question of the legitimacy of an individual's claim to property rights (e.g., a thief's consent would not be required before returning stolen property to the rightful owner). Hence, the collapse of CBA opens up the intellectual space for quite different rights-based approaches to public policy and legal questions, for example Dworkin (1978; 1980), Buchanan (1954; 1999), Ellerman (1992)—approaches that treat persons as ends-in-themselves rather than as factors in some overarching notion of "social welfare" or "social wealth" that "ought" to be maximized.

NOTES

1. Buchanan's reference is to Robbins (1932).
2. Many economists seem to believe—at least until challenged—that there is some objective (e.g., description and numeraire invariant) sense in which transfers of money are a "wash" that does not affect "social wealth" unlike transfers in apples or other goods.
3. The idea of a "different yardstick" is present in the idea of a *relative* price, the price of x in terms of y. The only price that has no information content is the "self-price" of the numeraire, one. That numeraire's price of one is only a definitional statement unlike the statement that John's valuation of an apple is one (dollar per apple).
4. That KH efficiency reduces to Pareto efficiency when the numeraire good is not involved in any of the transfers made in the potential Pareto-superior change is demonstrated mathematically in the Appendix of Ellerman (2009).

Chapter 10

A Summing Up

DIVERSITY

The common theme is best seen as a "cluster concept"—although "diversity" and "polycentricity" are fairly good labels for the collection of ideas and arguments that will be summarized by chapters.

According to the intellectual historian Arthur O. Lovejoy, one of the biggest shifts in Western thought in the nineteenth and twentieth centuries was away from the older static and uniform conceptions of the world to visions of change and diversity.

> There have, in the entire history of thought, been few changes in standards of value more profound and more momentous than that which took place when the contrary principle began widely to prevail—when it came to be believed not only that in many, or in all, phases of human life there are diverse excellences, but that diversity itself is of the essence of excellence. . . .
>
> [W]hat it is essential to remember is that the transformation has taken place and that it, perhaps, more than any other one thing has distinguished, both for better and worse, the prevailing assumptions of the mind of the nineteenth and of our own century from those of the preceding period in the intellectual history of the West. That change, in short, has consisted in the substitution of what may be called diversitarianism for uniformitarianism as the ruling preconception in most of the normative provinces of thought. (Lovejoy 1960, 293–94)

In Jane Jacobs's mature work on economies, diversity was such a central theme that she was indeed the "diva of diversity."

Biological metaphors are often a scourge in economics (e.g., social Darwinism), but Jacobs carefully drew upon biological ideas with some success. For instance, she saw Adam Smith's deepening of the division of labor as being akin to small mutations in DNA, while significant technological change was akin to recombinations of DNA as in sexual reproduction in a diverse population. Cities are the sites of change through repurposed and recombined technologies since people with very different knowledge jostle together in cities.

There are also two ways that biomass is increased: (1) existing organisms getting larger and (2) organisms having offspring. Since there are physical limits on the size and life span of organisms, the real principle of plenitude in biology is the reproduction of offspring. Hence, Jacobs was a "born-critic" of huge corporations which try to escape any bounds on size and longevity. She saw spin-offs and breakaways (where people leave to start a new firm) as the natural source of innovation. The opposite process of corporate empire-building through the acquisition of successful small businesses (or negative spin-offs) was a diversity-killing source of lethargy that deadened the springs of creativity and innovation.

Quite aside from Jane Jacobs, the author was involved in another recent development concerning the idea of diversity. Our era is seen as the "Information Age," father of which is rightly seen as Claude Shannon, who developed the mathematical theory of communication that is popularly known as "information theory" (a label that Shannon did not use). Shannon's theory was about the efficient coding of messages and communication through a channel, but it never said what "information" is other than the implication that it is measured by Shannon's formula for information content or entropy.

Recent developments in mathematical logic (Ellerman 2010) led to a new quantitative theory of information at the logical level that specifies the nature of information as diversity, distinctions, differentiations, and distinguishability (Ellerman 2017). All the Shannon definitions for simple, compound, relative, and mutual information content can be derived by a uniform requantifying transformation from the natural logical definitions. The basic logical formula for measuring information is quite old (Gini 1912); it is only the logical backstory that is new. In the field of biostatistics, the formula for logical information content or logical entropy is known as the Gini-Simpson index of biodiversity (Rao 1982). The interpretation of the biodiversity formula is that, in two independent random draws from a population of many species, it is the probability of getting *different* species. Thus, we may say with some confidence that the notion of diversity is quite fundamental to our Information Age.

EXIT VERSUS VOICE AND COMMITMENT

Many of the chapters in this book explore a duality. Albert Hirschman's famous duality was between the logic of exit (the market logic developed in economics) and the logic of voice and commitment developed in certain organizations. Among economic enterprises, the logic of commitment is perhaps best exemplified by the Japanese-style firm. Standard economic theory has made little headway in its agency theory toward understanding a commitment-based firm. "Most of the authors would agree that if you want to understand what goes on in Japanese boardrooms, you can throw most of the writings that go under the rubric 'agency theory' out of the window" (Dore and Whittaker 1994, 3).

Economics Nobel laureate, Herbert Simon, has even pointed out that economies of developed countries are best viewed as organizational economies (with thick organizations connected by thin markets) rather than as "market economies."

> The economies of modern industrialized society can more appropriately be labeled organizational economies than market economies. Thus, even market-driven capitalist economies need a theory of organizations as much as they need a theory of markets. The attempts of the new institutional economics to explain organizational behavior solely in terms of agency, asymmetric information, transaction costs, opportunism, and other concepts drawn from neo-classical economics ignore key organizational mechanisms like authority, identification, and coordination, and hence are seriously incomplete. (Simon 1991, 42)

Neoclassical economic theory is basically a theory of markets built around the logic of exit, not the logic of voice and commitment. In our current state of economic civilization, the reigning theory of economic firms is in the grip of some rather silly myths shamelessly promoted by economic and legal thinkers alike. For instance, in the large publicly traded corporations, the so-called members of the company, who officially have "voice," are the far-flung absentee shareholders who have little clue as to what is going on in the firm and who know that their only real recourse to dissatisfaction is to sell their shares (the "Wall Street Rule"). And the people who actually work in the firm and have some idea what is going on have no voice since they are seen as "outsiders" who have only monetary motivation, sell services as employees to the firm, and are always free to exit. Since that rather absurd legal structure wouldn't work very well, actual firms tend to operate differently.

> Organizations would be far less effective systems than they actually are if such (economic) rewards were the only means, or even the principal means, of motivation available. In fact, observation of behavior in organizations reveals other powerful motivations that induce employees to accept organizational goals and authority as bases for their actions. . . . (The) most important of these mechanisms (is): organizational identification. (Simon 1991, 34)

It is very rare but not impossible for a public thinker to break out of the current mythology and to point out its imaginary nature. For instance, in the rethinking that took place after the World War II in the United Kingdom, the conservative thinker Lord Eustace Percy laid down the challenge the system presents:

> Here is the most urgent challenge to political invention ever offered to the jurist and the statesman. The human association which in fact produces and distributes wealth, the association of workmen, managers, technicians and directors, is not an association recognised by the law. The association which the law does recognise—the association of shareholders, creditors and directors—is incapable of production and is not expected by the law to perform these functions. We have to give law to the real association, and to withdraw meaningless privilege from the imaginary one. (Percy 1944, 38)

At some time in the future, scholars will look back in wonderment at how the overwhelming bulk of economic, political, and legal thinkers of our time could shamelessly support the "imaginary" association and ignore the "real association."

PARALLEL EXPERIMENTATION

Duality is a great engine of human thought: series versus parallel, exit versus voice (and commitment), exploitation versus exploration, allocative efficiency versus X- or effort-efficiency, selection versus variation, social engineering versus piecemeal social change, shock therapy versus incrementalism, and so forth. Many of our tables have two columns for a duality plus a third column of labels.

One duality—series-parallel duality—runs throughout mathematics, engineering, and human affairs. Many problems can be conceptualized as searching over a tree (starting at the root). At each point, we have two options: to continue searching to greater depth along a branch of the tree, or to broaden the search to include one or more other branches of the tree.

Suppose one is facing a search tree in trying to find a solution to a problem. If one is quite sure that the solution lies along the branch that one is on, then a strategy of series experimentation is appropriate. Test the current proposed solution and then move along that branch, as it were, by improving that proposal. But if there is genuine uncertainty as to which branch may contain "the" solution or even "a" solution, then a strategy of parallel experimentation would be more appropriate. Try several options, prototype quickly to test the options, and communicate between the experiments since improvements in one option might also benefit other options. Eventually, a clear winner might emerge so that resources could then be concentrated on that option.

One might imagine a "series advocate" and a "parallel advocate" giving arguments for and against each strategy. For the series proponent, a multiplicity of experiments is wasteful duplication. Isn't it rational to put one's resources on the best option? Why not do everything in the One Best Way? Large prideful organizations tend to favor this reasoning. The organization's experts will decide on the best experiment or approach—otherwise the organization would appear "not to know what it's doing." It is safer to put one's resources on the knowledgeable choice rather than waste anything on what the authorities do not support. Scattering our resources among less-promising options will detract from the best chance of getting the breakthrough by putting all our resources on the most promising option. Applied to the social world, this is the viewpoint of the social engineer. As Jeffrey Sachs put it, why undertake "open experimentation" which could lead to "costly and dangerous wrong turns" (Sachs 1993, 5) when the experts in what has never happened before (the post-socialist transition) already knew the One Best Path?

Parallel experimentation is based on the opposite knowledge, the pragmatic or Socratic knowledge that one does not know—acknowledged ignorance. There is an old distinction between risk, where rough probabilities are known, and genuine uncertainty, where the probabilities are unknown and where one has only conflicting hunches. Parallel experimentation is based on genuine uncertainty.

CONTESTATION

Many of the themes in the book have a knowledge aspect. The best historical argument for contestation in the search for knowledge was John Stuart Mill's 1859 classic, *On Liberty* (1977). Today, the most blatant offenders against the principle of contestation are the large arrogant organizations such as the World Bank and the IMF in the field of economic policy. The best-known organizations that are officially dedicated to the pursuit of knowledge are the universities (as opposed to churches who already know the Truth). Somehow it is obvious to people in the universities that one does not label a theory by the name of the university. There is no "Harvard theory of general relativity" or "MIT theory of quantum mechanics." Otherwise, when other professors criticized the theories, then it would be seen as an attack on the universities as institutions. If other professors in the same university disagreed about the university's "Official Theory," then it would appear to the world that the university "doesn't know what it is talking about" and "can't even agree among themselves."

These are not subtle points, particularly about institutions that seek to improve knowledge and to advise others. Yet, these points consistently escape the leaders (and bureaucrats) in advisory institutions like the World Bank and the IMF, which cannot resist labeling certain theories or views as "the World Bank view" or "the IMF view." And as soon as a view is labeled as the official view of the organization, then the usual dynamics of suppressing dissent and contestation within the organization sets in. "How can we expect clients to agree with our advice if we can't even agree among ourselves?" Even the Public Relations departments of these institutions require consent before employees may publish outside any views that might embarrass the institution and make it appear "not to know what it is talking about." Offenders can even be charged with Ethical Violations (as in the infamous case of Bill Easterly who was hounded out of the World Bank), a category usually reserved for people caught embezzling money, getting kickbacks, or the like.

THE INDIRECT METHOD

The cliché-title of my 2005 book, *Helping People Help Themselves*, actually contains a conundrum. In any helper–doer relation, the heavier the footprint of the "helpers," the less the doers are helping themselves, and the more people actually help themselves, the less is the direct involvement of the helpers. This is the helping conundrum. Most helping organizations loathe to see the conundrum since successful helpers do themselves out of the job. The way out of the helping conundrum is to reconceive a successful helping relation as one that is essentially indirect. John Dewey emphasized this in his educational theory but saw the insight as being quite general.

> The best kind of help to others, whenever possible, is indirect, and consists in such modifications of the conditions of life, of the general level of subsistence, as enables them independently to help themselves. (Dewey and Tufts 1908, 390)

The indirect approach cuts across any field of human interaction as was emphasized even by a military historian.

> With deepening reflection, however, I began to realize that the indirect approach had a much wider application—that it was a law of life in all spheres: a truth of philosophy. Its fulfilment was seen to be the key to practical achievement in dealing with any problem where the human factor predominates, and a conflict of wills tends to spring from an underlying concern for interests. In all such cases, the direct assault of new ideas provokes a stubborn resistance, thus intensifying the difficulty of producing a change of outlook. . . . This idea of the

> indirect approach is closely related to all problems of the influence of mind upon mind—the most influential factor in human history. (Hart 1941, x)

In the chapter on the indirect method as well as in my 2005 book, I focus on the thinkers who understood some version of the helping conundrum and then promoted an indirect approach.

KNOWLEDGE AND DEVELOPMENT ASSISTANCE

The World Bank started out as a money bank but after the "knowledge management" revolution (or fad) of the 1980s and 1990s, the Bank aimed to also be a "Knowledge Bank." The Bank would "scan globally" to find the "best practices" and then would transmit that knowledge to the lagging regions and countries of the developing world. The first mistake in this approach was its directness, its aim to "transmit" knowledge to the developing countries backed by conditionalities in the money loans to the countries. The package of monetary aid and best-practice knowledge was typically

> adopted by aid-hungry governments in spite of continuing doubts of the policy makers themselves, resistance from some quarters within the government, onslaught against the "deal" from the opposition, and general distaste for the whole procedure. Naturally, doubts and reservations are not voiced at the moment of the aid compact; hence the delusion on the part of the donor that there has been a full meeting of minds. But soon after virtue has been "bought" through aid under these conditions, the reservations and resistances will find some expression-for example, through half-hearted implementation or sabotage of the agreed-to policies-and relations between donor and recipient will promptly deteriorate as a result. (Hirschman 1971, 205)

In addition to these problems in the directness of the approach, there were numerous problems in the idea of best practices that could be transplanted so easily. Even biological crops cannot always be transplanted easily, not to mention institutions and social practices. Often a large part of knowledge is unarticulated know-how (Ryle 1945) and personal knowledge (Polanyi 1962) that cannot be transmitted by the slides of World Bank trainers or embodied in the conditionalities of loan agreements. At best, the transmission of best practices had to be horizontal cross-learning between practitioners where the funding agency would play only the indirect role of facilitating the contact between practitioners. But that is something that funding agencies tend not to do: "What if they learned the 'wrong' lesson?" Even then the transmission of the best practice will involve a lot of reinvention. "Every alleged example of local implementation of central policy, if it results in significant social transformation, is in fact a process of local social discovery" (Schön 1971, 161). For these reasons, due to the many other reasons considered in the chapter on knowledge and development assistance, and the reasons connected to the disastrous advice given in the post-socialist transition (covered in later chapters), the World Bank was not able to reinvent itself as the Knowledge Bank.

RETHINKING GLOBALIZATION

In the World Bank, one of the constant mantras was for client countries to improve their "investment climate" so that foreign companies (generally from the developed world) would invest there. This chapter is based on a memo written while at the Bank that attempted to "complicate" the issue of investment climate—in addition to noting the imperialistic aspects of the mantra. There are quite different "investment climates" for workers, managers, current owners, and domestic investors in addition to foreign investors. Moreover, improving the investment climate for certain parties will worsen it for others.

One of the important dualities to understand is the contrast between social change coming from wiping the slate clean of the old and replacement by the new versus transformation of the old into the new. The mantra in favor of foreign investors seems to be based on the idea that the old cannot be transformed into the new (or, in other words, the advisory agency has little idea how to do that) so "salvation" must come from wiping the slate clean and importing replacement from abroad. This wiping-the-slate-clean mentality was particularly prominent in the advice given by the Western advisory agencies to the post-socialist countries. And that mentality comported with the shock therapy strategy that had such a detrimental effect on the populations it was supposed to help.

REVISITING THE PRIVATIZATION DEBATES

When socialism essentially collapsed in the late 1980s and early 1990s, then the massive problem arose of the post-socialist transition. The embedded reformers in the post-socialist countries as well as the area scholars from the West who studied those countries both had some knowledge of the difficulties of that transition and recommended incremental and experimental change. But the more academic economists of the West had no such impediment of knowing much about those countries, so they recommended cockamamie schemes of shock therapy and big bangery to jump over the transitional chasm in one "Great Leap Forward."

One of the more interesting historical facts to come out of the debacle of big bangery was how little the economics profession understood the institutional prerequisites of a decentralized market economy. Economists liken the transition to a country changing from driving on the left to driving on the right side of the road. On a given day, a whole new set of laws enacted by the legislature and by executive decree come into force, and then everyone wakes up the next morning and follows the new institutional framework (after seventy years of communism!). Entrepreneurs and decentralized markets would naturally spring up like weekend flea markets, and the transition would be complete. The academic economists were surprised and shocked when powerful people "didn't play by the new rules" and sacked what wealth the countries had for their own. The voucher privatization programs put all the assets on the cargo cult stock markets like marbles rolling around on a tabletop. Whoever had the heaviest thumb on the edge of the table could get the marbles rolling to them. The problem of the foxes having the run of the chicken coop was not the ridiculous design of the chicken coop by the Western experts; the problem was the rapacious nature of the foxes. They don't play by the textbook rules!

There had never before in history been a post-socialist transition, so the late 1980s and 1990s was a very interesting time for social scientists. What would Western economics, political science, and legal theory offer in the way of sound advice for the post-socialist countries? Now we can look back on those debates from the perspective of a quarter century.

One dividing line in the debates was, as noted, between the area specialists who knew something about the institutions in the socialist countries and who generally supported incremental change—as opposed to the more prominent theoretical and academic economists who relished the opportunity to wipe the slate clean of the socialist past in one "big bang" and to "install" the textbook institutions for a private property market economy. How often does such an opportunity present itself to ivory-tower academics?

Another dividing line was the older one between the generally progressive economists of neoclassical and Keynesian economics versus the more right-wing economists of the Austrian school (Hayek being the principal representative) who had previously opposed Bolshevik or Jacobin methods of institutional change in favor of incremental and piecemeal change. Whether it is surprising or unsurprising, the fact is that when it came to the social change from socialism to capitalism, the Austrian school either fell silent or supported the Jacobin methods of the market Bolsheviks. Ralf Dahrendorf, by no means a conservative or Austrian, published a 1990 book, *Reflections on the Revolution in Europe: In a Letter Intended to Have Been Sent to a Gentleman in Warsaw*, which deliberately echoed Edmund Burke's famous tract against the methods of the French Revolution that would be historically associated with the Jacobins. Dahrendorf recommended trial-and-error experimentation and pragmatism. The progressive big bangers from the West countered that if "the philosophy were one of open experimentation, I doubt that the transformation would be possible at all, at least without costly and dangerous wrong turns" (Sachs 1993, 5). And the Austrians were silent, if not supportive, of the shock therapists.

There were other dividing lines. In addition to the neoliberal thrust of the international development organizations (IMF and World Bank) and bilateral aid agencies, there was the strong and specific vision of the emigres from East Europe who left after communism was established in the 1940s and 1950s, and who then returned in the 1990s after having economically successful careers in the West. They expected to be received as returning heroes (they were against communism all along) and to be put into positions of power (they know how the Western system works). Moreover, they viewed all the accomplishments of the people under socialism as illegitimate—like goals scored during a timeout in a football match. Hence, their old family property, no matter how it had been developed in the intervening years, should be fully returned to them. The property rights (actual or de facto) that people had acquired under state socialism were illegitimate so they should be renationalized and redistributed in a proper way. Any other policy would just "reward" those who benefited under state socialism. The proper way to redistribute property rights was determined by neoliberal economic theory; put the rights "on the Market" so they will automatically find their "highest valued uses."

With many local variations, this vision was the controlling narrative for the post-socialist transition in Central and Southeast Europe (not to mention the countries further to the East). There always were alternative policies for the post-socialist transition. For instance, one alternative de-Soto-like strategy was to legally recognize the de facto property rights that ordinary people had acquired under state socialism to their places of living and their places of work. In that manner, ordinary people would meet the market economy and private property system as something that empowered them with legally defensible property rights—rather than as something that took away even their de facto rights.

THE LOGICAL FALLACY IN COST-BENEFIT ANALYSIS

One of the main legitimating tools of technocratic and nondemocratic decision-making is cost-benefit analysis which is technically based on the Kaldor-Hicks Principle in economics. Previously, cost-benefit analysis has been criticized on minor technical grounds that do not affect its normal applications or on broad humanistic grounds arguing for the importance of "equity" and distribution in addition to the economistic focus on "efficiency." But I show in the previous chapter (and in several previous publications) that there is a logical fallacy involved in the Kaldor-Hicks Principle and thus in cost-benefit analysis based on that principle.

A key part of the KH Principle is the statement that the compensation payments in a potential Pareto-superior change do not affect social wealth and are only a matter of distributional equity. That statement is simply that transfers in the numeraire do not affect to total amount of the numeraire (i.e., "social wealth" measured in terms of the numeraire). But that is a statement that is true by definition since the compensation payments are assumed to be in the numeraire. The statement is as vacuous as other definitional statements that only unpack the measurement or coordinate system being used such as: "The standard meter bar in Paris is one meter long," "The Earth does not move when its trajectory in space is plotted in geocentric coordinates," "Water boils at 100°C at sea level," "The X-axis crosses the Y-axis at the coordinates (0,0)," "A dollar buys a dollar's worth of goods," "Taking this yardstick as the standard, it is exactly one yard long," and so forth. Fallacious arguments based on these vacuous statements commit the "same yardstick fallacy"—as in "The Earth does not move!" (when motion is measured in geocentric coordinates), "There is no inflation" (since a dollar always buys a dollar's worth of goods), or "Compensation payments do not change social wealth" (since the payments are in the numeraire used to measure social wealth).

There is a simple example used to illustrate the KH Principle in a law and economics text (Friedman 2000) where the Pareto-superior change is the exchange of an apple for $0.75. When money is taken as the numeraire, then the transfer of the apple increases "social wealth" measured in terms of money and the transfer of the $0.75 does not affect social wealth. Hence, "efficiency" supports the apple transfer and leaves the money transfer as a distributional question of "equity." But one only needs to redescribe *exactly the same* Pareto-superior change with apples as the numeraire to reverse the "efficiency" and "equity" parts. Then it is the transfer of the $0.75 that increases the size of the "apple pie" while the transfer of the apple leaves the total "social wealth" measured in apples as the same. An apple's an apple for all that. Hence, the money transfer is then supported on "efficiency" grounds while the apple transfer is set aside as a distributional question of "equity." But it is the exact same situation simply redescribed by reversing the numeraire. Hence, "efficiency" recommendations of the KH Principle and cost-benefit analysis break down in incoherence.

When that same yardstick fallacy is avoided by choosing a numeraire good not involved in the potential Pareto-superior change, then both transfers increase "social wealth" so the analysis just collapses back to the Pareto Principle of catallactic economics or the Wicksellian unanimity of consent emphasized in James Buchanan's Public Choice School (Ellerman 2014). And since one's consent is only relevant in one's "sphere of consent," essentially one's person and property, the focus of analysis then shifts to one's human and property rights (Ellerman 1992).

Since cost-benefit analysis is one of the main methods of centralized, technocratic, and nondemocratic decision-making today, it seems appropriate to have a final chapter that shows that the Kaldor-Hicks Principle—upon which CBA rests—is based on a logical fallacy.

Bibliography

Abrams, M. H. 1953. *The Mirror and The Lamp: Romantic Theory and the Critical Tradition*. London: Oxford University Press.

Adler, Matthew D., and Eric A. Posner. 2001. *Cost-Benefit Analysis: Legal, Economic, and Philosophical Perspectives*. Chicago: University of Chicago Press.

Akerlof, George. 1984. *An Economic Theorist's Book of Tales*. New York: Cambridge University Press.

Akerlof, George, and Janet Yellen. 1986. *Efficiency Wage Models of the Labor Market*. Cambridge: Cambridge University Press.

Albert, Michel. 1993. *Capitalism Vs. Capitalism*. Translated by Paul Haviland. New York: Four Walls Eight Windows.

Allen, Max, Ed. 1997. *Ideas that Matter: The Worlds of Jane Jacobs*. Ontario: Ginger Press.

Anderson, Philip. 1999. "Seven Levers for Guiding the Evolving Enterprise." In *The Biology of Business*, edited by John Henry Clippinger, 113–52. San Francisco: Jossey-Bass.

Aoki, Masahiko. 1988. *Information, Incentives, and Bargaining in the Japanese Economy*. New York: Cambridge University Press.

Aoki, Masahiko. 1994. "The Japanese Firm as a System of Attributes: A Survey and Research Agenda." In *The Japanese Firm: Sources of Competitive Strength*, edited by Masahiko Aoki and Ronald Dore, 11–40. Oxford: Oxford University Press.

Arrow, Kenneth. 1962. "The Economic Implications of Learning by Doing." *Review of Economic Studies* 29 (June): 155–73.

Arrow, Kenneth. 1972. "Gifts and Exchanges." *Philosophy and Public Affairs* 1 (4): 343–62.

Arthur, Brian. 2009. *The Nature of Technology: What It Is and How It Evolves*. New York: Free Press.

Ashby, W. Ross. 1960. *Design for a Brain*. London: Chapman & Hall.

Ashby, W. Ross. 1963. *An Introduction to Cybernetics*. New York: John Wiley & Sons.

Augustine, Saint. 2006. *Confessions*. Translated by Garry Wills. New York: Penguin.

Axelrod, Robert, and Michael Cohen. 1999. *Harnessing Complexity: Organizational Implications of a Scientific Frontier*. New York: Free Press.

Bailey, Steve, and Steven Syre. 1996. "And Thermo Begat . . . : Thermo Electron Keeps Spinning Out Offspring." *Boston Globe*, March 19, 1996.

Bairoch, Paul. 1988. *Cities and Economic Development*. Chicago: University of Chicago Press.

Bateson, Gregory. 1972. *Steps to an Ecology of Mind*. New York: Ballantine.

Bauer, Peter T. 1981. *Equality, the Third World, and Economic Delusion*. Cambridge: Harvard University Press.

Bell, Martin, and Keith Pavitt. 1995. "The Development of Technological Capabilities." In *Trade, Technology, and International Competitiveness*, edited by Irfan ul Haque, 69–101. Washington DC: World Bank.

Benziger, Vincent. 1996. "The Chinese Wisely Realized That They Did Not Know What They Were Doing." *Transition* 7 (7–8 July–August): 6–7.

Berger, Peter. 1976. *Pyramids of Sacrifice*. Garden City: Anchor Books.

Berle, Adolf, and Gardiner Means. 1932. *The Modern Corporation and Private Property*. New York: MacMillan and Company.

Berlin, Isaiah. 1969. *Four Essays on Liberty*. Oxford: Oxford University Press.

Black, Bernard, Reinier Kraakman, and Anna Tarassova. 2000. "What Went Wrong With Russian Privatization." *Stanford Law Review* 52: 1–84.

Black, Bernard, Reinier Kraakman, and Jonathan Hay. 1996. "Corporate Law from Scratch." In *Corporate Governance in Central Europe and Russia: Insiders and the State*, edited by Roman Frydman, Cheryl W. Gray, and Andrzej Rapaczynski, 2:245–302. Budapest: Central European University Press.

Black, Jan Knippers. 1999. *Development in Theory and Practice: Paradigms and Paradoxes*. Boulder: Westview.

Blair, Margaret M. 1995. *Ownership and Control: Rethinking Corporate Governance for the Twenty-First Century*. Washington DC: The Brookings Institution.

Blasi, Joseph, Maya Kroumova, and Douglas Kruse. 1997. *Kremlin Capitalism: Privatizing the Russian Economy*. Ithaca: Cornell University Press.

Blinder, Alan S. 1995. "Should the Formerly Socialist Economies Look East or West for a Model?" In *Economics in a Changing World: Economic Growth and Capital and Labour Markets*, edited by Jean-Paul Fitoussi, 5:3–24. New York: St. Martin's Press.

Boadway, Robin. 1974. "The Welfare Foundations of Cost-Benefit Analysis." *Economic Journal* 84 (December): 926–39.

Boadway, Robin. 2000. "The Economic Evaluation of Projects." https://pdfs.semanticscholar.org/d452/054ec648937fff81b348aa4a14fa7dcd5e63.pdf.

Boadway, Robin, and Neil Bruce. 1984. *Welfare Economics*. Oxford: Basil Blackwell.

Boardman, Anthony E., David H. Greenberg, Aidan R. Vining, and David L. Weimer. 2011. *Cost-Benefit Analysis: Concepts and Practice*, 4th Ed. Upper Saddle River: Pearson Education.

Bondurant, Joan. 1958. *Conquest of Violence: The Gandhian Philosophy of Conflict*. Princeton: Princeton University Press.

Bork, Robert H. 1993. *The Antitrust Paradox*. New York: Free Press.

Brent, Robert J. 2006. *Applied Cost-Benefit Analysis*, 2nd Ed. Cheltenham: Edward Elgar.

Bretall, Robert. 1946. *A Kierkegaard Anthology*. Princeton: Princeton University Press.

Buber, Martin. 1965. *Between Man and Man*. New York: Macmillan and Company.

Buchanan, James M. 1954. "Social Choice, Democracy and Free Markets." *Journal of Political Economy* 62 (April): 114–23.

Buchanan, James M. 1999. *The Logical Foundations of Constitutional Liberty: The Collected Works of James M. Buchanan*, vol. 1. Indianapolis: Liberty Fund.

Buchanan, James M. 2005. *Why I, Too, Am Not a Conservative: The Normative Vision of Classical Liberalism*. Cheltenham: Edward Elgar.

Buchanan, Scott. 1970. *Embers of the World*. Santa Barbara: Center for the Study of Democratic Institutions.

Burckhardt, Jacob. 1998 (orig. 1898). *The Greeks and Greek Civilization*. New York: St. Martin's Griffin.

Burke, Edmund. 1937. "Reflections on the French Revolution: In a Letter Intended to Have Been Sent to a Gentleman in Paris." In *The Harvard Classics: Edmund Burke*, edited by Charles Eliot, 143–378. New York: Collier.

Burnyeat, Myles. 1987. "Wittgenstein and Augustine *De Magistro*." *Proceedings of the Aristotelian Society Supplementary Volume* LXI: 1–24.

Business Roundtable. 2019. "Statement on the Purpose of a Corporation." *Business Roundtable*. https://opportunity.businessroundtable.org/wp-content/uploads/2019/08/BRT-Statement-on-the-Purpose-of-a-Corporation-with-Signatures.pdf.

Byrd, William A., and Qingsong Lin. 1990. "China's Rural Industry: An Introduction." In *China's Rural Industry: Structure, Development, and Reform*, edited by William A. Byrd and Qingsong Lin, 3–18. Washington DC: Oxford University Press for the World Bank.

Campbell, Donald E. 1995. *Incentives: Motivation and the Economics of Information*. New York: Cambridge University Press.

Campbell, Harry, and Richard Brown. 2003. *Benefit-Cost Analysis*. Cambridge: Cambridge University Press.

Campos, Jose Edgardo, and Hilton L. Root. 1996. *The Key to the Asian Miracle: Making Shared Growth Credible*. Washington DC: The Brookings Institution.

Candy, Philip. 1991. *Self-Direction for Lifelong Learning*. San Francisco: Jossey-Bass.

CERFE, and Urban Habitat. 1995. *Review of Current Global Trends in Economic and Social Development*. Rome: Global Urban Observatory.

Chandler, Alfred. 1990. *Scale and Scope: The Dynamics of Industrial Capitalism*. Cambridge: Harvard University Press.

Chang, Ha-Joon. 2002. *Kicking Away the Ladder*. London: Anthem Press.

Chipman, John S., and James C. Moore. 1978. "The New Welfare Economics 1939-1974." *International Economic Review* 19 (3 October): 547–84.

Chomsky, Noam. 1966. *Cartesian Linguistics*. New York: Harper & Row.

Clark, Rodney. 1979. *The Japanese Company*. New Haven: Yale University Press.

Coffee, John C. 1996. "Institutional Investors in Transitional Economies: Lessons from the Czech Experience." In *Corporate Governance in Central Europe and Russia: Volume 1 Banks, Funds, and Foreign Investors*, edited by Roman

Frydman, Cheryl W. Gray, and Andrzej Rapaczynski, 111–86. London: Central European University Press.

Collins, James C., and Jerry I. Porras. 1994. *Built to Last*. New York: Harper Business.

Confucius. 1938. *The Analects of Confucius*. Translated by Arthur Waley. New York: Vintage.

Coser, Lewis. 1956. *The Functions of Social Conflict*. New York: Free Press.

Cudworth, Ralph. 1996. *A Treatise Concerning Eternal and Immutable Morality*. Cambridge: Cambridge University Press.

Dabrowski, Marek, Stanislaw Gomulka, and Jacek Rostowski. 2001. "Whence Reform?: A Critique of the Stiglitz Perspective." *Journal of Policy Reform* 4 (4): 291–324.

Dahrendorf, Ralf. 1990. *Reflections on the Revolution in Europe: In a Letter Intended to Have Been Sent to a Gentleman in Warsaw*. New York: Random House.

Darwin, Charles. 2009. *The Origin of Species*, 6th Ed. Cambridge: Cambridge University Press.

Datta, Dhirendra Mohan. 1961. *The Philosophy of Mahatma Gandhi*. Madison: University of Wisconsin Press.

David, Paul A., and Dominique Foray. 1994. "Dynamics of Competitive Technology Diffusion Through Local Network Structures: The Case of EDI Document Standards." In *Evolutionary Economics and Chaos Theory*, edited by Loet Leydesdorff and Peter Van den Besselaar, 63–78. New York: St. Martin's Press.

Dawkins, Richard. 1996. *Climbing Mount Improbable*. New York: W. W. Norton & Company.

De Grazia, Alfred. 1975. *Eight Bads–Eight Goods: The American Contradictions*. Garden City: Anchor Books.

De Soto, Hernando. 1989. *The Other Path: The Invisible Revolution in the Third World*. New York: Harper & Row.

De Soto, Hernando. 2000. *The Mystery of Capital*. New York: Basic Books.

Deci, Edward, and Richard Ryan. 1985. *Intrinsic Motivation and Self-Determination in Human Behavior*. New York: Plenum Press.

Deming, W. Edwards. 1982. *Out of the Crisis*. Cambridge: MIT Center for Advanced Engineering Study.

Deming, W. Edwards. 1994. *The New Economics for Industry, Government, Education*. Cambridge: MIT Center for Advanced Engineering.

Dennett, Daniel. 1995. *Darwin's Dangerous Idea: Evolution and the Meanings of Life*. New York: Touchstone.

Dewey, John. 1916. *Democracy and Education*. New York: Free Press.

Dewey, John. 1939. *Freedom and Culture*. New York: Capricorn.

Dewey, John, and James Tufts. 1908. *Ethics*. New York: Henry Holt.

Dore, Ronald. 1987. *Taking Japan Seriously*. Stanford: Stanford University Press.

Dore, Ronald, and Hugh Whittaker. 1994. "Introduction." In *Business Enterprise in Japan: Views of Leading Japanese Economists,* edited by Kenichi Imai and Ryutaro Komiya, 1–15. Cambridge: MIT Press.

Dorf, Michael, and Charles Sabel. 1998. "A Constitution of Democratic Experimentalism." *Columbia Law Review* 98: 267.

Downs, Anthony. 1967. *Inside Bureaucracy*. Boston: Little, Brown and Company.

Drèze, Jean, and Nicholas Stern. 1987. "The Theory of Cost-Benefit Analysis." In *Handbook of Public Economics*, vol. II, edited by Alan Auerbach and Martin Feldstein, 909–89. Amsterdam: North-Holland.

Drucker, Peter. 1954. *The Practice of Management*. New York: Harper & Row.

Drucker, Peter. 1973. *Management: Tasks, Responsibilities, Practices*. New York: Harper & Row.

Dworkin, Ronald. 1978. *Taking Rights Seriously*. Cambridge: Harvard University Press.

Dworkin, Ronald. 1980. "Why Efficiency?" *Hofstra Law Review* 8 (Spring): 563–90.

Eatwell, John, Murray Milgate, and Peter Newman. 1989. *The New Palgrave: Allocation, Information, and Markets*. New York: W. W. Norton & Company.

EBRD. 1993. *Management and Employee Buy-Outs in Central and Eastern Europe-an Introduction*. London: EBRD.

Eigen, Manfred. 1992. *Steps Towards Life*. Oxford: Oxford University Press.

Eisenhardt, Kathleen. 1989. "Agency Theory: An Assessment and Review." *Academy of Management Review* 14 (1): 57–74.

Ellerman, David. 1984. "Entrepreneurship in the Mondragon Cooperatives." *Review of Social Economy* XLII (December): 272–94.

Ellerman, David. 1988. "The Legitimate Opposition at Work: The Union's Role in Large Democratic Firms." *Economic and Industrial Democracy: An International Journal* 9 (4 November): 437–53.

Ellerman, David. 1992. *Property & Contract in Economics: The Case for Economic Democracy*. Cambridge: Blackwell.

Ellerman, David. 1993. "Management and Employee Buy-Outs in Central and Eastern Europe: Introduction." In *Management and Employee Buy-Outs as a Technique of Privatization*, edited by David Ellerman, 13–30. Ljubljana: Central and Eastern European Privatization Network.

Ellerman, David. 1995. *Intellectual Trespassing as a Way of Life: Essays in Philosophy, Economics, and Mathematics*. Lanham: Rowman & Littlefield.

Ellerman, David. 1998. "Voucher Privatization with Investment Funds: An Institutional Analysis." *Policy Research Paper No. 1924*. Washington DC: World Bank.

Ellerman, David. 2001. "Lessons from East Europe's Voucher Privatization." *Challenge: The Magazine of Economic Affairs* 44 (4 July–August): 14–37.

Ellerman, David. 2003a. "Policy Research on Migration and Development." *World Bank Policy Research Working Paper No. 3117*. Washington DC: World Bank.

Ellerman, David. 2003b. "On the Russian Privatization Debates: What Has Been Learned a Decade Later?" *Challenge* 46 (3 May–June): 6–28. https://doi.org/10.1080/05775132.2003.11034201.

Ellerman, David. 2005. *Helping People Help Themselves: From the World Bank to an Alternative Philosophy of Development Assistance*. Ann Arbor: University of Michigan Press.

Ellerman, David. 2009. "Numeraire Illusion: The Final Demise of the Kaldor-Hicks Principle." In *Theoretical Foundations of Law and Economics*, edited by Mark D. White, 96–118. New York: Cambridge University Press.

Ellerman, David. 2010. "The Logic of Partitions: Introduction to the Dual of the Logic of Subsets." *Review of Symbolic Logic* 3 (2 June): 287–350.

Ellerman, David. 2014. "On a Fallacy in the Kaldor-Hicks Efficiency-Equity Analysis." *Constitutional Political Economy* 25 (2 June): 125–36.

Ellerman, David. 2017. "Logical Information Theory: New Foundations for Information Theory." *Logic Journal of the IGPL* 25 (5 October): 806–35. https://doi.org/10.1093/jigpal/jzx022.

Ellerman, David, Ales Vahcic, and Tea Petrin. 1991. "Privatization Controversies East and West." *Communist Economies and Economic Transformation* 3 (3): 283–98.

Ellerman, David, and Vladimir Kreacic. 2002. "Transforming the Old into a Foundation for the New: Lessons of the Moldova ARIA Project." *Policy Research Working Paper No. 2866*. Washington DC: World Bank.

Elster, Jon. 1983. *Sour Grapes: Studies in the Subversion of Rationality*. Cambridge: Cambridge University Press.

Elster, Jon, Claus Offe, and Ulrich K. Preuss. 1998. *Institutional Design in Post-Communist Societies: Rebuilding the Ship at Sea*. Cambridge: Cambridge University Press.

Erikson, Erik. 1969. *Gandhi's Truth: On the Origins of Militant Nonviolence*. New York: W. W. Norton & Company.

Farber, Leslie. 1976. *Lying, Despair, Jealousy, Envy, Sex, Suicide, Drugs, and the Good Life*. New York: Basic Books.

Feynman, Richard. 1985. *Surely You're Joking Mr. Feynman*. New York: W. W. Norton & Company.

Fitzgerald, F. Scott. 1945. "The Crack-Up." In *The Crack-Up*, edited by Edmund Wilson, 68–72. New York: New Directions.

Flynn, John J. 1973. "Corporate Democracy: Nice Work If You Can Get It." In *Corporate Power in America*, edited by Ralph Nader and Mark J. Green, 94–110. New York: Grossman Publishers.

Follett, Mary Parker. 1992 (1926). "The Giving of Orders." In *Classics of Public Administration*, edited by Jay Shafritz and Albert Hyde, 66–74. Pacific Grove: Brooks/Cole.

Freeman, Richard, and James Medoff. 1984. *What Do Unions Do?* New York: Basic Books.

Freire, Paulo. 1970. *Pedagogy of the Oppressed*. New York: Continuum.

Frey, Bruno. 1997. *Not Just for the Money: An Economic Theory of Personal Motivation*. Cheltenham: Edward Elgar.

Friedman, David D. 2000. *Law's Order: What Economics Has to Do with Law and Why It Matters*. Princeton: Princeton University Press.

Froebel, Friedrich W. 1954. "Froebel." In *Three Thousand Years of Educational Wisdom*, edited by Robert Ulich, 523–76. Cambridge: Harvard University Press.

Gandhi, Mohandas K. 1957. *An Autobiography: The Story of My Experiments with Truth*. Boston: Beacon Press.

Gandhi, Mohandas K. 1961. *Non-Violent Resistance (Satyagraha)*. New York: Schocken.

Garrison, Ray. 1979. *Managerial Accounting*. Dallas: Business Publications Inc.
Gell-Mann, Murray. 1994. *The Quark and the Jaguar: Adventures in the Simple and the Complex*. New York: W. H. Freeman.
Gini, Corrado. 1912. *Variabilità e Mutabilità*. Bologna: Tipografia di Paolo Cuppini.
Glaeser, Edward, Hedi Kallal, Jose Scheinkman, and Andrei Shleifer. 1992. "Growth in Cities." *Journal of Political Economy* 100: 1126–52.
Glick, Mark. 2018. "The Unsound Theory Behind the Consumer (and Total) Welfare Goal in Antitrust." *Antitrust Bulletin* 63 (4): 455–93. https://doi.org/10.1177/0003603X18807802.
Goldberg, Victor. 1980. "Relational Exchange: Economics and Complex Contracts." *American Behavioral Scientist* 23 (3 January and February): 337–52.
Gooch, G. P. 1959. *English Democratic Ideas in the Seventeenth Century*. New York: Harper & Row.
Gould, Stephen Jay. 1987. *An Urchin in the Storm: Essays about Books and Ideas*. New York: W. W. Norton & Company.
Goyder, George. 1961. *The Responsible Company*. Oxford: Basil Blackwell.
Haas, Ernst B. 1990. *When Knowledge Is Power: Three Models of Change in International Organizations*. Berkeley: University of California.
Handy, Charles. 1993. *Understanding Organizations*, 4th Ed. London: Penguin.
Harding, Harry. 1987. *China's Second Revolution: Reform after Mao*. Washington DC: Brookings Institution.
Hart, B. H. Liddell. 1941. *The Strategy of Indirect Approach*. London: Farber and Farber.
Hart, B. H. Liddell. 1967. *Strategy*, 2nd Revised Ed. New York: New American Library.
Hartl, D. L., and A. G. Clark. 1997. *Principles of Population Genetics*. Sunderland: Sinauer.
Hawkins, David. 2000. *The Roots of Literacy*. Boulder: University Press of Colorado.
Hayek, Friedrich A. 1978. *New Studies in Philosophy, Economics and the History of Ideas*. Chicago: University of Chicago Press.
Hayek, Friedrich A. 1984. *The Essence of Hayek*. Stanford: Hoover Institution Press.
Hicks, John R. 1939. "The Foundations of Welfare Economics." *Economic Journal* 49 (196): 696–712.
Hicks, John R. 1975. "The Scope and Status of Welfare Economics." *Oxford Economic Papers* 27 (3): 307–26.
Hirsch, Fred. 1976. *Social Limits to Growth*. Cambridge: Harvard.
Hirsch, P., S. Michaels, and R. Friedman. 1987. "'Dirty Hands' versus 'Clean Models': Is Sociology in Danger of Being Seduced by Economics?" *Theory and Society* 16 (3 May), 317–36.
Hirschman, Albert O. 1958. *The Strategy of Economic Development*. New Haven: Yale University Press.
Hirschman, Albert O. 1965. *Journeys toward Progress*. New York: Anchor Books.
Hirschman, Albert O. 1967. *Development Projects Observed*. Washington DC: Brookings Institution.

Hirschman, Albert O. 1970. *Exit, Voice, and Loyalty: Responses to Decline in Firms, Organizations, and States*. Cambridge: Harvard University Press.

Hirschman, Albert O. 1971. *A Bias for Hope: Essays on Development and Latin America*. New Haven: Yale University Press.

Hirschman, Albert O. 1973. *Journeys Toward Progress*. New York: W. W. Norton & Company.

Hirschman, Albert O. 1992. *Rival Views of Market Society*. Cambridge: Harvard University Press.

Hirschman, Albert O. 1995. "Social Conflicts as Pillars of Democratic Market Societies." In *A Propensity to Self-Subversion*, 231–48. Cambridge: Harvard University Press.

Hirschman, Albert O., and Charles E. Lindblom. 1971. "Economic Development, Research and Development, and Policy Making: Some Converging Views." In *A Bias for Hope,* edited by Albert O. Hirschman, 63–84. New Haven: Yale University Press.

Humboldt, Wilhelm von. 1969. *The Limits of State Action*. Cambridge: Cambridge University Press.

Humboldt, Wilhelm von. 1997. "The Nature and Conformation of Language." In *The Hermeneutics Reader*, edited by Kurt Mueller-Vollmer, 99–105. New York: Continuum.

Hyman, Stanley Edgar. 1966. *The Tangled Bank: Darwin, Marx, Frazer and Freud as Imaginative Writers*. New York: Grosset & Dunlap.

Imbs, Jean, and Romain Wacziarg. 2003. "Stages of Diversification." *American Economic Review* 93 (1 March): 63–86.

Ionescu, Ghita, and Isabel de Madariaga. 1972. *Opposition: Past and Present of a Political Institution*. Harmondsworth: Penguin.

Irvin, George. 1978. *Modern Cost-Benefit Methods*. London: Macmillan and Company.

Jacobs, Jane. 1961. *The Death and Life of Great American Cities*. New York: Vintage.

Jacobs, Jane. 1969. *The Economy of Cities*. New York: Random House.

Jacobs, Jane. 1980. *The Question of Separatism: Quebec and the Struggle over Sovereignty*. New York: Random House.

Jacobs, Jane. 1984. *Cities and the Wealth of Nations: Principles of Economic Life*. New York: Random House.

Jacobs, Jane. 1992. *Systems of Survival: A Dialogue on the Moral Foundations of Commerce and Politics*. New York: Vintage Books.

Jacobs, Jane. 2000. *The Nature of Economies*. New York: Modern Library.

Jacobs, Jane. 2004. *Dark Age Ahead*. New York: Random House.

Janik, Allan, and Stephen Toulmin. 1973. *Wittgenstein's Vienna*. New York: Touchstone.

Janis, Irving L. 1972. *Victims of Groupthink*. Boston: Houghton Mifflin.

Jefferson, Thomas. 2004 (orig. 1779). "A Bill for Establishing Religious Freedom." In *Jefferson: Political Writings*, edited by Joyce Appleby and Terence Ball, 390–92. Cambridge Texts in the History of Political Thought. Cambridge: Cambridge University Press.

Kagono, Tadao, and Takao Kobayashi. 1994. "The Provision of Resources and Barriers to Exit." In *Business Enterprise in Japan*, edited by Kenichi Imai and Ryutaro Komiya, 89–102. Cambridge: MIT Press.

Kaldor, Nicholas. 1939. "Welfare Propositions of Economics and Interpersonal Comparisons of Utility." *Economic Journal* 49 (195): 549–52.

Kamii, Constance. 1973. "Pedagogical Principles Derived from Piaget's Theory: Relevance for Educational Practice." In *Piaget in the Classroom*, edited by Milton Schwebel and Jane Raph, 199–215. New York: Basic Books.

Kanigel, Robert. 1997. *The One Best Way: Frederick Winslow Taylor and the Enigma of Efficiency*. New York: Viking.

Kant, Immanuel. 1963. "What Is Enlightenment?" In *Kant on History*, edited by Lewis White Beck, 3–10. New York: Macmillan and Company.

Kant, Immanuel. 1991. "Idea for a Universal History with a Cosmopolitan Purpose." In *Kant Political Writings*, edited by Hans Reiss, 41–53. New York: Cambridge University Press.

Kauffman, Stuart. 1995. *At Home in the Universe*. New York: Oxford University Press.

Keynes, John Maynard. 1933. "National Self-Sufficiency." In *The Collected Writings of John Maynard Keynes*, edited by Donald Moggeridge, 21:233–46. London: Cambridge University Press.

Keynes, John Maynard. 1936. *The General Theory of Employment, Interest, and Money*. New York: Harcourt, Brace & World.

Kierkegaard, Søren. 1989. *The Concept of Irony with Continual Reference to Socrates*. Edited by Edna Hong and Howard Hong. Princeton: Princeton University Press.

Kierkegaard, Søren. 1992. *Concluding Unscientific Postscript to Philosophical Fragments*, vol. I. Edited by Edna Hong and Howard Hong. Princeton: Princeton University Press.

King, Martin Luther. 2010. *Stride Toward Freedom*. Boston: Beacon Press.

Klein, Burton H. 1977. *Dynamic Economics*. Cambridge: Harvard University Press.

Klein, Burton H. 1984. *Prices, Wages and Business Cycles: A Dynamic Theory*. New York: Pergamon Press.

Klein, Burton H., and William Meckling. 1958. "Application of Operations Research to Development Decisions." *Operations Research* 6: 352–63.

Kline, Stephen J., and Nathan Rosenberg. 1986. "An Overview of Innovation." In *The Positive Sum Strategy: Harnessing Technology for Economic Growth*, edited by Ralph Landau and Nathan Rosenberg, 275–305. Washington DC: National Academy Press.

Kohn, Alfie. 1993. *Punished by Rewards*. Boston: Houghton Mifflin.

Kohr, Leopold. 1978. *The Breakdown of Nations*. New York: E. P. Dutton.

Koppl, Roger, Abigail Devereaux, Jim Herriot, and Stuart Kauffman. 2018. "A Simple Combinatorial Model of World Economic History." *ArXiv*. https://arxiv.org/ftp/arxiv/papers/1811/1811.04502.pdf.

Kornai, Janos. 1990. *The Road to a Free Economy. Shifting from a Socialist System: The Example of Hungary*. New York: W. W. Norton & Company.

Kreps, David. 1997. "Intrinsic Motivation and Extrinsic Incentives." *American Economic Review* 87: 359–65.

Kripke, Saul A. 1980. *Naming and Necessity*. Cambridge: Harvard University Press.

Landes, David S. 1998. *The Wealth and Poverty of Nations: Why Some Are So Rich and Some So Poor*. New York: W. W. Norton & Company.

Lane, Robert E. 1991. *The Market Experience*. New York: Cambridge University Press.

Lao-Tzu. 1989. *Te-Tao Ching*. Translated by Robert Henricks. New York: Ballantine.

Lau, Lawrence, Ying-Yi Qian, and Gerard Roland. 2000. "Reform without Losers: An Interpretation of China's Dual-Track Approach to Transition." *Journal of Political Economy* 108 (1): 120–43.

Lawrence, Elizabeth. 1970. *The Origins and Growth of Modern Education*. Baltimore: Pelican.

Lawrence, Peter. 1979. *Road Belong Cargo: A Study of the Cargo Movement in the Southern Madang District New Guinea*. Atlantic Highland: Humanities Press.

Layard, Richard, and Stephen Glaister. 1994. *Cost-Benefit Analysis*, 2nd Ed. Cambridge: Cambridge University Press.

Lefcourt, Herbert. 1976. *Locus of Control*. Hillsdale: Erlbaum/Wiley.

Leibenstein, Harvey. 1966. "Allocative Efficiency versus X-Efficiency." *American Economic Review* 56 (3): 392–415.

Leibenstein, Harvey. 1984. "The Japanese Management System: An X-Efficiency Game Theory Analysis." In *The Economic Analysis of the Japanese Firm*, edited by Masahiko Aoki, 331–57. Amsterdam: Elsevier.

Lepper, Mark R., and David Greene. 1978. *The Hidden Costs of Rewards: New Perspectives on the Psychology of Human Motivation*. Hillsdale: Erlbaum/Wiley.

Levy, Leonard. 1985. *Emergence of a Free Press*. New York: Oxford University Press.

Lilienthal, David E. 1964. "The Road to Change." *International Development Review* 6 (December).

Lin, Yutang. 1948. *The Wisdom of Laotse*. New York: Modern Library.

Lindblom, Charles. 1965. *The Intelligence of Democracy: Decision Making Through Mutual Adjustment*. New York: Free Press.

Lindblom, Charles. 1990. *Inquiry and Change*. New Haven: Yale University Press.

List, Friedrich. 1885. *The National System of Political Economy*. London: Longmans, Green, and Co. http://www.economics.mcmaster.ca/ugcm/3ll3/.

Lloyd, G. E. R. 1996. *Adversaries and Authorities: Investigations into Ancient Greek and Chinese Science*. Cambridge: Cambridge University Press.

Lloyd, Richard. 1993. "Pilot Privatizations and Management/Employee Buy-Outs in Russia 1991-92." In *Management and Employee Buy-Outs as a Technique of Privatization*, edited by David Ellerman, 150–58. Ljubljana: Central and Eastern European Privatization Network.

Logue, John, Sergey Plekhanov, and John Simmons. 1995. *Transforming Russian Enterprises: From State Control to Employee Ownership*. Westport: Greenwood Press.

Lovejoy, Arthur O. 1960. *The Great Chain of Being: A Study of the History of an Idea*. New York: Harper Torchbooks.

Lucas, Robert E. 1988. "On the Mechanics of Economic Development." *Journal of Monetary Economics* 22 (1 July): 3–42.

Lutz, Mark. 1999. *Economics for the Common Good*. London: Routledge.

Madison, James. 2008. "Federalist Paper 51." In *Alexander Hamilton, James Madison, and John Jay: The Federalist Papers*, edited by Lawrence Goldman, 256–60. New York: Oxford University Press.

Mankiw, N. Gregory. 2003. "Review of: Reinventing the Bazaar (Book by John McMillan)." *Journal of Economic Literature* XLI (March): 256–57.

Marglin, Stephen. 1990. "Losing Touch: The Cultural Conditions of Worker Accommodation and Resistance." In *Dominating Knowledge: Development, Culture, and Resistance*, edited by Frederique Marglin and Stephen Marglin, 217–82. Oxford: Clarendon.

Marshall, Alfred. 1920. *Principles of Economics.* New York: Macmillan and Company.

Marshall, Alfred. 1961. *Principles of Economics*, 9th Ed. Ninth (variorum) edition. London: MacMillan and Company.

Mason, Alpheus Thomas. 1946. *Brandeis: A Free Man's Life*. New York: Viking Press.

Mason, Edward S., and Robert E. Asher. 1973. *The World Bank Since Bretton Woods.* Washington DC: Brookings Institution.

Matson, Floyd. 1966. *The Broken Image: Man, Science and Society*. Garden City: Anchor Books.

McClintock, David. 2006. "How Harvard Lost Russia." *Institutional Investor*, January 24, 2006.

McClintock, Robert. 1982. "Reaffirming a Great Tradition." In *Invitation to Lifelong Learning*, edited by Ronald Gross, 46–78. Chicago: Follett.

McGregor, Douglas. 1948. "The Staff Function in Human Relations." *Journal of Social Issues* 4 (3): 5–22.

McGregor, Douglas. 1960. *The Human Side of Enterprise*. New York: McGraw-Hill.

McGregor, Douglas. 1966. *Leadership and Motivation.* Cambridge: MIT Press.

McGregor, Douglas. 1967. *The Professional Manager.* Edited by Caroline McGregor and Warren Bennis. New York: McGraw-Hill.

McMillan, John. 2002. *Reinventing the Bazaar: A Natural History of Markets.* New York: W. W. Norton & Company.

Michels, Robert. 1962. *Political Parties: A Sociological Study of the Oligarchical Tendencies of Modern Democracy*. New York: Collier.

Mill, John Stuart. 1977. "On Liberty." In *Collected Works of John Stuart Mill*, vol. 18, 213–310. Toronto: University of Toronto Press.

Milton, John. 1957a (orig. 1644). "Areopagitica." In *John Milton: Complete Poems and Major Prose*, edited by Merritt Hughes, 716–49. New York: Odyssey Press.

Milton, John. 1957b (orig. 1659). "To Remove Hirelings Out of the Church." In *John Milton: Complete Poems and Major Prose*, edited by Merritt Hughes, 856–79. New York: Odyssey Press.

Mishan, E. J., and Euston Quah. 2007. *Cost-Benefit Analysis*, 5th Ed. London: Routledge.

Mokyr, Joel. 1990. *The Lever of Riches: Technological Creativity and Economic Progress*. New York: Oxford.

Morita, Akio. 1986. *Made in Japan.* New York: E. P. Dutton.

Morley, John. 1877. *On Compromise*. London: Chapman & Hall.

Murrell, Peter. 1992. "Conservative Political Philosophy and the Strategy of Economic Transition." *Eastern European Politics and Societies* 6 (1): 3–16.

Murrell, Peter. 1995. "The Transition According to Cambridge, Mass." *Journal of Economic Literature* XXXIII (March): 164–78.

Nellis, John. 1999. "Time to Rethink Privatization in Transition Economies?" *IFC Discussion Paper No. 38*. Washington DC: International Finance Corporation.

Nellis, John. 2007. "Chapter 2: Leaps of Faith: Launching the Privatization Process in Transition." In *Privatization in Transition Economies: The Ongoing Story (Contemporary Studies in Economic and Financial Analysis, Volume 90)*, edited by Ira W. Lieberman and Daniel J. Kopf, 81–136. Bingley: Emerald Group Publishing. https://doi.org/10.1016/S1569-3759(07)00002-2.

Nelson, Richard R. 1961. "Uncertainty, Learning and the Economics of Parallel Research and Development Efforts." *Review of Economics and Statistics* 43 (November): 351–64.

Nelson, Richard R., and Sidney Winter. 1982. *An Evolutionary Theory of Economic Change*. Cambridge: Harvard University Press.

Nonaka, Ikujiro, and Hirotaka Takeuchi. 1995. *The Knowledge-Creating Company*. New York: Oxford University Press.

Nussbaum, Martha. 1994. *The Therapy of Desire: Theory and Practice in Hellenistic Ethics*. Princeton: Princeton University Press.

Nussbaum, Martha. 1997. *Cultivating Humanity: A Classical Defense of Reform in Liberal Education*. Cambridge: Harvard University Press.

Nussbaum, Martha. 2001. "The Costs of Tragedy: Some Moral Limits of Cost-Benefit Analysis." In *Cost-Benefit Analysis: Legal, Economic, and Philosophical Perspectives*, edited by Matthew D. Adler and Eric A. Posner, 169–200. Chicago: University of Chicago Press.

Oakeshott, Michael. 1991. *Rationalism in Politics and Other Essays*, Expanded Ed. Indianapolis: Liberty Fund.

Ortega y Gasset, Jose. 1961. *Meditations on Quixote*. New York: W. W. Norton & Company.

Ortega y Gasset, Jose. 1966. *Mission of the University*. New York: W. W. Norton & Company.

Pagels, Heinz. 1988. *The Dreams of Reason: The Computer and the Rise of the Sciences of Complexity*. New York: Bantam.

Parfit, Derek. 1984. *Reasons and Persons*. Oxford: Clarendon.

Pearce, D. W. 1983. *Cost-Benefit Analysis*, 2nd Ed. London: Macmillan and Company.

Percy, Eustace. 1944. *The Unknown State: 16th Riddell Memorial Lectures*. London: Oxford University Press.

Perrow, Charles. 1972. *Complex Organizations: A Critical Essay*, 3rd Ed. New York: McGraw-Hill.

Peters, Thomas J. 1992. *Liberation Management*. New York: Knopf.

Peters, Thomas J., and Robert H. Waterman. 1982. *In Search of Excellence*. New York: Warner Books.

Pfeffer, Jeffrey. 1994. *Competitive Advantage Through People*. Boston: Harvard Business School Press.

Piaget, Jean. 1955. *The Language and Thought of the Child*. Translated by Marjorie Gabain. New York: Meridian.

Pigou, Arthur C. 1960. *The Economics of Welfare*, 4th Ed. London: Macmillan and Company.

Polanyi, Michael. 1951. *The Logic of Liberty*. Chicago: University of Chicago Press.

Polanyi, Michael. 1962. *Personal Knowledge: Towards a Post-Critical Philosophy*. Chicago: University of Chicago Press.

Polanyi, Michael. 1966. *The Tacit Dimension*. Garden City: Doubleday.

Pollock, W. J. 2004. "Wittgenstein on the Standard Metre." *Philosophical Investigations* 27 (2): 148–57.

Popper, Karl R. 1962. *The Open Society and its Enemies*, vols. I and II. New York: Harper & Row.

Porter, Michael E. 1990. *The Competitive Advantage of Nations*. New York: Free Press.

Posner, Richard. 1972. *Economic Analysis of Law*. Boston: Little, Brown and Company.

Posner, Richard. 1983. *The Economics of Justice*. Cambridge: Harvard University Press.

Posner, Richard. 1990. *The Problems of Jurisprudence*. Cambridge: Harvard University Press.

Posner, Richard. 2001. "Cost-Benefit Analysis: Definition, Justification, and Comment on Conference Papers." In *Cost-Benefit Analysis: Legal, Economic, and Philosophical Perspectives*, edited by Matthew D. Adler and Eric A. Posner, 317–41. Chicago: University of Chicago Press.

Pratt, John W., and Richard J. Zeckhauser. 1991. *Principals and Agents: The Structure of Business*. Boston: Harvard Business School Press.

Prendergast, Canice. 1999. "The Provision of Incentives in Firms." *Journal of Economic Literature* XXXVII (March): 7–63.

Provine, William B. 1971. *The Origins of Theoretical Population Genetics*. Chicago: Chicago University Press.

Provine, William B. 1986. *Sewall Wright and Evolutionary Biology*. Chicago: University of Chicago Press.

Putnam, Robert. 1993. *Making Democracy Work*. Princeton: Princeton University Press.

Rao, C. R. 1982. "Gini-Simpson Index of Diversity: A Characterization, Generalization and Applications." *Utilitas Mathematica* B 21: 273–82.

Raymond, Eric. 2001. *The Cathedral and the Bazaar: Musings on Linux and Open Source by an Accidental Revolutionary*, Revised Ed. Sebastopol: O'Reilly & Associates.

Reddaway, Peter, and Dmitri Glinski. 2001. *The Tragedy of Russia's Reforms: Market Bolshevism Against Democracy*. Washington DC: United States Institute of Peace Press.

Richardson, Henry S. 2001. "The Stupidity of the Cost-Benefit Standard." In *Cost-Benefit Analysis: Legal, Economic, and Philosophical Perspectives,* edited by Matthew D. Adler and Eric A. Posner, 135–67. Chicago: University of Chicago Press.

Robbins, Lionel. 1932. *The Nature and the Significance of Economic Science*. London: Macmillan and Company.

Rockafellar, R. Tyrrell. 1970. *Convex Analysis*. Princeton: Princeton University Press.

Rodrik, Dani. 2007. *One Economics; Many Recipes*. Princeton: Princeton University Press.

Rogers, Carl R. 1951. *Client-Centered Therapy*. Boston: Houghton Mifflin.

Rogers, Carl R. 1969. *Freedom to Learn*. Columbus: Charles Merrill.

Rogers, Everett. 1983. *Diffusion of Innovations*, 3rd Ed. New York: Free Press.

Rohr, Janelle. 1989. *The Third World: Opposing Viewpoints*. Edited by Bruno Leone. San Diego: Greenhaven Press.

Romer, Paul. 1986. "Increasing Returns and Long-Run Growth." *Journal of Political Economy* 94 (5 October): 1002–37.

Rosenberg, Nathan, and L. E. Birdzell. 1986. *How the West Grew Rich: The Economic Transformation of the Industrial World*. New York: Basic Books.

Ross, Stephen. 1973. "The Economic Theory of Agency: The Principal's Problem." *American Economic Review* 63: 134–39.

Rousseau, Jean-Jacques. 1979 (orig. 1762). *Emile or On Education*. Translated by Allan Bloom. New York: Basic Books.

Ruskin, John. 1985 (orig. 1862). *Unto This Last*. London: Penguin.

Rutgaizer, Valery. 1989. *Аренда Предприятия (Leasing of an Enterprise in Russian)*. Moscow: Knowledge.

Ryle, Gilbert. 1945. "Knowing How and Knowing That." *Proceedings of the Aristotelian Society* XLVI (June): 1–16.

Ryle, Gilbert. 1949. *The Concept of Mind*. New York: Barnes & Noble.

Ryle, Gilbert. 1967. "Teaching and Training." In *The Concept of Education*, edited by R. S. Peters, 105–19. London: Routledge & Kegan Paul.

Sabel, Charles. 1994. "Learning by Monitoring: The Institutions of Economic Development." In *Rethinking the Development Experience: Essays Provoked by the Work of Albert O. Hirschman*, edited by Lloyd Rodwin and Donald Schön, 231–74. Washington DC: Brookings Institution.

Sabel, Charles, and Sanjay Reddy. 2007. "Learning to Learn: Undoing the Gordian Knot of Development Today." *Challenge* 50 (5): 73–92. https://doi.org/10.2753/0577-5132500505.

Sachs, Jeffrey. 1993. *Poland's Jump to the Market Economy*. Cambridge: MIT Press.

Sagan, Carl. 1996. *The Demon-Haunted World: Science as a Candle in the Dark*. New York: Random House.

Sah, Raaj, and Joseph Stiglitz. 1985. "Human Fallibility and Economic Organization." *American Economic Review* 75 (2 May): 292–97.

Samuelson, Paul A. 1961. "The Evaluation of 'Social Income': Capital Formation and Wealth." In *The Theory of Capital*, edited by F. A. Lutz and D. C. Hague, 32–57. London: Macmillan and Company.

Samuelson, Paul A. 1976. *Economics*, 10th Ed. New York: McGraw-Hill.

Schelling, Thomas C. 1984. *Choice and Consequences: Perspectives of an Errant Economist*. Cambridge: Harvard.

Schön, Donald A. 1971. *Beyond the Stable State*. New York: W. W. Norton & Company.

Schön, Donald A. 1983. *The Reflective Practitioner*. New York: Basic Books.

Schumpeter, Joseph A. 1962. *Capitalism, Socialism and Democracy*. New York: Harper Torchbooks.

Schwartz, Benjamin I. 1978. "The Rousseau Strain in the Contemporary World." *Daedalus* 107 (3 Summer): 193–206.

Schwenk, C. R. 1984. "Devil's Advocacy in Managerial Decision Making." *Journal of Management Studies* 21 (2 April): 153–68.

Schwenk, C. R. 1989. "A Meta-Analysis of the Comparative Effectiveness of Devil's Advocacy and Dialectical Inquiry." *Strategic Management Journal* 10 (3): 303–06.

Scitovsky, Tibor. 1941. "A Note on Welfare Propositions in Economics." *Review of Economic Studies* 9: 77–88.

Scitovsky, Tibor. 1976. *The Joyless Economy: An Inquiry into Human Satisfaction and Consumer Dissatisfaction*. Oxford: Oxford University Press.

Scott, James C. 1998. *Seeing Like a State: How Certain Schemes to Improve the Human Condition Have Failed*. New Haven: Yale.

Scott, W. Richard. 1998. *Organizations: Rational, Natural, and Open Systems*, 4th Ed. Upper Saddle River: Prentice Hall.

Sen, Amartya. 1982. *Choice, Welfare and Measurement*. Oxford: Basil Blackwell.

Sen, Amartya. 1999. *Development as Freedom*. Oxford: Oxford University Press.

Seneca. 1969. *Letters from a Stoic*. Translated by Robin Campbell. London: Penguin.

Shannon, Claude E. 1948. "A Mathematical Theory of Communication." *Bell System Technical Journal* 27: 379–423; 623–56.

Shaw, George Bernard. 1961. *Back to Methuselah*. Baltimore: Penguin.

Shleifer, Andrei, and Robert Vishny. 1998. *The Grabbing Hand: Government Pathologies and Their Cures*. Cambridge: Harvard University Press.

Simon, Herbert. 1991. "Organizations and Markets." *Journal of Economic Perspectives* 5 (2 Spring): 25–44.

Smith, Adam. 1994. *The Wealth of Nations*. New York: Modern Library.

Smith, Jeffery A. 1988. *Printers and Press Freedom: The Ideology of Early American Journalism*. New York: Oxford University Press.

Smullyan, Raymond. 1977. *The Tao Is Silent*. San Francisco: Harper & Row.

Squire, L. R. 1987. *Memory and Brain*. New York: Oxford University Press.

Squire, Lynn, and Herman G. van der Tak. 1975. *Economic Analysis of Projects*. Baltimore: Johns Hopkins Press.

Stiglitz, Joseph E. 1974. "Incentives and Risk Sharing in Sharecropping." *Review of Economic Studies* 41 (April): 219–55.

Stiglitz, Joseph E. 1994. *Whither Socialism?* Cambridge: MIT Press.

Stiglitz, Joseph E. 2001. "Whither Reform? —Ten Years of the Transition." In *Joseph Stiglitz and the World Bank: The Rebel Within*, edited by Ha-Joon Chang, 127–71. London: Anthem Press.

Stiglitz, Joseph E., and David Ellerman. 2001. "Not Poles Apart: 'Whither Reform?' And 'Whence Reform?'" *The Journal of Policy Reform* 4 (4): 325–38. https://doi.org/10.1080/13841280108523424.

Stone, Deborah. 1997. *Policy Paradox: The Art of Political Decision Making*. New York: W. W. Norton & Company.

Strang, Gilbert. 1986. *Introduction to Applied Mathematics*. Wellesley: Wellesley-Cambridge Press.

Stokey, Edith, and Richard Zeckhauser. 1978. *A Primer for Policy Analysis*. New York: W. W. Norton & Company.

Sunstein, Cass. 2018. *The Cost-Benefit Revolution*. Cambridge: MIT Press.

Tanese, Reiko. 1989. "Distributed Genetic Algorithms." In *Proceedings of the 3rd International Conference on Genetic Algorithms, Arlington Virginia*, 434–39. San Mateo, California: M. Kaufmann Publishers.

Tawney, Richard H. 1954. *Religion and the Rise of Capitalism*. New York: Mentor Books.

Tawney, Richard H. 1964. *The Radical Tradition*. New York: Minerva Press.

Tawney, Richard H. 1966. *Land and Labor in China*. Boston: Beacon Press.

Teece, David. 1998. "Design Issues for Innovative Firms: Bureaucracy, Incentives and Industrial Structure." In *The Dynamic Firm: The Role of Technology, Strategy, Organization, and Regions*, edited by Alfred Chandler, Peter Hagström, and Örjan Sölvell, 134–65. Oxford: Oxford University Press.

Thompson, W. R. 1933. "On the Likelihood That One Unknown Problem Exceeds Another in View of the Evidence of Two Samples." *Biometrika* 25: 275–94.

Titmuss, Richard. 1970. *The Gift Relationship*. London: Allen and Unwin.

Tobin, James. 1990. "One or Two Cheers for the 'Invisible Hand.'" *Dissent* (Spring): 229–236.

Tung, L. L., and A. R. Heminger. 1993. "The Effects of Dialectical Inquiry, Devil's Advocacy, and Consensus Inquiry Methods in a GSS Environment." *Information & Management* 25: 33–41.

Ulich, Robert, Ed. 1954. *Three Thousand Years of Educational Wisdom*. Cambridge: Harvard University Press.

Versényi, Laszlo. 1963. *Socratic Humanism*. New Haven: Yale University Press.

Von Alven, William. 1964. *Reliability Engineering*. Englewood Cliffs: Prentice-Hall.

Waddington, C. H. 1977. *Tools for Thought*. New York: Basic Books.

Waismann, Friedrich. 1967. *Ludwig Wittgenstein Und Der Wiener Kreis*. Oxford: Basil Blackwell.

Warsh, David. 1991. "In E. Europe, Major Differences in Privatization Yield to General Improvement." *Washington Post*, May 15, 1991.

Warsh, David. 2018. *Because They Could: The Harvard Russia Scandal (and NATO Enlargement) after Twenty-Five Years*. Scott's Valley, California: CreateSpace Independent Publishing.

Watzlawick, Paul. 1976. *How Real Is Real?* New York: Vintage.

Wedel, Janine. 1998. *Collision and Collusion*. New York: St. Martin's Press.

Weick, Karl. 1979. *The Social Psychology of Organizing*. New York: Random House.

Weiss, Andrew, and Georgiy Nikitin. 1998. "Performance of Czech Companies by Ownership Structure." Washington DC: World Bank.

Weitzman, Martin. 1992. "On Diversity." *Quarterly Journal of Economics* 107 (2 May): 363–405.

Weitzman, Martin. 1993. "How Not to Privatize." In *Privatization Processes in Eastern Europe*, edited by Mario Baldassarri, Luigi Paganetto, and Edmund S. Phelps, 249–69. New York: St. Martin's Press.

Weitzman, Martin. 1998. "Recombinant Growth." *Quarterly Journal of Economics* 113 (2 May): 331–58.

Weitzman, Martin, and Chenggang Xu. 1994. "Chinese Township-Village Enterprises as Vaguely Defined Cooperatives." *Journal of Comparative Economics* 18: 121–45.

Westbrook, Robert. 1991. *John Dewey and American Democracy*. Ithaca: Cornell University Press.

Whyte, William Foote, and Kathleen King Whyte. 1991. *Making Mondragon*, 2nd Revised Ed. Ithaca: ILR Press.

Wiener, Norbert. 1954. *The Human Use of Human Beings*. Garden City: Doubleday Anchor.

Wiener, Norbert. 1961. *Cybernetics: Or Control and Communication in the Animal and the Machine*, 2nd Ed. Cambridge: MIT Press.

Wiener, Norbert. 1993. *Invention: The Care and Feeding of Ideas*. Cambridge: MIT Press.

Williams, Christopher. 1981. *Origins of Form*. New York: Architectural Book Publishing Co.

Wills, Garry. 1994. *Certain Trumpets: The Call of Leaders*. New York: Simon & Schuster.

Wilson, Haken. 1994. "Restructuring Large Enterprises in Preparation for Privatization: A Case Study." In *Russia: Creating Private Enterprises and Efficient Markets*, edited by Ira Lieberman and John Nellis, 159–69. Washington DC: World Bank.

Wortman, Tunis. 1966 (orig. 1800). "A Treatise Concerning Political Enquiry." In *Freedom of the Press from Zenger to Jefferson: Early American Libertarian Theories*, edited by Leonard Levy, 230–84. Indianapolis: Bobbs-Merrill.

Wright, Sewall. 1932. "The Roles of Mutation, Inbreeding, Crossbreeding, and Selection in Evolution." *Proceedings of the Sixth International Congress of Genetics* 1: 356–66.

Wright, Sewall. 1986. *Evolution: Selected Papers*. Edited by William B. Provine. Chicago: University of Chicago Press.

World Bank. 1996. *The World Bank Participation Sourcebook*. Washington DC: World Bank.

Young, Owen D. 1927. "Dedication Address." *Harvard Business Review* V (4 July): 385–94.

Zerbe Jr., Richard O., and Allen S. Bellas. 2007. *A Primer for Benefit-Cost Analysis*. Cheltenham: Edward Elgar.

Index

About the Author

David P. Ellerman retired in 2003 to academia after ten years at the World Bank, where he was the economic adviser and speechwriter for the chief economist Joseph Stiglitz. He is currently an associate researcher at the School of Social Science, University of Ljubljana, Slovenia, a visiting scholar in the Department of Philosophy, University of California at Riverside, and a Gordon Fellow at the Institute for Advanced Study, Stellenbosch, South Africa.

For two years prior to joining the World Bank in 1992, Dr. Ellerman was the founder and president of EOS/Ljubljana d.o.o. in Ljubljana, Slovenia (with offices in Rijeka, Croatia, and Prague), which provided consulting for the ownership by managers and workers.

In his prior university teaching, Dr. Ellerman taught over a twenty-year period in the Boston area in five disciplines: economics, mathematics, computer science, operations research, and accounting. He was educated at Massachusetts Institute of Technology (Philosophy of Science, 1965), and at Boston University from where he has two master's degrees, one in philosophy and one in economics, and a doctorate in mathematics. Dr. Ellerman has published many articles in scholarly journals in economics, logic, mathematics, physics, philosophy, and law (see website), as well as several books, the most recent ones being:

Helping People Help Themselves: From the World Bank to an Alternative Philosophy of Development Assistance. Foreword by Albert O. Hirschman. University of Michigan Press, 2005. South Asia edition published by Tulika Press, New Dehli, India, 2006.

Intellectual Trespassing as a Way of Life: Essays in Philosophy, Economics, and Mathematics. Rowman & Littlefield Inc. 1995.

Property and Contract in Economics: The Case for Economic Democracy. Cambridge MA: Basil Blackwell Inc. 1992.

The Democratic Worker-Owned Firm. London: Unwin-Hyman Academic. 1990. Revised and published in Chinese as *The Democratic Corporation* 1997, Xinhua Publishing House, Beijing. Original book reprinted by Routledge Revivals, 2015.

David P. Ellerman
Website: http://www.ellerman.org

www.ingramcontent.com/pod-product-compliance
Ingram Content Group UK Ltd.
Pitfield, Milton Keynes, MK11 3LW, UK
UKHW020840290926
15470UKWH00004B/1461

9 781793 623720